REASON AND THE RULE OF FAITH

Conversations in the Tradition with John Paul II

Edited by
Christopher J. Thompson
and
Steven A. Long

University Press of America,® Inc.
Lanham · Boulder · New York · Toronto · Plymouth, UK

Copyright © 2011 by
University Press of America,® Inc.
4501 Forbes Boulevard
Suite 200
Lanham, Maryland 20706
UPA Acquisitions Department (301) 459-3366

Estover Road
Plymouth PL6 7PY
United Kingdom

All rights reserved
Printed in the United States of America
British Library Cataloging in Publication Information Available

Library of Congress Control Number: 2010936060
ISBN: 978-0-7618-3963-7 (paperback : alk. paper)
eISBN: 978-0-7618-5393-0

∞™ The paper used in this publication meets the minimum
requirements of American National Standard for Information
Sciences—Permanence of Paper for Printed Library Materials,
ANSI Z39.48-1992

In Memoriam

Avery Cardinal Dulles, S.J.
August 24, 1918—December 12, 2008

Requiescat in Pacem

TABLE OF CONTENTS

Preface	v
Acknowledgments	vii
Introduction	ix

SECTION ONE: **The Intellectual Landscape Encountered by the Catholic Intellectual**

Chapter One: Philosophy and Theology 17
Avery Cardinal Dulles, S.J. (†)

Chapter Two: The Thomistic Meta-Structure of Pope John Paul II's Doctrinal Initiatives 25
Steven A. Long, Ph.D.

Chapter Three: Is Aquinas's *Summa* Only About Grace? 43
Romanus Cessario, O.P.

Chapter Four: Analogy, Necessity, and an Editor's Anxiety 55
John F. Boyle, Ph.D.

Chapter Five: From Scholasticism to Personalism 63
Avery Cardinal Dulles, S.J. (†)

SECTION TWO: **Questions on the Nature and Importance of Truth for the Catholic Intellectual**

Chapter Six: The Natural Knowledge of God in *Fides et Ratio* 73
Guy Mansini, O.S.B.

Chapter Seven: Redeemed Reason, Natural Law, and the Competency of the Magisterium 85
Lawrence J. Welch, Ph.D.

Chapter Eight: Figurative and Properly Literal Discourse in Scripture and Theology 101
Christopher J. Malloy, Ph.D.

Chapter Nine: *Fides et Ratio* and the English Catholic Revival: Classic Apologists on Faith and Reason 119
David Paul Deavel

Table of Contents

SECTION THREE: **Person, Freedom and the Good in Contemporary Intellectual Culture**

Chapter Ten: Lest the Cross of Christ Be Emptied of Its Power: Negative Moral Norms in the Moral Life — 135
Christopher J. Thompson, Ph.D.

Chapter Eleven: *Veritatis Splendor* and the Fundamental Option: Seeking Guidance from Thomas's Doctrine of Infused Cardinal Virtue — 143
William Mattison, Ph.D.

Chapter Twelve: The Political Common Good and the Perfection of Human Freedom — 159
John Goyette, Ph.D.

Chapter Thirteen: Our Merits, God's Gifts — 167
W. Matthews Grant, Ph.D.

Chapter Fourteen: Edith Stein and *Fides et Ratio* — 177
Catherine Jack Deavel, Ph.D.

Chapter Fifteen: Man as *Imago Dei* and *Capax Dei*: Man's Specific Obediential Potency for Grace and Glory — 197
Lawrence Feingold, Ph.D.

Bibliography — 217
Index of Names — 225
Contributors — 229

PREFACE

These essays mark the fruition of several days of conversations conducted on three separate occasions during the summers of 2003, 2005, and 2007. These "Habits of Mind" seminars were generously sponsored by the Center for Catholic Studies at the University of St. Thomas and were designed to foster *habitus*, or habits which sought to form committed Catholic intellectuals in community—with each other and with the wider Church of which they serve as teachers, scholars, and apprentices of the tradition. We were blessed with the company of *Magistri:* the late Cardinal Avery Dulles, S.J., graciously conducted one session and Fr. Romanus Cessario, O.P., led two gatherings. We dedicate these efforts to the memory of His Eminence, Cardinal Dulles, in gratitude to God for all that he inspired in us, and to all those who have given of themselves that we might come to ponder more deeply the mysteries of our Catholic faith.

Christopher Thompson & Steven Long
Saint Paul, Minnesota
January, 2010

ACKNOWLEDGEMENTS

We wish to thank the Center for Catholic Studies at the University of St. Thomas, especially Don J. Briel, for extending both hospitality and resources toward making these and so many occasions in Catholic higher education possible, especially for his generous efforts in securing support for these seminars through the "Beyond Career to Calling" Grant from the Lilly Endowment, Inc. Heartfelt gratitude, as well, is due to The Saint Paul Seminary School of Divinity, especially Monsignor Aloysius Callaghan, Rector, for his dedicated work and support for the intellectual life of the seminary. Nancy Sannerud deserves special kudos for her persistence in bringing this project to a happy conclusion. Alexandra Theis and Susan Moro should also be acknowledged for their assistance. Finally, we are grateful to The Chapelstone Foundation for their on-going support for this and similar projects.

INTRODUCTION

In his *Three Rival Versions of Moral Enquiry*, Alasdair MacIntyre noted the importance of what he called "tradition guided inquiry," a form of intellectual formation that aims to develop a conversation among contemporaries and the tradition from which they draw their inspiration. Such a form of inquiry is to be contrasted with two other habits of mind that have so often characterized the academy. The first he identified as the Genealogical tradition. Nietzschean in inspiration, this form of inquiry aims to "unmask"—and thereby undermine— what are alleged to be biases parading as intellectual foundations. The second is the Encyclopaedic approach which aims toward an all-encompassing, comprehensive view of what has gone before, with no particular intellectual conviction serving as the vantage point from which one evaluates and judges rival claims. Genealogists seek to undermine tradition while Encyclopaedists seek to passively chronicle it.

Neither approach is sufficient for Catholic intellectuals dedicated to the living, magisterial tradition of the Church. And so these essays seek neither to undermine nor merely chronicle the intellectual achievements of recent decades. Instead, they draw their inspiration foremost from St. Thomas Aquinas, the premier tradition guided enquirer, and the doctrinal tradition he inspired. More specifically, they draw upon the monumental achievements of the late Pope John Paul II: *Veritatis Splendor* and *Fides et Ratio*. These two works serve as the magisterial foundation upon which a renewal of Thomistic guided enquiry may flourish in the third millennium. In varying degrees of expression and modes of elucidation, these essays together form a sustained effort to provide for the next generation of scholars a vital encounter with the Catholic intellectual tradition as set in motion by the work of John Paul II. It is our firm conviction that these encyclicals taken together form not the conclusion at the close of a pontificate as much as the inaugural call to future promise and growth.

Crafted with an eye toward accessibility across disciplines, these essays were generated in a spirit of *convivium*, of mutual support for the further service of the Church and her intellectual achievements. Scholars new to the vocation and seasoned mentors gathered for several days to share not merely written work but living ideas. Sessions consisted of extended meditations offered by the late Avery Cardinal Dulles, S.J., and Fr. Romanus Cessario, O.P., while Professors Steven A. Long, John F. Boyle, and Lawrence Feingold provided keynote addresses. These efforts were meant to serve not as conclusions but as catalysts for those gathered for our conversations as well as the next generation of committed Catholic intellectuals. The remaining essays signal the signs of great achievement and promise for the Church.

Cardinal Avery Dulles' essay, *Philosophy and Theology,* inaugurates the first section concerning "foundational contexts" and considers the relationship between philosophy and theology and identifies at least four modes in which philosophical inquiry is conducted in relationship to the discipline of theology. Reflecting particularly on John Paul II's *Fides et Ratio*, he considers philosophy "as conducted under the aegis of faith," as well as philosophy as the *ancilla theologiae*. In the end he raises the question whether there might be a level of discourse which transcends the distinction between philosophy and theology. "I would like to think," he says, "that there could be such a thing as integral wisdom, which studies the whole or reality with the tools of philosophy and theology together." He concludes his reflections with a consideration of the importance of a life of Christian witness in evangelization.

Steven A. Long, in his keynote address, *The Thomistic Meta-Structure of John Paul II's Doctrinal Initiatives*, proposes that many of John Paul II's doctrinal initiatives may be characterized in terms of "classical Thomism." Along the way he challenges those who believe that the absence of any explicit mention of the normativity of St. Thomas signals a departure for his importance for the Catholic magisterial tradition. On the contrary, Long argues, "as an historical and doctrinal matter it is uniquely the Thomistic school that warned of precisely the errors corrected by these encyclicals as speculative effects flowing from earlier grave mistakes within theology." He completes this thesis by illustrating the historical and intellectual etiology of the "autonomism" John Paul II names in *Veritatis Splendor*, turning explicitly to the controversies occasioned by Molina's sixteenth-century denial that our freedom has its first cause in God.

Romanus Cessario, O.P., in *Is Aquinas' 'Summa' Only About Grace?* considers the reception of St. Thomas, especially in the post-conciliar *milieu*, giving special attention to the treatment of Thomas among Rahnerians. His concern is that "this enthusiasm for making Aquinas fit comfortably into the post-Heideggerian world risks a conflation of nature and grace and a blurring of important distinctions. . . ." On the contrary, Fr. Cessario reminds the reader, Saint Thomas does not think it is unbecoming to speak of created natures, including human nature, in terms of its own integrity, its own dynamics. It is upon this basis, Cessario argues, that St. Thomas speaks of a "*gratia elevans*," by which human beings can reach out for God.

John Boyle asserts in his keynote address, *Analogy, Necessity, and an Editor's Anxiety*, that "Precision in understanding of the created order provides precision in theological analysis," and from this vantage presses the importance of analogy in engaging in authentic theological reasoning as *scientia*. He challenges those who see St. Thomas as principally a model of *method* in theology, but not content, and directs us to consider carefully the problems described in *Fides et Ratio*: the importance of metaphysics understood as the science of things in their being and essence; the claim that the human mind can know the truth. Because theology is dependent upon analogy, he suggests, it is, in turn, dependent upon the health of philosophy.

In his second essay, *From Scholasticism to Personalism*, Cardinal Avery Dulles, S.J., turns our attention to Karol Wojtyla's efforts "to retrieve Scholasticism in a personalist key." The former method focuses upon the tools of abstraction and prefers universal concepts rather than particular perceptions of experiences. Personalism, by distinction, while not necessarily rejecting scholastic principles, focuses on the concrete or existential approach. "Nature does not make decisions," Cardinal Dulles notes, "but persons do." In addition to these distinctions, one must keep in mind the elements of the controversies in the 1940's surrounding the proper understanding of the relationship between nature and grace. All of this serves to provide the context for the tasks taken up in *Fides et Ratio* by John Paul II and permeates the Holy Father's approach to the relationships of faith and reason, theology and philosophy. In concluding, Cardinal Dulles remarks that *Fides et Ratio* "represents a retrieval of Scholasticism in light of modern personalism" and directs our attention to the importance of personal witness in apologetics and the task of evangelization in today's culture.

Section two focuses on issues of truth and opens with an essay by Fr. Guy Mansini, O.S.B., in which he considers the issues surrounding the capacity of the human being to know God. In his essay, *The Natural Knowledge of God in Fides et Ratio,* Fr. Mansini argues that in *Fides et Ratio* human reason does not succeed outside the context of supernatural grace—even to a natural knowledge of God. "This is not some Milbankian conflation of reason and faith," he cautions, "but the thesis that reason needs faith to attain to the knowledge of God of which reason is naturally capable." He asserts, moreover, that the necessity of faith for reason to achieve its aim of knowing God "is a peculiarly modern need," and he develops his reflections around the compelling claim that not only revelation but reason itself has its own history and dynamic. In its post-lapsarian exercise, especially in its encounter with death, reason reaches for the answers that only faith can provide.

Lawrence Welch continues the theme of the relationships of reason and faith, with special focus on *Veritatis Splendor.* In his essay, *Redeemed Reason, Natural Law and the Competency of the Magisterium,* he takes the reader beyond the initial parameters of the relations of faith and reason, and directs us to consider how this broader issue impacts one's approach to the truth of the moral life and the magisterium, specifically the latter's ability to teach infallibly concrete moral norms pertaining to the natural law. How one understands the competency of the magisterium is bound up with, among other things, "whether we understand that Christ is really revealed to us as the full revelation of the true identity of the rational creature that is man." He challenges those who suggest that the magisterium cannot teach infallibly concrete moral norms of the natural law, and argues that the natural law itself needs to be more adequately understood as contained within Divine providence and the Trinitarian Revelation; as such, "it is thoroughly theological" and cannot be explained in isolation from revelation.

Christopher Malloy explores the issues surrounding the nature of "truth", giving special attention to figurative and properly literal discourse in scripture and theology. In *Figurative and Properly Literal Discourse in Scripture and Theology,* he explores the claim within *Fides et Ratio* concerning philosophy's capacity to develop universally communicable discourse and conceptual language—or truth. From the vantage of St. Thomas' treatment of figurative and analogical discourse, he then turns his attention to matters of contemporary exegesis (source criticism) and elements of the theological discourse of Hans Urs von Balthasar. Some source critics, he argues, blur the appropriate distinctions between metaphor and analogy and in this way they do a disservice to the theological community. Similar challenges are brought to bear upon the work of von

Balthasar. Both source critics and von Balthasarians, he suggests, ought to come to terms with the rigor of Saint Thomas' distinctions between figurative and proper discourse.

David Paul Deavel addresses issues of communicating truth in contemporary culture, turning specifically to the claim in *Fides et Ratio* that theological work in the church is at the service of the proclamation of the faith in catechesis. In his essay, *Fides et Ratio and the English Catholic Revival,* Deavel traces in broad outline some of the notable apologists of the early and mid-twentieth century: Robert Hugh Benson, Ronald Knox, Frank Sheed and Maisie Ward. In many ways, he suggests, these influential apologists anticipated many of the elements that John Paul II employs in his "daring" treatment of faith and reason in *Fides et Ratio*.

The third and final section of essays focuses upon the questions surrounding the human person, human freedom and the achievement of the good life, beatitude. In *Lest the Cross of Christ Be Emptied of its Power* Christopher Thompson meditates upon the role of negative moral norms in the pursuit of excellence. Because negative norms bind differently upon consciences in contrast to positive injunctions, they figure differently on the horizon of Christian witness. In this way, he suggests, the defense of intrinsically evil acts provided in the first two sections of *Veritatis Splendor* naturally leads the reader to the subject taken up in the third section: martyrdom. "Negative moral norms," he states, "far from diminishing our dignity, actually announce our fundamental splendor and power."

William Mattison reflects on the pursuit of the good life and considers the status of infused virtues. In his essay, *Veritatis Splendor and the Fundamental Option*, Mattison investigates the "fundamental option" in moral theology and argues that such an approach runs parallel to a misinterpretation of St. Thomas' doctrine of infused cardinal virtue. Thomas' doctrine of infused cardinal virtue both illuminates the issues and provides the remedy for the inadequacies in fundamental option moral theory.

John Goyette continues to take up the question of the good life, giving special attention to its public character. In his essay, *The Political Common Good and the Perfection of Human Freedom*, Goyette addresses the problem of human freedom and contrasts the contemporary emphasis on human autonomy as creating its own values or moral norms with the perspective of human freedom found in *Veritatis Splendor* in which human autonomy is only rightly understood as having both its origin and end in God. Goyette advances the conversation beyond a consideration of individuals and their relationship to God as origin and end and argues that "although [individual] human freedom is ultimately ordered towards God as a final end, it is also ordered towards more proximate final end, the common good of the political community."

Matthews Grant directs our attention toward the subtle questions concerning our good, meritorious actions and God's grace. In *Our Merits, God's Gifts,* Grant focuses our attention on the relations between faith and reason, yet precisely from the vantage of divine and human agency. By defending the notion that our natural reason can support a model of co-operation between divine action and human freedom, he provides a necessary and appropriate context for the role of philosophy with respect to theology. Special attention is given to certain features of the cosmological argument for the existence of God, whereby he both secures the foundations for our dependence upon God's causality and our free, meritorious actions. "Thus, philosophy, without exhausting all the mystery surrounding divine grace and human freedom, appears to converge with Catholic doctrine concerning our merits as God's gifts."

Catherine Jack Deavel takes up the questions of human empathy, giving special attention to the works of Edith Stein—one of the twentieth-century philosophers explicitly cited in *Fides et Ratio* as engaging in "courageous research." In *Edith Stein and Fides et Ratio*, Jack Deavel argues that Stein's reflections on empathy especially can serve as an important resource and model for meeting the tasks to which John Paul II has called philosophers in *Fides et Ratio*, specifically: the recovery of the sapiential dimension of philosophy, the affirmation that human reason can know objective truth, and metaphysics. Stein's account of empathy provides insight into many of the dimensions of the search for meaning as well as the essential role of community, the latter facilitating her turn from strict phenomenological method toward the Christian philosophical tradition. "In her mature work," Jack Deavel concludes, "in which she turns to the integration of phenomenology and Thomism and reflects directly on truths of faith, Stein offers a practical model of the relation of philosophy and theology."

In the last essay of the section, Larry Feingold takes up the issue of the *imago dei* and our *capax dei*. In his keynote address, *Man as Imago Dei and Capax Dei: Man's Specific Obediential Potency*, Feingold takes up one of the fundamental and perennial problems in Christian tradition: that of our created human nature and our capacity to receive supernatural gifts. The essay is in many ways a *precis* of his larger work, *The Natural Desire to See God According to St. Thomas Aquinas* (Rome, 2001), for which he has received much attention since our seminars. In so far as it treats of many of the central themes of both *Veritatis Splendor* and *Fides et Ratio*, and does so in light of the tradition of St. Thomas, it forms a suitable concluding context to the aims of our overall efforts in these seminars and essays.

In conclusion, we hope we inspire others to recognize in these pages the work of dedicated men and women who place their gifts at the service of the tradition. In a spirit of gratitude for what has come before and hopeful promise for what lies ahead, we look forward to the rich harvest God has in store for those who serve Him in the Catholic intellectual community.

SECTION ONE

THE INTELLECTUAL LANDSCAPE
ENCOUNTERED BY THE
CATHOLIC INTELLECTUAL

Chapter One

Philosophy and Theology

Avery Cardinal Dulles, S.J. († 2008)

Among academic disciplines, philosophy and theology have a particular affinity with each other because both are concerned with ultimate meaning and transcendent truth. Both deal with the nature and order of reality as a whole and with the final purpose of human existence. They grapple with similar, even identical, questions: Why is there something rather than nothing? What is the place of human beings in God's plan? Whence do we come, why do we exist, what must we do, and what may we hope for?

Intimately related though they are, the two disciplines differ in their method and to some extent in their object. Philosophy ponders naturally knowable truth by the natural light of reason. It makes inferences from things known by common human experience, which is available to believers and nonbelievers alike. Theology, by contrast, uses human reason assisted by the added light of faith to understand the truth that God has revealed. But since truth is always compatible with truth, the findings of philosophy and theology must, in the end, agree.

The question often arises: how is philosophy related to faith? I am sure that is a very actual question for all of you who teach philosophy in Catholic institutions or to Catholic students. It would be a mistake, I believe, to insist on any one answer to that question. Philosophy can be cultivated in a variety of relationships with faith and theology. I find convenient to distinguish four situations, giving rise to four states of philosophy.

I

The first state is one of philosophy untouched by Christian faith. All the philosophy produced before the time of Christ would fit into this category. The Greeks, in particular, rose to great heights in the time of Plato and Aristotle, to mention but two pre-Christian philosophers. Many Christians have sought to write philosophical works that in no way depend upon the truth of Christian revelation. Such reasoning at its best can establish many truths that are important for Christian faith; for example, the capacity of the human mind to attain abiding truth and to transcend shifting phenomena; and the possibility of demonstrating the existence and attributes of God, the spirituality and immortality of the human soul, and the obligation to do good and avoid evil. The Catholic Church teaches that truths such as these can be proved by natural reason, without dependence on Christian faith. (The Church does not teach that these proofs have been constructed by nonbelievers, but only that it is possible for them to be so constructed.)

Philosophy of this type does not deliver a complete and self-contained system. It ends up with some pressing questions that, according to its champions, cannot be solved without revelation. Maurice Blondel, for example, ended his philosophical dissertation on *Action* with the open question as to whether or not there is a supernatural. Others would say (in the spirit of the early Karl Rahner, S.J.) that philosophy can raise the question of a possible revelation, but that it cannot say whether God will freely disclose himself, still less what that revelation will contain. Will God's final word be one of condemnation or of pardon and absolution?

II

In a second state, philosophy is in dialogue with Christian faith. In a Christian civilization such as that of the West since the fourth century, it is almost impossible for philosophy not to be influenced by faith. It is forced to grapple with questions on which believers have taken a definite position, but it does not allow religious faith to dictate the answers to philosophical questions.

This second category is a very broad one because it makes room for philosophers who are variously disposed toward the Christian religion. Three subcategories may be distinguished.

Some are relatively orthodox; they are convinced that philosophy delivers results fully compatible with Christian faith. This would be the case with Malebranche, Leibniz, Kierkegaard, and Marcel.

A second subcategory contains those who remain Christian but who bend the doctrines of faith to some degree to bring them into conformity with their philosophy. Examples might be furnished by Locke, Kant, and Hegel, who were believers but not by most standards orthodox.

The third subcategory would be those who were in dialogue with Christianity but who came to oppose it on philosophical grounds. As examples, one might think of Feuerbach and Marx, Comte and Nietzsche, Heidegger and Sartre. Even though they were atheists, their views about God, the world, and human destiny were profoundly influenced by their exposure to Christianity, the religion they had deserted.

Philosophers never begin their work in a cultural vacuum. Judeo-Christian ideas and values have so permeated the culture of the West that no philosopher can ignore them. They establish the framework in which philosophers think about the dignity and rights of the human person, freedom and responsibility, the human nostalgia for the transcendent and the divine, and many such themes. Even philosophers who do not want to be Christian deal with themes like these in ways closer to Christianity than any pre-Christian thinkers.

It can, of course, be debated whether the influence of Christian culture on philosophy is favorable or detrimental. A nonbeliever might try to escape any such influence as far as possible. But it has to be admitted that philosophy has developed to greater heights in the West than elsewhere in the world. The stimulus of Christianity has contributed significantly to that development.

III

In its third state, philosophy operates under the aegis of faith. The philosopher is confessedly a believer, who will not admit any contradiction between philosophy and what God has revealed through the Church. But at the same time, he or she recognizes a difference of method between the disciplines and does not wish to behave as a theologian. Writing strictly as a philosopher, he affirms only what can be established by philosophical methods. This is what John Paul II in his encyclical, *Fides et Ratio,* describes as Christian philosophy (§76).[1] As an example, one might also think of Jacques Maritain.

Minimally, faith operates as a negative norm. The philosopher knows that his discipline cannot prove anything contrary to the word of God. If philosophy seems to be inclined to assert this, it must have gotten off the track. Revelation therefore prevents philosophers from making mistakes they might otherwise make. It alerts them to errors such as atheism, pantheism, polytheism, materialism, determinism, etc.

As John Paul II remarks, the contribution of faith is not merely negative. It makes a twofold positive contribution, subjective and objective. Subjectively, faith purifies the heart of the philosopher, rendering him more perceptive. It overcomes the pride and presumptuousness that so often blind philosophers, and at the same time gives them the courage to tackle problems that might seem too daunting. Objectively, it gives a view of the universe that commends itself to human reason. It suggests answers to properly philosophical problems that are in principle accessible to reason, but which philosophers might not be able to find without the hints given by revelation. I like to compare this situation to a textbook in mathematics that has the answers to the problems in the back of the book. Knowing the answers helps is no substitute for solving the problem; however it can help the student find the right solution. So, too, revelation suggests answers to philosophical problems that philosophers might not be able to find on their own.

Examples from the field of natural theology come readily to mind. Assisted by biblical revelation, philosophy is able to establish that there is only one God; that God is wise, loving, and personal; that he is eternal, infinite, immutable, etc. The arguments that philosophers make from the nature of God as *ipsum esse subsistens* do not depend intrinsically on any premises from revelation. They are philosophically valid but would not have occurred to philosophers without the extrinsic help of revelation.

So likewise in the field of anthropology, philosophy is able to show that the human being has a spiritual soul that is naturally immortal. In a Christian civilization, philosophers can find a solid philosophical basis for asserting the dignity and rights of the individual person, the freedom of the will, the capacity to commit sin and to merit rewards, etc. The contemporary debate about abortion too often overlooks the foundation for the rights of the unborn in reason. The problem is treated almost exclusively as a religious issue, indeed as a sectarian one.

The field of cosmology offers many instances of philosophy operating under the aegis of faith. As Christians, we believe that the world was freely created by

God and this belief has suggested to philosophers arguments that the world does not exist by necessity, as the ancient Greeks supposed, but only because of a free decision of God's will. The universe, therefore, is radically contingent. It lacks any reason for existence in itself.

The question of evolution has been a focus of heated debate. Here, again, Christian philosophers are called to make a contribution. Does intelligent design on the part of a Creator mean that God has to intervene at particular points in the process, or can a process that looks like sheer chance from below be identical with the execution of a divine plan? Scientists, philosophers, and theologians all have something to say in this area, but they can do better in collaboration than if they revive the wars of the past.

IV

The fourth situation of philosophy is within theology. John Paul II, turning to this situation in *Fides et Ratio* (§77) reflects on the term *ancilla theologiae*. At this point philosophers put their skills at the service of theology for the purpose of better understanding the data of revelation. The Greek Fathers and the early councils, as we know, made extensive use of philosophical terms and categories in order to ponder mysteries such as the Trinity, the Incarnation, the Eucharist, and predestination. While contributing their skills to theology, Christian philosophers enriched their own discipline. The idea of subsistent relations, important for the doctrine of the Trinity, could not have arisen apart from theology. The same may be said for the concept of transubstantiation, much used in Eucharistic theology. Although these concepts first arise within philosophical theology, they have implications outside of theology. The theory of causality was perfected, for example, by the Christian doctrine of creation—a causal operation that presupposes nothing on the part of the recipient. Modern personalist philosophy has derived great benefit from theology. Personalist philosophy, for example, builds on the distinction between person and nature that was developed in theology.

At this fourth level, the distinction between philosophy and theology is more difficult to maintain. The philosophical theologian must be adept in both fields but still keep them apart. The same individual can speak now as a philosopher and now as a theologian. St. Thomas Aquinas, O.P., for example, wrote a number of purely philosophical works, such as his commentaries on Aristotle and his *De ente et essentia*. Francisco Suárez, S.J., produced the first Christian textbook on metaphysics, a purely philosophical work. Karl Rahner, S.J., composed some purely philosophical works, such as his *Spirit in the World*, and Karol Wojtyla did likewise in his *The Acting Person*.

V

The question may now be raised—and I put it only as a question—whether there is a level of discourse that transcends the distinction between philosophy and theology, blending them into one. As usually understood, theology deals with the contents of Christian revelation rather than with reality as a whole; philosophy deals with reality as a whole, but only without the light of faith. Believers have a hard time putting their faith into brackets and saying only what they could say if they lacked the help of revelation. For this reason I would like to think that there could be such a thing as integral wisdom, which studies the whole of reality with the tools of philosophy and theology together.

This kind of overarching worldview with the combined resources of reason and revelation does not lack a certain foundation in the Bible. In the very first paragraph of *Fides et Ratio*, John Paul II points out that similar questions are asked in the sacred literature of Israel and in that of India, China, and Greece. In chapter 2, he notes that the Wisdom literature of the Old Testament picks up themes from that of Egypt and Mesopotamia. The first stage of divine revelation occurs in the book of nature, which, when read with the proper tools of human reason, can lead to knowledge of the Creator (*FR*, §19). But at a certain point human reason runs up against its limits and needs the added light of the gospel in order to transcend them. If it refuses this further revelation, reason becomes proud and turns into foolishness, as Paul points out in the opening chapter of Romans.

John Paul II seems to be pressing for a recovery of the broad concept of theology espoused by some of the early Christian thinkers. Clement of Alexandria, for example, declared that he had found in the gospel "the true philosophy," and that "we call philosophers those who love the wisdom that is creator and mistress of all things, that is, knowledge of the Son of God" (*Stromata*, *FR*, §38). Their philosophy, while it no longer restricts itself to the unaided light of reason, still seeks the wisdom that is the goal of philosophy itself.

Vatican II hints at this broader vision of wisdom. In the Pastoral Constitution *Gaudium et Spes*, the Council declares that faith does not simply disclose a number of revealed truths; it "casts a new light on everything, manifests God's design for man's total vocation, and thus directs the mind toward solutions that are fully human" (*GS*, §11). In its closing message "To Men of Thought and Science," Vatican II exhorted intellectuals to see real science and real faith as friends of one another. "Have confidence in faith," it declared, "this great friend of intelligence. Enlighten yourselves with its light in order to take hold of truth, the whole truth." [2]

Throughout *Fides et Ratio* John Paul II urges philosophers not to take refuge in merely linguistic or historical studies but to grapple with the great metaphysical questions that have always been the concern of the wise. As philosophy comes to deal with the true, the beautiful, and the good in their full range, it enters into closer relations with revealed religion.

VI

Before closing, I would like to say a few words about philosophy and the new evangelization. Paul VI, in launching the program, spoke of the need for an evangelization of cultures, because cultural situations can dispose people to be unreceptive to the gospel. The prevalent culture in the West, and increasingly throughout the world, is consumerist. Consumerism, though hardly a philosophical system, has philosophical roots that go back several centuries.

Influenced by the agnosticism of the Kantian school, people have lost confidence in the possibility of gaining real knowledge about anything that transcends what the senses can perceive. They consequently write off religious convictions as arbitrary decisions of the will, rooted perhaps in the unconscious or in ideology, but in any case unsupported by rational grounds. Religion is regarded as something like music—a hobby for those who are inclined to it. In this context people look for satisfactions here and now. The majority seek to pile up wealth and material goods that will secure such satisfactions.

Pope John Paul II in *Fides et Ratio* calls attention to a variety of contemporary philosophical deviations, such as subjectivism, relativism, historicism, scientism, and pragmatism. Because people doubt that it is possible to get to any solid truth in matters of religion, their religion is permeated with these errors. Subjectivism means an acceptance of the idea that there is no objectively binding truth, but that people may content themselves with finding what is true for them, as though each of us had a different truth. Historical or cultural relativism means that ideas are always culture-bound. The wisdom of the past is no longer valid for today because it was conditioned by a cultural framework that no longer exists. The teaching of Scripture and tradition, therefore, can no longer be treated as having more than historical interest. Scientism means the presumption that true knowledge and progress are achievable only by exact measurement and rigorous calculation, which are thought to be the methods of science. Pragmatism means that truth is not to be found in abstract theory but in applicability, what actually pays off, what William James called "cash value." Religion can be useful if it makes people happy and induces them to become better citizens, but it can also lead to hatred and violence, as is obvious in our day. Religion is therefore judged by purely secular criteria.

These errors, rather than others that are strictly theological, are the principal obstacles to religious faith and to the new evangelization. For this reason I would plead with you who are philosophers to take on these tendencies and expose their superficiality. I hope that as Christian and Catholic philosophers you will feel a sense of responsibility to secure the foundations of faith.

The new evangelization, to be successful, must be accompanied by a new apologetics. To clear the way for an effective proclamation of the gospel, philosophers must help to dispel the climate of opinion that makes people antecedently dismiss any such proclamation as incredible. Philosophers might also help to work out a theory of testimony. Paul VI and John Paul II agreed that the modern world is more influenced by witness than by argument. Most people, however, lack an adequate epistemology of testimony. What are the qualities that make a witness credible? The old textbooks spoke of competence and truthfulness, but further work is needed to show what witnesses are competent to be bearers of divine revelation, and what kind of truth is to be sought in the gospel. Some good work has been done in this field, but I doubt that it is known to most teachers and to their students.

While philosophy can make an essential contribution to the new evangelization, I would like to add a word of caution. Philosophy by itself cannot account for the whole process of coming to the faith. The key element in any conversion is the grace of God which enlightens the mind and attracts the will. To sort out the respective contributions of nature and grace requires a cooperative effort on the part of philosophers and theologians together. We must not be content to perpetuate a kind of departmental isolation that makes adherents of the two disciplines strangers to each other. This conference should help in a modest way to overcome the estrangement.

NOTES

1. Pope John Paul II, *Fides et Ratio* (September 14, 1998), §76 at http://www.vatican.va/holy_father/john_paul_ii/encyclicals/documents/hf_jpii_enc_1510 1998_fides-et-ratio_en.html.

2. Abbot, Walter M., S.J., ed., *The Documents of Vatican II: in a New and Definitive Translation, with Commentaries and Notes by Catholic, Protestant and Orthodox authorities.* Trans. Joseph Gallagher (New York: Herder & Herder, Association Press, 1966), 731.

CHAPTER TWO

THE THOMISTIC META-STRUCTURE OF POPE JOHN PAUL II'S DOCTRINAL INITIATIVES

Steven A. Long. Ph. D.

INTRODUCTION

It's a joy and honor to greet you at the start of this conference on the vocation of the Catholic intellectual, "Habits of the Mind." As Catholics we enjoy the legacy of a strong doctrine of the divine Providence. This should console you for the mammoth speculative extravaganza you are about to suffer during this after-dinner hour. If God were only slightly less omnipotent than He is, I would be worried whether He could sustain anyone's habits of mind through such after-dinner commentary. It reminds me of Bertrand Russell's comment, when a friend breathlessly said to him, "I didn't know that your yacht is as big as it is!" Russell responded, "Oh no, my yacht is every bit as big as it is!" God is every bit as omnipotent as He is—and this lecture every bit as ambitious—and so, tonight you are really in for it.

This evening I will argue that the content—and even more importantly, what I call the "meta-structure"—of John Paul II's doctrinal initiatives may best be characterized in terms of classical Thomism. However, this account must be preceded by the removal of some obstructive scenery from the pathway to our topic. I will first remove the obstructive scenery—about which, more in a moment—and then I will turn directly to my argument about the character of John Paul II's doctrinal initiatives.

I. OBSTRUCTIVE SCENERY: AN INCORRECT NARRATIVE HISTORY OF THOMISM

The obstructive scenery is a common but incorrect narrative history of Thomism in the postconciliar epoch. According to this history, the papal predilection for Thomism has in the postconciliar period become an embarrassed shadow of itself, and the story of Thomism is presented as that of a theological and philosophic school progressively marginalized and abandoned. For many who read history in this way, the real tale is reduced to canon law. Once, we are told, there were more exacting requirements imposed by the Church upon those who teach in Catholic institutions, obliging them to follow the spirit and doctrine of Thomas both in theology and in philosophy. But now it is only in theology that Thomas's teaching is mentioned in canon law, and indeed, even this mention often is thought to be chiefly a venerable but worn-out honorific title with no very significant effect upon the cutting edge of theological development. This is the depiction that I want briefly to clear away, before progressing further. It is a depiction that boasts some erudite advocates. Professor Pereira of Fordham University has published an essay—"Thomism and the Magisterium: From *Aeterni Patris* to *Veritatis Splendor*"—arguing that *Veritatis Splendor* is noteworthy for promulgating the "abrogation" of the canonic "imposition of Thomism."[1] Since *Veritatis Splendor* is by my reckoning the single most Thomistic papal encyclical since *Aeterni Patris* over one hundred years ago, this claim of Professor Pereira has captured my attention.

A proper response to his argument must of course begin and end by noting what Prof. Pereira himself acknowledges: that Pope John Paul II himself speaks of the doctrine of Thomistic metaphysics as of the prime synthetic truth of Christian philosophy. Granted that there is no philosophy simply of the Church—as though the Church were commissioned by Our Lord to preach Thomism to the world as saving doctrine—there nonetheless is a philosophy in the Church, a point that has been well made by Cardinal Biffi (in the first volume of *Doctor Communis*). The principles and structure of being are presupposed by divine revelation. As Fr. Jan Walgrave, O.P., the great Newman scholar, has noted, it is not possible to understand Sacred Scripture without presupposing philosophic principles and categories.[2]

So no one—least of all Professor Pereira—disputes the historic predilection of the papacy for Thomism, although Prof. Pereira does suggest that there are now too many Thomisms for us easily to identify the real artifact. Undeniably there are boundary issues regarding the delineation of any philosophic school. But the claim that the term "Thomism" is equivocal often is trotted out as an obliging show pony by those who know very well precisely what it is that they don't like about Thomism. For example, it is clear enough what Professor Pereira doesn't like about Thomas's teaching, and he communicates this to us the way that only an accomplished essayist can. He cites his master Suárez after having lauded as inspiration for his essay Fr. José Hellin, S.J., whom he describes in the very first footnote as "the greatest Suárezian of our times." Professor Pereira dislikes the doctrine of the real distinction of essence and existence, about which one has no doubt that he concurs with Suárez that this doctrine is "ridiculous and entirely unintelligible."[3] Granted the divergences in Thomistic interpretation, there are points about which no one who knows the text is in doubt, and that Thomas teaches a real distinction of essence and existence is one of these points.

Hence the difficulty posed by the narrative history I criticize tonight is not that no one can figure out what Thomism is. The question is only this: does the absence of express mention of the normativity of Thomas's philosophy in the new code of canon law constitute a retreat from the high tide of papal acknowledgment of Thomism? Further, what does the pope intend when he writes in *Veritatis Splendor* (§29), "Certainly the Church's Magisterium does not intend to impose upon the faithful any particular theological system, still less a philosophical one."

One might question the interpretation of canon law offered by Professor Pereira. He construes the lack of express mention of Thomistic philosophy in the new code of canon law as implying the lapse of the antecedent papal support for Thomism. But the new code of Canon Law promulgated by Pope John Paul II in 1983 (*Codes Iuris Canonici*, 1983) does (§ 251) mention that philosophic studies must be based upon the "philosophical heritage that is perennially valid." One who reads this phrase in the light of prior papal teaching (for example, in this century, *Lumen Ecclesiae* by Paul VI, or the allocution by John Paul II in 1980 on the centenary of *Aeterni Patris*) will realize it is at least highly probable that this "perennially valid" heritage is intended to include doctrines such as that of the real distinction of essence and existence—a doctrine highly lauded by several pontiffs including Pope John Paul II.

Further, the express reference in canon law to teaching the theology of Thomas presupposes his philosophy, because his theology necessarily depends upon antecedent affirmations deriving from his philosophy. Only someone unacquainted with Thomas's theology could suppose it to be wholly separable from his philosophy. Given the exertions of papal teaching asserting Thomism's distinctive and universal value, this seems to be an unlikely depiction of papal intent. Finally, the passage from *Veritatis Splendor* about non-imposition of any theological or philosophical system would also war against the stress in canon law noted by Prof. Pereira upon the normativity of Thomistic theology for theological instruction.

Professor Pereira is not unaware of these conundrums. He even quotes the exuberant praise of John Paul II for Thomas's teaching. Pereira quotes the Pope concerning Thomas' universalism, saying that it is:

> Openness to reality in all its parts and dimensions, without reduction or particularisms (without the absolutization of single aspects).... This openness has its basis and its origin in the fact that the philosophy of St. Thomas is a philosophy of existence, that is, of the *actus essendi* ("act of existence"), whose transcendental value is the most direct way to rise up to the knowledge of Subsistent Existence and Pure Act, which is God. For such a reason, this philosophy can absolutely be called the proclamation of existence, a hymn in honor of the existent.[4]

Professor Pereira further proceeds to quote the Holy Father's praise of St. Thomas's doctrine of the *actus essendi* or act of existence:

> All the richness of the content of reality has its origin in the "act of existence." It has in an anticipatory manner, so to speak, the right to all that is true with reference to reality. Inversely, all comprehension of reality...has full right of citizenship in the "philosophy of existence," independently of who has approved such an advancement of understanding and irrespective of the philosophical school to which he belongs.[5]

So let's leave aside canonic arguments and note only what Prof. Pereira himself admits: namely, that this pope, like the last several popes, teaches that of all the analogates of Christian philosophy, Thomas's is the most exalted and universal—the most open to all that is of worth wherever it derives—because his teaching is paridigmatically open to being and to the principles of being. The pope is not speaking in a merely private capacity, but as summarizing the Petrine attitude to Aquinas's legacy.

This is all we need to handle criticisms like those of Professor Pereira, because philosophy is not chiefly a matter of canonic imposition, but of teaching. And although the modality in which the Petrine predilection for Thomism is expressed may be altered (in the prudential alignments consequent upon the Second Vatican Council), the substance of that predilection appears unchanged. Even if one cedes the premise that the Church's canon law no longer distinctively recommends Thomas's philosophy—a proposition that seems to me historically amnesiac—even so, the substantive theological commitment of the Church is not reducible to its mere canonic expression.

But what of the words of *Veritatis Splendor*? It is true that this encyclical states that, "Certainly the Church's Magisterium does not intend to impose upon the faithful any particular theological system, still less a philosophical one." This is true. Nor does anyone need to make formal profession acknowledging the principle of non-contradiction in order to receive baptism; nor is it mandatory—despite the essentiality of the doctrine of the trinity—that one even be capable of counting to three. Nor are the rules of grammar either in any vulgar tongue—or even Latin itself—absolute requirements for access to the sacraments: a proposition that answers to that ancient disputed question: whether even freshmen undergraduates can be saved. In fact, the Church has always made way for the baptism of idiots and the mentally impaired. Clearly, the height of doctrinal intelligence is not the minimal requirement for communion. But surely this is not a sign that the Church no longer realizes a need either for philosophy in general or for the philosophy of Aquinas in particular. These lines from *Veritatis Splendor* constitute rather a slender reed upon which to hang the claim that the Church herself—to the degree that she has recourse to philosophy—does not principally have recourse to that philosophy that the past ten or fifteen pontificates—including this one—most highly praise.

But everything I've said thus far was said by Thomas Aquinas in one sentence, several hundred years ago (in his work *Contra Retrahentes*, 13): "It is unseemly and rather ridiculous for theologians to cite canon lawyers as theological authorities, or to be occupied with points of legal detail." Having removed the argument from extrinsic denomination of canon law against this pontificate's dominating preference for the teaching of Aquinas, this brings us back to the issue of the Thomistic character of this pontificate's doctrinal initiatives.

II. THE THOMISTIC META-STRUCTURE OF THIS PONTIFICATE'S DOCTRINAL INITIATIVES

What I really want to propose at the outset of this conference is—to use a Bonaventurian turn of phrase—that we "taste and see" the synthesis of high Thomism that characterizes this pontificate's major doctrinal initiatives. Toward this end I wish to propose not only that there are several quite expressly Thomistic propositions lurking in these encyclicals, but something far more striking: that the whole "meta-structure" of John Paul II's teaching has been masterfully and profoundly Thomistic from beginning to end. This meta-structure of papal teaching is best considered in relation to the objects of papal criticism on the one hand, and the geneology of these objects on the other. Theology and philosophy, like other disciplines, have what one may with Karl Popper call a "problem situation," that is, a function of prior speculative history. It is in relation to the deep problem situation of theology—considered from an intra-Catholic and Thomistic vantage point—that the character of this pontificate's doctrinal initiatives are best assessed.

So, what are the objects criticized, and what is their geneology? It is fairly clear that in his encyclicals John Paul II adversely identifies, criticizes, and corrects a postmodern theological pluralism and moral relativism. The encyclicals clearly confute extreme autonomism and place freedom in an intellectualist and providentialist context wherein it is divinely ordered to be perfected in and by the truth. The metaphysical definition given by St. Thomas of natural law—that it is nothing other than a rational participation of the eternal law—is prominently asserted within *Veritatis Splendor* (e.g., *Veritatis Splendor*, §43). This encyclical also rejects moral proportionalism as among the harmful effects caused by excessive stress upon the autonomy of the rational agent.

Positively, these encyclicals clearly teach that there is a natural truth—distinct from revealed truth—which concerns the good of the human person. They also insist upon the mediative function for theology of a metaphysical appropriation of this natural truth;[6] upon its importance for knowledge of the moral good;[7] and indeed as noted above upon the character of this law as participating eternal law. The Thomistic provenance of all this is more than clear, even when it is not accompanied by citations to the text of Thomas itself, as it often is. Along similar lines, the Congregation for the Doctrine of the Faith's instruction *Dominus Jesus* reaffirms the absolute character of the deposit of faith. It seeks to protect the integrity of revelation from its threatened absorption within a relativized dialectical context—the context of postmodern theological pluralism—which has for some theologians and philosophers replaced metaphysical objectivity and natural truth.

A careful reading of *Veritatis Splendor* and *Fides et Ratio* manifests the presence of three overarching positive theses: 1) the theonomic character of natural law as participating the eternal law; 2) the affirmation of metaphysical objectivity—of the knowability of being and nature; and 3) the vindication of the dignity and relative integrity of nature as a normative metaphysical principle that necessarily mediates our knowledge of divine revelation. The objects that these encyclicals criticize—the errors corrected—correlate as negations of these positive teachings: first, the error of excessive autonomism negates the theocentric character of natural law;[8] secondly, the errors of metaphysical agnosis, fideism, and rationalism negate metaphysical objectivity; and thirdly, the erroneous negation of nature as a normative mediating principle within theology negates the mediative role of nature in theology.[9]

Now, these three errors corrected by the encyclicals have a history, and indeed they have causes. If we hypothesize that the pope is looking through Thomist spectacles, what would these spectacles bring to light as the causes of the theological and philosophic errors considered above? What is their etiology? Where do they come from?

Clearly there are extra-Catholic or secular sources of origination one might look to for these errors. The second—the negation of realist metaphysics—has its home in Kantian, Hegelian, Humean, and positivist sources.[10] But the intra-Catholic sources are most prominent for the first and third of these errors, namely excessive autonomism, and the negation of nature as a metaphysically normative mediating principle in Catholic theology.

From a Thomistic vantage point, it is more than conspicuous that these errors seem essentially related to the two most profound and extensive theological controversies of the classical Thomist School in its many-storied history within the Church. These controversies are, first, the famed late sixteenth century dispute over the nature of human freedom and its relation to divine causality and Providence; and second, the nature/grace dispute that raged before the Second Vatican Council over whether the natural order of ends is possessed of a relative integrity in its own right or whether—as Henri de Lubac argued—it is even apart from grace directly ordered to supernatural beatitude.

The chief error that any Thomist would—and did—predict, inasmuch as human freedom comes to be viewed as a liberty of indifference to divine providence, is an error of excessive autonomism transforming human judgment into a jurisdiction outside divine providence and the eternal law. And the error which any Thomist contemplating the nature/grace controversy would—and did—predict, was the loss of nature as a normative theological principle, and the consequent reduction of nature from being preamble to grace, to being a pure nought whose content will relativistically fluctuate according to the intra-theological dialectic of the moment.

I do not claim that the present pope overtly sympathizes with the Thomistic School in these earlier disputes. I do claim: a) that these are the most extensive and fundamental theological disputes in the history of Thomism; b) that prominent exponents of the classical Thomist School did strongly warn that excessive autonomism and the relativization and historicization of theological method and teaching are necessarily implied by the doctrines about freedom and nature that the Thomists opposed in these disputes; c) that these implications have become widespread with equal pace, *pari passu*, alongside the doctrines about freedom and nature that Thomists oppose; and finally d) that John Paul II has acted directly, clearly, and forcefully to clean up what—to a Thomist—look like the effects of an earlier theological train wreck.

A wise Thomistic pontiff, looking at the brood of troubles spawned by these improvident teachings, would not reach his hand back into the hornet's nest of the original controversies, which were obscure and difficult at the time, and which with the passage of time have grown only more difficult of access. Rather, he would take it upon himself to close down the highway of implications that flow from these teachings, so that traffic along these pernicious routes will eventually die out and be supplanted by the happy commerce of the Catholic tradition. This Thomistic masterstroke is exactly what Pope John Paul II has performed in *Veritatis Splendor* and *Fides et Ratio*.

Of course, any authentic school of Catholic theology and philosophy might produce an account congruent with these encyclicals. But as an historical and doctrinal matter it is uniquely the Thomistic school that warned of precisely the errors corrected by these encyclicals as speculative effects flowing from earlier grave mistakes within theology. It was Fr. Labourdette, O.P., editor of *Revue Thomiste*, who publicly feared lest theology as *scientia* would be replaced by a babble of relativized and historicized "approaches", and lest "pluralism" be a code word for the abandonment of every conceptual advance won for theology by St. Thomas's theological contemplation. It was Garrigou-Lagrange, O.P., who in the twentieth century warned that a non-intellectualist and non-Providentialist account of human freedom had near-Pelagian roots, and would necessarily retard basic elements of the spiritual life in preference for excessive autonomy.[11] Even those who think there to be too many Thomisms to say what Thomism is, cannot bring themselves to make-believe that Labourdette and Garrigou-Lagrange are not unequivocal representatives of a well-delineated Thomist School—what Prof. Pereira himself—expressly mentioning Garrigou-Lagrange— calls "the enduring school of classical Thomism."

III. A THOMISTIC ETIOLOGY OF THE ERRORS CRITICIZED BY *VERITATIS SPLENDOR* AND *FIDES ET RATIO*

In the remainder of my remarks, I will try briefly to present a thumbnail Thomistic etiology or causal analysis—a Thomistic doctrinal pre-history, as it were—of moral autonomism and of the negation of nature as a normative principle within theology. Of course, this violates the protocol according to which no one can possibly know what Thomism is. But like the view that no one can know where New York is, the simplest answer is to go there.

A. Doctrinal Etiology of Moral Autonomism

As to moral autonomism, we now know the thing in question all too well—the claim that the freedom of the person cannot be subject to universal norms or a higher law without losing its own spontaneity and inner excellence, so that it itself must create its own unique and unrepeatable "values." Such an autonomism is essentially a Nietzchean parody, with the Last Man playing the role of übermensch. But how does it have its roots in Catholic theological judgment, let alone preconciliar theological judgment?

From the vantage point of Thomism, the remote conditioning for moral autonomism begins with Molina's sixteenth-century denial that the perfection of our acts of freedom has its first cause in God.[12] If we view this controversy in its principles, we first see a controversy over the question whether freedom is a rational power, such that our liberty is a function of the rational specification of the will by its formal object, the universal good. According to St. Thomas, no finite good may compel the will, because the intellect presents the finite good to the will as a good that is limited and therefore in some respect "not-good." Since every finite good may be considered in some way "not-good," no finite good may command the will, which retains a dominating indifference with respect to any finite good even while embracing it. This does not mean that the will is able to act without divine aid, nor that if we knew God as God we would be "free" to abandon Him. According to St. Thomas, the human will is defined as free relative to its finite contingent objects (*De malo*, q. 16, a.7.ad 15) and not because it stands outside the divine causality.[13]

Viewed under a different aspect, the controversy about God and the will concerns the "couplet" of the metaphysical principles of act and potency—whether these are genuinely metaphysical principles that apply to the human person and hence to the nature of human freedom in relation to divine causality, or whether they pertain instead only to lower physical beings, or do not pertain at all.[14] So viewed, this is the first controversy between autonomist personalism and Thomism, and is mirrored by more recent similar controversies.[15]

Considered from the most formal and metaphysical perspective, the question is whether God is genuinely the first cause of every perfection of being. If so, then God must be the first cause of the perfection of our free acts of self-determination, and this is indeed the teaching of Aquinas. Hence he writes in *De malo*, q. 3, a. 2 ad 4, that "when anything moves itself, this does not exclude its being moved by another, from which it has even this that it moves itself. Thus it is not repugnant to liberty that God is the cause of the free act of the will."[16]

Thomas famously argues (*ST* I-II, q. 109, a. 1, resp.) that no creature, no matter how noble, can even proceed to its act unless it first be moved by God, and that the action of any created being depends upon God in two ways, "first inasmuch as it is from Him that it has the form whereby it acts; secondly, inasmuch as it is moved by Him to act."[17]

One recalls the famous formulation of Molina[18]—who disputed the teaching of St. Thomas on these points—in the *Concordia* that the will is free only when, all requirements being retained, the will can indeed act otherwise.[19] This proposition—true of all terrestrial causes—is impossible with respect to the hypothetical but immutable divine willing of created effects. For what changes with this hypothetical but immutable divine willing—owing to the divine simplicity—is not God, but rather only the creature itself. *Thus one cannot retain the requirement that God cause the creature freely to act while the creature is not causes freely to act, because this is a contradiction in terms.*

The relation of the absolutization of human freedom to an excessive moral autonomy is necessary and direct. It is a constant of natural theology that God's providence extends as far as his power and that God is omnipotent.[20] Hence

Thomas writes "For since every agent acts for an end, the ordering of effects towards that end extends as far as the causality of the first agent extends."[21] And again: "Hence all things that exist in whatsoever manner are necessarily directed by God towards the end";[22] and again: "it necessarily follows that all things, inasmuch as they participate being, must to that extent be subject to divine providence."[23] In the very article wherein Thomas defines natural law as nothing other than a participation of the eternal law (*ST* I-II, q. 91, a. 2) he expressly conditions subjection to the eternal law on prior subjection to divine providence: "Since all things subject to Divine providence are ruled and measured by the eternal law, as was stated above; it is evident that all things partake somewhat of the eternal law."[24]

If we remove the positive substance of man's free acts from the transcendent divine causality, it will follow as a necessary corollary that the positive substance of these free acts is alike removed from divine providence. And that which lies outside divine providence is not subject to the direction of eternal law. From this point onward, that which for St. Thomas defines the natural law—namely, that it is a rational participation in the eternal law—will become something extraneous and alien.[25] If we deny that the human will receives its natural motion, and the application of its natural motion in any particular free determination, from God, then we establish a realm of being and perfection—that of human action—to which the divine causality, and hence the divine government, does not extend.[26] On this supposition, finite human creatures roam the earth creating *ex nihilo* the added perfection or reality of their free determinations, entirely outside of the divine causality, the divine providence, and the eternal law. The volitional agent is thus removed from the divine jurisdiction in being removed from the divine causality. This directly implies a way of understanding the natural law that Thomas's philosophy and theology prohibit—a way which treats nature and natural law not as manifestations of divine government but as demarcating a zone of independence from divine governance.[27]

Nature and reason go from being manifestations and expressions of normative divine order, to being antipodes of divine order to which one may appeal in order to "safeguard" human freedom from divine authority. God moves from being the author and perfector of human liberty and virtue, to being a threat to authentic human freedom and an alien distortive influence upon morality. The symmetry of these implications with Kantian autonomism is arresting. Yet unlike the express rationalism of Kant, these implications flow from a Catholic effort to grapple with a most central issue of natural theology: that of the reconciliation of divine causality and human freedom.

It will be discerned that in this movement we transit from a view of what Pope John Paul II wisely calls participated theonomy to a view of natural law as a zone of rational autonomy from divine governance.[28]

Having made of human liberty a demiurgic divinity, it becomes understandable that its worshippers feel obliged to protect the theophany of this strange god. Thus we are not surprised to hear the words of Joseph Füchs—the famed continental author on the natural law—who argues that the idea that

> The human person is illuminated by a light that comes, not from one's own reason . . . but from the wisdom of God in whom everything is created . . . cannot stand up to an objective analysis nor prove helpful in the vocabulary of Christian believers.[29]

He further holds that:

> Neither the Hebrew Bible nor the New Testament produces statements that are independent of culture and thus universal and valid for all time; nor can these statements be given by the church or its magisterium. Rather, it is the task of human beings—of the various persons who have been given the requisite intellectual capacity—to investigate what can and must count as a conviction about these responsibilities.[30]

Russell Hittinger has commented about Füchs that

> It follows from his own doctrine that while God creates, he does not govern the human mind. The human mind is a merely natural light, to which there corresponds a merely natural jurisdiction over ethics.[31]

But how or why should utterly unmoved volitional first movers—autonomous demiurges—receive a natural law not first caused by themselves? Nor are we shocked to discover the late Bernard Häring, or Karl Rahner, or any of the usual Teutonic suspects, holding forth to the same effect and denying the ontological competency of the Church herself to define particular moral norms.

This is the very artery of autonomist traffic decisively closed down by *Veritatis Splendor*. This encyclical makes luminously clear that man's freedom is a created and rational liberty, and that it is providentially governed so as to be perfected in and by the truth rather than constituting an autonomous jurisdiction immune from divine governance and law. The Thomistic authors of the Dominican submission to the *Congregatio de Auxiliis*, if they had to craft an encyclical to address the dangerous moral implications of the erroneous view of freedom they criticized—implications which I think it may truthfully be said that they predicted—would write: *Veritatis Splendor*.

B. Doctrinal Etiology of the Negation of the Normativity of Nature Within Theology

The case is similar with respect to the loss of any normative concept of nature as essential to the integrity of theology. In devising his way beyond the apologetically motivated and overly abstract veneer of scholastic manualism, Thomists argue that Henri de Lubac—orthodox beyond peradventure of doubt— unwittingly authored a doctrine equally distortive of Catholic life: namely, his teaching that human nature is in itself and apart from supernatural grace directly ordered to the beatific vision.[32]

As with the question of God's causality of free acts, I cannot presume here fully to engage this issue at its appropriate level of complexity.[33]

Here my object is simply to point out the implications of De Lubac's teaching from a Thomistic vantage point. According to St. Thomas, natures are known by powers, powers are known by acts, acts are known by their objects, and objects are known in relation to their ends. Thus if human nature is directly ordered to supernatural beatitude apart from grace—De Lubac's renowned thesis—human nature becomes nothing other than an exigency for the divine, a pure function of the transcendent God, undefinable and absolutely unintelligible apart from the divine mystery.

It is here that we must do a Thomistic thing: we must make a distinction. Because although in this order of providence, in which man is created in grace, all ends are only ends at all because they are ordered to the *finis ultimus* of supernatural beatitude, nonetheless nature itself is distinguishable from the order of providence to which it now is subject. Were this not so, the doctrine of the Incarnation would make no sense: the Word's assumption of human nature would be an assumption of we-know-not-what, the assumption of a mere vacuole waiting to be filled. Although it is certainly true that in the given actual synthesis of divine providence nature is vain apart from grace, it is not true that there is no distinguishable order of ends proportioned to nature apart from the graced providential ordering to supernatural beatitude.[34]

Aquinas clearly argues (in *ST* I, q. 75, a. 7, ad 1) that man and angel are specifically different because they have different proportionate natural ends even though they share the same supernatural beatific end—which clearly implies that there is a natural order of ends definable in precision from supernatural grace. In his *Quaestiones Quodlibetales,* Thomas expressly teaches that God could have created man in a state of pure nature (e.g., *Quod.* I, q. 4, a.3, resp.). Further, in *De malo*, q. 5, art. 1, ad 15, Thomas writes that, had man not been created in sanctifying grace, then the deprivation of the beatific vision would be not a punishment but merely a defect. As he puts it:

> Man endowed with only natural powers would be without the divine vision if he were to die in this state, but nevertheless the debt of not having it would not be applicable to him. For it is one thing not to be bound to have, which does not have the nature of punishment but of defect only, and it is another thing to be bound not to have, which does have the nature of punishment.

Clearly, if the natural desire for God were simply the same thing as graced desire for supernaturally beatific vision, then it would follow that to be perpetually deprived of this end proper to nature would be a punishment. But St. Thomas teaches exactly the contrary.

This point is not a remote and merely exegetic one. In this controversy with De Lubac, Thomists[35]—such as Fr. Labourdette, O.P., of the *Revue Thomiste*, Fr. M.-J. Nicolas, O.P.,[36] and Fr. Garrigou-Lagrange, O.P.,[37]—feared lest the character of theology and philosophy as scientia be impugned or denied in the life of the Church. Thomists—very conspicuously, Fr. Labourdette—argued that if the normativity of natural order were removed from theology that theology would dissolve into a relativized historicity. Lacking any normative conception of natural order as such, Catholics would find themselves thrust into a chasm between the necessarily absolute mission and teaching of the magisterium and a soup of dialectical relativism lacking any language in which to affirm natural law and integrity as immutably essential components of Christian life. Within such a context, lacking any normative concept of nature, the assertions of the magisterium would travel the abyss only to be heard on the other side as raw assertions of ecclesial power.

De Lubac's thesis cuts away at the prime Thomistic thesis that nature is the preamble to grace, for his teaching implies the reduction of nature to a placeholder awaiting total redefinition in and by grace. From being the methodic root of our speech and distinctions, the first creation, and the preamble of grace, human nature becomes a cipher wholly constituted by revealed theology. Man's relative natural transcendence is absolutized into an ordering directly to the inner reality of God, and the role of our meditation upon the first creation in fathoming the life of grace is rendered not a preamble to, but instead purely a postscript of, divine revelation.[38] Hence the followers of De Lubac even today befittingly follow him in arguing that in theological instruction the treatise on the trinity should precede the treatise *De Deo uno*, because natural knowledge of God is no longer in their view methodologically and epistemically prior within theological contemplation.

The problem is that this teaching leaves to human nature only what is generated by intra-theological dialectic. The effective nullification of human nature as a normative principle within theology leads to the absorption of theological dialectic within either a rationalism relativized by the lack of natural foundation, or a fideist absolutism closed to the human intelligence. It is precisely the urgent need to correct these baneful effects that spurred and brought forth the encyclical *Fides et Ratio*.

While even today it is a widely taught commonplace that the Second Vatican Council validated De Lubac's account of nature and grace, we find a different resonance in the insistence of the prologue to *Fides et Ratio* that theology requires two wings, those of nature and of grace, and that it requires a speculative metaphysical appropriation of nature [§83]. Of the role of the metaphysical appropriation of nature in relation to theology, *Fides et Ratio* affirms that:

> Metaphysics thus plays an essential role of mediation in theological research. A theology without a metaphysical horizon could not move beyond an analysis of religious experience, nor would it allow the *intellectus fidei* to give a coherent account of the universal and transcendent value of revealed truth.[39]

Clearly it is one thing to affirm that God reveals man to himself; it is something else to say that the revelation of man's higher destiny in grace does not presuppose the relative integrity of created nature. *Fides et Ratio* affirms (§34) that revelation is not opposed to "the truths which philosophy perceives" and that the fullness of truth is found in natural and revealed knowledge, the unity of whose truth is [§34] a "fundamental premise of human reasoning as the principle of non-contradiction makes clear." The same encyclical affirms that nature is indeed the preamble to grace, that it is knowable in precision therefrom, and cites as true [§75] the Thomistic maxim that grace does not destroy nature but rather perfects it.[40] It is not inconceivable that the pope wrote this with no motive with respect to De Lubac's thesis, or even positively approving it: but the logical incompatibility is patent. Likewise many orthodox Catholic scholars today prefer placing the treatise on the trinity (*De Deo Trino*) in advance of the treatise on the one God (*De Deo uno*)—and so favor quickly bypassing the mediating function of the metaphysical appropriation of nature *vis a vis* revelation. But the theological teaching advanced in *Fides et Ratio* stands to the contrary and is not a private initiative—even though, *pace* Professor Pereira, it is after all merely the province of theological teaching rather than of canon law.

IV. CONCLUSION: THE NEW THOMIST MILLENNIUM

This pontificate has authoritatively corrected the errors of moral autonomism, and of free-floating theological dialectics severed from the metaphysical appropriation of nature. John Paul II has given us a map of the future. The theology and philosophy of the future will be metaphysically realist; it will embrace the first creation of nature as preamble to grace; and it will yield a moral theology which is centered on the graced development of the life of theological, infused, and acquired virtues in accord with man's natural and graced participations in eternal law. Perhaps, *mirabile dictu*—wonder to behold—the profound convergence of these concerns with classical Thomism is a mere accident. But whatever the papal motivation behind this work of doctrinal articulation, in this new millennium—and for this Thomist—it counts as a terrestrial epiphany of the heavenly "Triumph of St. Thomas" so well depicted in art, and as a sign of the authentic renewal of the Catholic life for the sake of which the Second Vatican Council was called.

NOTES

1. Jose Pereira, "Thomism and the Magisterium: From *Aeterni Patris* to *Veritatis Splendor*," Logos: *A Journal of Catholic Thought and Culture* 5, no. 3 (Summer 2002): 146—183. Hereafter, Pereira.

2. Jan H. Walgrave, O.P., *Unfolding Revelation: The Nature of Doctrinal Development* (Philadelphia: Westminster, 1972).

3. Francisco Suárez, S.J., *Disputationes Metaphysicae*, disp. 31, sect. 12, n. 5. *Opera omnia*, vol. 26 (Paris: Vivès, 1866), 285. The translation and this citation I take from Prof. Pereira's essay.

4. John Paul II, *In Pontificia Universitate S. Thomae Aquinatis, saeculo expleto a datis Encyclicis Aeterni Patris*. Cited in Pereira, 29.

5. Ibid.

6. Cf. *Fides et Ratio* §83: "Metaphysics thus plays an essential role of mediation in theological research. A theology without a metaphysical horizon could not move beyond an analysis of religious experience, nor would it allow the intellectus fidei to give a coherent account of the universal and transcendent value of revealed truth."

7. *Fides et Ratio* (§83) affirms that metaphysical realism reaching to the affirmation of God is "a requirement for knowing the moral good," and speaks of, "the need for a philosophy of genuinely metaphysical range, capable, that is, of transcending empirical data in order to attain something absolute, ultimate and foundational in its search for truth. This requirement is implicit in *sapiential* and analytical knowledge alike; and in

particular it is a requirement for knowing the moral good, which has its ultimate foundation in the Supreme Good, God himself."

8. In *Veritatis Splendor* there are 17 references to autonomy in the text, almost all critically referring to excessive autonomy, as well as five other adjectival uses of the term

9. One may note that the second and third error seem reciprocally to imply one another. If being and nature are unknowable, then nature as a normative principle is gone; and, if nature as a knowable principle is gone, then there is nothing to know. This is the point where the extra-Catholic and intra-Catholic sources of these errors meet. Nonetheless, our primary focus is upon the first and third rather than the second error.

10. Although clearly Blondel's famous definition of truth not as "the conformity of mind with being" but of "mind with life," approximates this error from the Catholic side. For the conformity of mind with life is certainly healthful in God alone, in Whom life is the subsistent universal good. Any other sense of "life" as supreme good will be analogical and founded on this—which of course presupposes the very metaphysical *adequatio intellectus et rei* that Blondel's early formulations obscure.

11. Cf. R. Garrigou-Lagrange, O.P., *Reality*, trans. Patrick Cummins, O.S.B., (St. Louis: Herder, 1958).

12. A more comprehensive expression of my reading of these issues may be found in "Providence, liberté et loi naturelle," *Revue Thomiste* 102 (2002): 355—406.

13. *De malo*, q. 16, a. 7, ad 15: *"Et hoc quidem quantum ad scientiam patet ex his quae supra dicta sunt. Sicut enim se habet divina scientia ad futura contingentia, sic se habet oculus noster ad contingentia quae in praesenti sunt, ut dictum est. Unde sicut certissime videmus Socratem sedere cum sedet, nec tamen propter hoc sequitur quod sit simpliciter necessarium; ita etiam ex hoc quod Deus videt omnia quae eveniunt, in seipsis, non tollitur contingentia rerum. Ex parte autem voluntatis considerandum est, quod voluntas divina est universaliter causa entis, et universaliter omnium quae consequuntur modum necessitatis et contingentiae. Ipsa autem est supra ordinem necessarii et contingentis, sicut est supra totum esse creatum. Et ideo necessitas et contingentia in rebus distinguuntur non per habitudinem ad voluntatem divinam, quae est causa communis, sed per comparationem ad causas creatas, quas proportionaliter divina voluntas ad effectus ordinavit; ut scilicet necessariorum effectuum sint causae intransmutabiles, contingentium autem transmutabiles."* "And in regard to knowledge this is clear from what was said above (in the Reply to 14): for just as divine knowledge is in relation to future contingent events, so our eye is in relation to contingent things that occur here and now, as was said (in the Response); hence just as we most certainly see Socrates sitting while he is sitting, but nonetheless it does not follow from this that his sitting is absolutely necessary, so also from the fact that God sees in themselves all the things that take place, the contingency of things is not done away with. And as regards the will we must take into account that the divine will is universally the cause of being and universally of all the things that follow on this, hence even of necessity and contingency; but His will itself is above the order of the necessary or contingent just as it is above all created being. And therefore necessity and contingency in things are distinguished not in relation to the divine will, which is a universal cause, but in relation to created causes which the divine will has ordered proportionately to the effects, namely in such a way that the causes of necessary effects are unchangeable, and of contingent effects changeable." All Latin texts are taken from Thomas Aquinas, *Corpus Thomisticum: S. Thomae de Aquino Opera Omnia* (Pamplona:University of Navarre, 2000) at http://www.corpusthomisticum.org.

14. In this sense, this is the first controversy in which antinomian personalism rears its head to declare that it is not subject to metaphysical principles but supercedes these. Ever since, Thomists have found themselves attempting to reason personalists away from metaphysical separatism into the acknowledgement that the rational creature is a *creature*

rather than the metaphysically unintelligible demiurge of the various species of continental rationalism.

15. Compare, for example, the efforts to impose a quasi-Balthasarean putatively "personalist" notion of receptivity as necessarily a positive perfection of act in rational creatures because it is such in the Trinity—a *petitio principii* which is all too close to panentheism for those who know the philosophic implications of predicating of creatures what is true only of God.

16. "*Similiter cum aliquid movet se ipsum, non excluditur quin ab alio moveatur, a quo habet hoc ipsum quod se ipsum movet; et sic non repugnat libertati quod Deus est causa actus liberi arbitrii.*" The antecedent text of this response to the fourth objection is also very much to the purpose: "*Ad quartum dicendum, quod cum dicitur aliquid movere se ipsum, ponitur idem esse movens et motum; cum autem dicitur quod aliquid movetur ab altero, ponitur aliud esse movens et aliud motum. Manifestum est autem quod cum aliquid movet alterum, non ex hoc ipso quod est movens, ponitur quod est primum movens; unde non excluditur quin ab altero moveatur, et ab altero habeat similiter hoc ipsum quod movet.*"—"To the fourth it should be said that when it is said that something moves itself, that the same thing is mover and moved. But when it is said that something is moved by another, the moved is taken to be one thing and the mover another. But it is clear that when something moves another, from this it is not taken to follow that it is the first mover: wherefore it is not excluded that from another it is itself moved and from this other it has even this, that it moves." Thence the lines follow that "when something moves itself, this does not exclude that it is moved by another from which it has even this, that it moves itself. And thus it is not repugnant to liberty that God is the cause of the free act of the will."

17. *ST* I-II, q. 109, a.1, resp. "*Manifestum est autem quod, sicut omnes motus corporales reducuntur in motum caelestis corporis sicut in primum movens corporale; ita omnes motus tam corporales quam spirituales reducuntur in primum movens simpliciter, quod est Deus. Et ideo quantumcumque natura aliqua corporalis vel spiritualis ponatur perfecta, non potest in suum actum procedere nisi moveatur a Deo. Quae quidem motio est secundum suae providentiae rationem; non secundum necessitatem naturae, sicut motio corporis caelestis. Non solum autem a Deo est omnis motio sicut a primo movente; sed etiam ab ipso est omnis formalis perfectio sicut a primo actu. Sic igitur actio intellectus, et cuiuscumque entis creati, dependet a Deo quantum ad duo, uno modo, inquantum ab ipso habet formam per quam agit; alio modo, inquantum ab ipso movetur ad agendum.*" "All movements, both corporeal and spiritual, are reduced to the absolutely First Mover, Who is God. And hence no matter how perfect a corporeal or spiritual nature is supposed to be, it cannot proceed to its act unless it be moved by God. Now this motion is according to the plan of His providence, and not by a necessity of nature, as the motion of the body of the heavens. *But not only is every motion from God as from the First Mover, but all formal perfection is from Him as from the First Act. Hence the action of the intellect, or of any created being whatsoever, depends upon God in two ways: first, inasmuch as it is from Him that it has the form whereby it acts; secondly, inasmuch as it is moved by Him to act.*" [my emphasis]

18. For the work which is the font of it all, see Luis de Molina, S.J., *Liberi arbitrii cum gratiae donis, divina praescientia, providentia, praedestinatione et reprobatione concordia* (A Reconciliation of Free Choice with the Gifts of Grace, Divine Foreknowledge, Providence, Predestination and Reprobation) (First Edition, Lisbon 1588; Second Edition, Antwerp 1595).

19. Cf. Molina's *Concordia*, q. 14, a. 13, disp. II.

20. See for instance *ST* I, q. 22, a. 2, resp.: "For since every agent acts for an end, the ordering of effects towards that end extends as far as the causality of the first agent ex-

tend. Whence it happens that in the effects of an agent something takes place which has no reference towards the end, because the effect comes from some other cause outside the intention of the agent. But the causality of God, Who is the first agent, extends to all beings not only as to the constituent principles of species, but also as to the individualizing principles; not only of things incorruptible, but also of things corruptible. Hence all things that exist in whatsoever manner are necessarily directed by God towards the end."

21. *ST* I, q. 22, a. 2, resp.: "*Cum enim omne agens agat propter finem, tantum se extendit ordinatio effectuum in finem, quantum se extendit causalitas primi agentis.*"

22. Ibid. "*Unde necesse est omnia quae habent quocumque modo esse, ordinata esse a Deo in finem.*"

23. Ibid. "*necesse est omnia, inquantum participant esse, intantum subdi divinae providentiae.*"

24. A point he makes in *ST* I-II, q. 92, a. 2, ad 1.

25. If the volitional act is not subject to divine causality, it is alike not subject to divine providence. This inference is absolute. St. Thomas does not, of course, envision this causality as violent or external. Rather, the divine causality of the acts of the will is precisely that whereby they are naturally constituted as volitional acts. God causes necessary things necessarily, and contingent things contingently, and the will is denominated as "free" because it is not an operative power prefixed to only one effect, but has for its formal object the universal good as specified by reason. Thomas holds that no finite good may compel the rational will, so that the will is objectively free with respect to its natural finite objects. Yet he also maintains that the rational will cannot proceed to its own act of free self-determination unless moved from potency to act with respect to this act of free self-determination by God.

26. The citations possible for this doctrine of St. Thomas are numerous. But, for instance, see *Summa contra gentiles*.3b.89-90. The title of Chapter 89, is quite clear: "That the Movement of the Will, and Not Only the Power of the Will, is Caused by God."

27. For St. Thomas, the rational creature both passively and actively participates the eternal law. It passively participates this law because its very own nature, act, object, and end are established by the eternal law and received from God as first cause. Yet unlike the case of lower creatures who are participate the divine government in a merely passive way—precisely *because* the rational creature is created, sustained, and actuated as such— it actively participates the eternal law and shares in its own government. Because its passive participation includes the possession of reason, the rational creature receives its ordering from God not merely passively but rationally and *preceptively*, as giving it *reasons* to do and not to do. Cf. *ST* I-II, q. 91, a. 2.

28. Cf. also Martin Rhonheimer, *Natural Law and Practical Reason*, trans. by Gerald Malsbary (New York: Fordham University Press, 2000), 321—322.

29. Josef Füchs, S. J., *Moral Demands and Personal Obligations*, trans. by Brian McNeil (Washington, D.C.: Georgetown University Press, 1993), 157.

30. Ibid., at 55.

31. Russell Hittinger has aptly summed up the problem. He wryly notes the problem of "Cartesian minds somehow under Church discipline." See Russell Hittinger, "Natural Law and Catholic Moral Theology" in *A Preserving Grace*, ed. by Michael Cromartie (jointly published—Washington, DC: Ethics and Public Policy Center; Grand Rapids, MI: Errdmans Publishing Co., 1997): 1—30.

32. Cf. Henri de Lubac, *Surnaturel etude historiques* (Paris: Aubier, 1946); *Augustinisme et théologie modern* (Paris: Aubier, 1965), 242—251; *Le Mystere du surnaturel* (Paris: Aubier, 1965), noteworthy for its criticism of the Dominican commentator tradition, pp. 87-88, 142, 179-189; J. Laporta *La Destinée de la nature humane selon Thomas d'Aquin* (Paris: J. Vrin, 1965). Laporta devotes an appendix to arguing that St. Thomas

does not use the language of obediential potency in his account of the supernatural destiny of man (pp. 133—146).

33. I have tried elsewhere in the pages both of the *International Philosophical Quarterly* and of *The Thomist* ("Obediential Potency, Human Knowledge, and the Natural Desire for God," *International Philosophical Quarterly* 37 (1997), 45—64; "On the Possibility of a Purely Natural End for Man: A Response to Denis Bradley," *The Thomist* 64 (2000) 211—237) to articulate the richness of the doctrine of obediential potency as exemplifying *par excellence* the teaching of the Second Vatican Council that in Christ man is revealed to himself. Were human nature of itself and apart from grace ordered to beatitude, grace would become merely another means for the perfection of an antecedent tendency. Whereas, to the contrary, man's remote capacity to be aided to know God is one of which we have sufficiently profound experience and knowledge only owing to God's active agency on the human soul, aiding and elevating it. This is a profound theme about which Thomas's texts provide an incredibly rich doctrine which is lost when we unwarrantedly refuse his express insistence that the concept of obediential potency applies to the relation of nature to grace. One notes especially Thomas's language of *ST* III, q. 1, a. 3, ad 3, regarding the "greatest grace," the "grace of union", which clearly is invoking the idea of obediential potency in speaking of a double capability *of* human nature, one according to the order of natural power, and the other according to the order of divine power.

34. De Lubac's error is largely consequent on failing to grasp St. Thomas's use of the concept of obediential potency. The remote "orderability" founded on a thing's nature in relation to God's agency is the idea of obediential potency. If it were what the Franciscan school, and later De Lubac and then Gilson, thought it to be—a mere extrinsic susceptibility to miraculous transmutation—then it would be impossible for it to be central in understanding the relation of grace to nature, for then elevating grace would transmute rather than perfect: the one created would not be the one redeemed. But although nature is "passive" in both miraculous transmutation and obediential potency proper, the two are distinct—or, if one wishes to call both obediential potencies, then the two are very distinct types of obediential potency. It is worth reiterating what is asserted in note §19 above, namely Thomas's clear distinction between natural power and the power of nature in relation to the active agency of God with respect to the highest grace, the grace of union. Clearly Thomas is here applying the idea of obediential potency to the relation of nature and grace. It also bears pointing out that for Thomas the natural desire for God is *modalized* according to the order of Providence in which it is found, such that in this given order of Providence—wherein we are called to supernatural beatific vision as sons and daughters of God—we know through revelation that supernatural beatific vision is possible to us, so that the natural desire for God is elevated in grace to embrace the beatific end.

35. See the fine essay by Aidan Nichols, O.P., titled "Thomism and *La Nouvelle Théologie*" *The Thomist* 64 (2000): 1—19, for an excellent exposition of the outlook of the Thomistic participants in this controversy. Of course, the controversy was not merely with De Lubac, but with a number of theologians of whom De Lubac was in some respects the exemplar. Nichols writes that in the early part of this controversy "Those specifically mentioned, all Jesuits, were Bouillard, Hans Urs von Balthasar, Gaston Fessard, de Lubac, Pierre Teilhard de Chardin, but above all Daniélou." But especially after the publication of *Surnaturel*, with its radical thesis regarding nature and grace, De Lubac's work became the focal point of criticism. Moreover, as Nichols notes, "though de Lubac is never mentioned by name in "Les orientations présentes de la pensée religieuse" it was *his* already impressive body of work that Daniélou was implicitly putting forward as the model for French theology in the future." It is not mistaken to see the entire controversy

as focalized and defined by the dispute regarding De Lubac's thesis.

36. Cf. M.-M. Labourdette, O.P., and M.-J. Nicolas, O.P., "L'analogie de la vérité et l'unité de la science théologique," *Revue Thomiste* 55 (1947): 417—466; see also M.-M. Labourdette, O.P., "La théologie, intelligence de la foi," *Revue Thomiste* 46 (1946): 5—44.

37. R. Garrigou-Lagrange, O.P.,"La nouvelle théologie, où va-t-elle?" *Angelicum* (1946): 126—145.

38. Of course, there is a valid sense in which fallen nature reveals far less of its wounded host than does elevated nature in the state of grace. But the order of knowledge and the order of being are not identical. In the order of being, what nature is conditions both how it can fall, and how it can under the active agency of God rise, as well as to some degree how it can be known. In the order of knowledge, we cannot help but be aided or retarded by our actual condition or state as knowers, while nonetheless *what* we know—the nature—provides an essential determination for our judgment (in whatever state we find it): if one likes, a preamble to a more complete theological contemplation.

39. See Pope John Paul II's *Fides et Ratio, L'Osservatore Romano* Weekly Edition in English, 14 October 1998.

40. Cf. *Fides et Ratio*, §75, referring to the birth of philosophy, and which deserves the following extensive quotation: "We see here philosophy's valid aspiration to be an autonomous enterprise, obeying its own rules and employing the powers of reason alone. Although seriously handicapped by the inherent weakness of human reason, this aspiration should be supported and strengthened. As a search for truth within the natural order, the enterprise of philosophy is always open—at least implicitly—to the supernatural. Moreover, the demand for a valid autonomy of thought should be respected even when theological discourse makes use of philosophical concepts and arguments. Indeed, to argue according to rigorous rational criteria is to guarantee that the results attained are universally valid. This also confirms the principle that grace does not destroy nature but perfects it: the assent of faith, engaging the intellect and will, does not destroy but perfects the free will of each believer who deep within welcomes what has been revealed."

CHAPTER THREE

IS AQUINAS' *SUMMA* ONLY ABOUT GRACE?

Romanus Cessario, O.P.

The philosophical and theological achievement of Thomas Aquinas continues to exercise a significant influence on the development of contemporary Roman Catholic theology. And even though some assert that, in the wake of the Second Vatican Council, Aquinas holds a less firm claim to his title of Common Doctor than was the case before 1962, theologians of various persuasions are still considering ways to legitimize their use of the Thomist epithet.[1] This remains especially true of the professional adherents of the German Jesuit Karl Rahner. Thus today, a large number of academic theologians favor a transcendental reading of Aquinas; in fact, the only familiarity some persons gain with Aquinas's texts and thought comes through the prism of modern German philosophy.[2]

While this turn of events has affected many different areas of theology, it has made a special impact on the way a large number of contemporary theologians conceive the relationship between human nature and sanctifying grace. In fact, not a few students of theology assume that conspicuous parallels exist between what Aquinas and Rahner have to say about the content of the many varied questions in the treatise *De Gratia* that have traditionally commanded the attention of Catholic theologians.[3] I fear, however, that this enthusiasm for making Aquinas fit comfortably into the post-Heideggerian world risks a conflation of nature and grace and a blurring of important distinctions, such as the one between formal and efficient causality, that theologians in the past have painstakingly developed to talk about our participation in the divine nature. And so this paper proposes to argue that one can neither maintain that Aquinas upholds an inclusivist doctrine of "grace as uncreated and formal-created," such as some attribute to Karl Rahner,[4] nor argue that this allegedly Rahnerian construal of divine grace throws an interpretative light on the structure of the *Summa Theologiae*. I intend to proceed first by examining the claim of the American Dominican Thomas F. O'Meara that grace forms an underlying theological theme of the *Summa Theologiae*, and secondly by suggesting how Thomists can still talk about grace and efficient causality without adopting the post-Cartesian presumption that efficient causes necessarily mean extrinsic causes.[5]

In an article on the theological structure of the *Summa Theologiae*, O'Meara addresses a question whose remote origins stretch back to the earliest eras of theological inquiry.[6] "Two conceptions remain proper to the human species," wrote the fourth-century Alexandrian theologian, Didymus the Blind, "one comes from our fleshly bodies, and the other from the divine spirit."[7] First, O'Meara seeks to address the relationship between nature and grace, between the natural order and the supernatural. Secondly, he wants to examine this question in the context of searching out the theological themes that control Aquinas's major endeavor in systematic theology, the *Summa Theologiae*. As the title of his article suggests, O'Meara is disposed to argue that the *Summa* illustrates an inclusivist doctrine of divine grace.

In order to advance his thesis, O'Meara proposes grace as one of the prominent theological structures in the *Summa*. "The goal of the following pages," he writes, "is to observe the role in the *Summa Theologiae* of that reality called 'grace'" (132). Secondly, although O'Meara claims that his interest lies elsewhere than in "another study on the formal pattern of the *Summa Theologiae*" (132), he nonetheless considers himself as working in continuity with the tradition inaugurated by M.D. Chenu in his groundbreaking work, *Towards Understanding St. Thomas*.[8] O'Meara questions "aspects of Chenu's model" (132) for the *Summa*, but at the same time, he clearly shares the distinguished French theologian's basic sympathies and outlook. Especially does O'Meara follow Chenu when the latter criticizes certain scholastic commentaries for reducing the *Summa* "to a sort of sacred metaphysics seasoned with allusions to the spiritual."[9] As a result, instead of delineating a "static work of logical classification" (133), O'Meara wants to identify the theological threads—his own metaphor—that stitch together the entire work. "Grace," he states, "is one such theological thread" (133). Because he wants to depict a configuration that makes up a reality and, at the same time, to define syntax capable of interpreting a body of knowledge, O'Meara pursues his investigation in a way that suggests the distinction French intellectuals make between "structurel" and "structural." From a certain perspective, O'Meara's theological style emulates theology written after the fashion of literary analysis.

Although O'Meara eschews Aristotelian metaphysics as a source for the unity of the *Summa*, he nonetheless seems less wary of the role that an ontology of self-communication can play in developing a Christian doctrine on grace. Thus, he argues that "grace" appears everywhere in the *Summa Theologiae*.[10] "Since grace grounds the divine being as well as its word and life to us," concludes O'Meara, "it would have been surprising if this realm of *quiddam supernaturale* (I-II, q. 110, a. 1) had not unfolded a wider presence" (152). I suggest, however, that this form of inclusive ontology, which does not discriminate sufficiently the various levels of efficient causality that characterize the divine activity *ad extra*, provides a Procrustean bed for the *Summa Theologiae*. Indeed Aquinas would have felt certain reservations concerning the notion of grace as the communication of God's inner being *simpliciter*. Given the importance that Aquinas attaches to divine efficient causality, such an exclusive emphasis on formal causality imports a reductionism foreign to his philosophical and theological sensibilities.

Aquinas himself signals the requirements divine efficient causality imposes on any attempt to set forth, as the *Summa* purports to do, a teaching about God. In fact, we find Aquinas's understanding of efficient causality reflected in the very structure of the *Summa* itself.[11] As I shall point out, the commentatorial tradition clearly appreciates this fact when, for example, John of St-Thomas identifies the various moments of divine final and efficient causation as the basis for the principal divisions of the *Summa*.[12] Nor does such an *éclaircissement* constitute a return to "sacred metaphysics." On the contrary, it points out a fundamental Christian truth about God's action *ad extra*. "Grace is caused in man by the presence of the divinity," writes Aquinas, "as light in the atmosphere by the presence of the sun" (IIIa, q. 7, a. 13). We should first of all recall that Aquinas uses this broad analogy in the context of discussing the relationship of Christ's created habitual grace to the grace of union, that is, to explain how Christ's divinity affects the substantial holiness of his human nature. Accordingly, this image is meant principally to identify the blessed Trinity as the principal efficient cause of Christ's created grace.

In the singular instance of the incarnation, the three Persons of the blessed Trinity together cause the assumption of an individual human nature, even though the term of this assumptive action is and must be the Person of the Logos/Son, who alone among the Persons of the Trinity communicates a personal subsistence to the man Jesus Christ.[13] But this hypostatic union occurs only in the unique case of the incarnate Logos. For the blessed Trinity is present to every other human person, not through a communication of personal subsistence, but through created activities of knowledge and love that God alone can initiate and sustain. Customarily we think of this as God coming to dwell in us, for instance, as in the doctrine of the Trinitarian missions. To be more theologically precise, we should rather consider each sanctified human person as one who is elevated to share in God's life and this through knowing and loving each one of the divine Persons. This elevation, moreover, represents something entirely distinct from that creative presence of God to every creature, including human and angelic creatures, which Aquinas deliberately refers to as *"per essentiam, potentiam et praesentiam."*[14] Aquinas's use of the sun as an image only points to the fact that sanctifying grace has the power to affect everything that exists, but it is not meant to blur the real distinctions that differentiate the other modes—"substance, power, and presence"—whereby God as agent cause remains present to his creation.

O'Meara unquestionably interprets the image of the sun as a controlling metaphor, for it leads him to inquire to what extent undifferentiated grace appears throughout the *Summa*. Towards this end, the author examines principal sections of the *Summa Theologiae* in order to ascertain whether "grace" actually appears there, but first he provides a working definition of "grace" to which, he claims, the "teachings of Christianity bear witness" (134). Although the author cites several phrases from *Summa Theologiae* Ia-IIae, q. 110 where Aquinas talks explicitly about the grace of the new law, O'Meara provides no direct citation for his working definition of grace, *viz.,* "a reality and force in and above nature calling and moving persons to a life described as one participating in the divine and supernatural" (134). A reader familiar with the *Summa Theologiae* will recognize some of the terms that O'Meara employs, but his explanations of these terms seem idiosyncratic. For instance, in order to explain *"bonitas denominans"* in *Summa Theologiae* Ia, q. 6, a. 4, O'Meara speaks about "the sparks which are openings to the properly divine world" (135). In the text cited, Aquinas only argues that created goodness, like any perfection, analogically resembles the divine goodness.[15] To give another example, O'Meara glosses the first twenty-six questions of the *Summa Theologiae* thus: "God is essentially a dynamo of personal activities" (137). In these ways, he introduces an element of analogical imagination into his argument, but this literary manoeuvre unfortunately results in some very broad and unfocused claims about the relations between God and the creature.

It is not my principal purpose, however, to challenge every line of O'Meara's Thomistic exegesis. As I have suggested, the author clearly approaches the text of Aquinas with a preference for literary allusions. All in all, it seems to me that O'Meara reads Aquinas along the lines of what George Vandevelde has recently called the "grammar of grace" in Karl Rahner's theology.[26] It comes as no surprise, then, that O'Meara reduces every reference to the divine in Aquinas to a single principle of explanation. Again, "grace under various terms," concludes O'Meara, "is present in the entire *Summa Theologiae*, and not just in its allotted segment, qq. 109-114 of the I-II" (148). As suggestive as this proposal may be for bringing Aquinas into contact with certain styles of contemporary theological discourse, the thesis remains substantially incomplete. As with any reductionist approach to the *Summa*, it fails to take full enough account of the way in which Aquinas orders the various parts of his textbook for beginners. I propose that, in order to render an adequate Christian account of how God really acts in the world, both in creation as well as in salvation history, Aquinas recognized the need to complement his analysis of intrinsic formal causality with a thorough discussion of extrinsic efficient causes as well.

Let me begin with an historical anecdote. In the summer of 1267, Thomas Aquinas was sent to serve the papal curia of Clement IV then located at Viterbo. As a result of the translations provided by William of Moerbeke, St. Thomas came into close contact with Byzantine theology, including the neo-Platonic theme of the "*exitus-reditus.*"[27] During this same period Aquinas also began his *Summa Theologiae*. Given the principal divisions of the work, we can readily understand Chenu's conviction that Thomas developed the "*exitus-reditus*" theme as a result of this increased exposure to Eastern thought. Thus, in the prologue, *Summa Theologiae* Ia, q. 2, Thomas writes:

> We now intend to set forth this divine teaching by treating,
>   first, of God;
>   secondly, of the journey to God of reasoning creatures;
>   thirdly, of Christ, who, as man, is our road to God.
>
> The treatment of God will fall into three parts:
>   first, his nature;
>   secondly, the distinction of persons in God;
>   thirdly, the coming forth from him of creatures.

The concluding paragraph, of course, covers the main divisions of the *prima pars*. And similar divisions introduce the other major parts of the *Summa*, i.e., *prima-secundae, secunda-secundae, tertia*.

We turn momentarily from the structure of the *Summa* to the idea of Aristotelian science that guided Aquinas's theological method. Since the twelfth century and the progressive introduction of the works of Aristotle comprising the *logica nova* (above all, the two *Analytica*), theological methodology had acquired new importance and self-consciousness.[28] The question was: in what respect does theology measure up to the Aristotelian canon of scientific knowing as that canon is expressed in the *Analytica Posteriora*? For scientific knowing involves both the universal and the necessary; it denotes a knowledge of what cannot be other than the case and of the necessary connection between cause and effect.[29] Christian theology, by contrast, centers upon a God who remains utterly free in his address to human freedom, as it tries to render an account of the intersection and dialogue of divine and human freedoms, which is salvation-history. The methodological question for theology can be posed more precisely: how can there be a scientific account (one that matches up to Aristotle's scientific ideal) about what endures as contingent, free, gracious, and historical?

The beginning of a solution to this question of theological methodology looks to find a course between theology as "sacred history," where the intelligible connection between the mysteries constitutes simply narrative chronology as in Hugh of St. Victor's *De Sacramentis*, and theology as *necessitarian emanationism* as in Plotinus's *Enneads*. Aquinas himself confronted this issue in two ways: "*in actu signato*" in the methodological treatment of *Summa Theologiae* Ia, q.1, a.1 and "*in actu exercito*" in the very structure of the *Summa Theologiae* itself as he planned it. Even if we allow that Aquinas did adopt the *exitus-reditus* scheme from later neo-Platonism, nevertheless he develops it, building the nuance of his own analogical understanding into the scheme.

As I have already mentioned, the renaissance commentator on St. Thomas, John of St-Thomas (1589-1644), also considered this scheme important for understanding the mind of Aquinas and his purpose in ordering the questions of his *Summa*. But John of St-Thomas offers another explanation of the theological design it represents. In his *Cursus Theologicus*, the author argues that Aquinas divides his material in the *Summa Theologiae* according to a threefold consideration of the divine causality, namely, "as effective principle, as finalizing beatitude, as restoring Savior."[20] John of St-Thomas, in other words, regards the diverse exercises of divine causality as a theological plan that guides the development of the *Summa Theologiae*. In his view, Aquinas deliberately combines considerations of efficient and final causality in order to specify three general modes of causation that guide the development of his *Summa*.[21]

John of St-Thomas, then, at least signals a caution in applying Chenu's scheme too rigidly. Both "exitus" and "reditus" require further delineation in terms of the different kinds of causality that govern the diverse movements represented in the *Summa Theologiae*.[22] For this reason, some critics even suggest that Chenu's interpretation either gives an over-simplified explanation of Thomas's master plan or misrepresents altogether the general structure of the *Summa Theologiae*. In any event, some remarks about efficient causality will serve both to nuance the question of the "exitus-reditus" theme and to illumine the way that Aquinas treats divine grace in his theology. When Aquinas affirms that grace is the only perfection that makes God exist in the human person as an object known and loved, he simply seeks to articulate a theological reason for the two conceptions about which St. John speaks: "But to all who received him, who believed in his name, he gave power to become children of God; who were born, not of blood nor of the will of the flesh nor of the will of man, but of God" (Jn 1: 12,13). We can easily recognize both formal and efficient causality evident here in the context of finality.

In fact, it seems perhaps more accurate to view "exitus-reditus" in the pattern of the *Summa* not as a singular circular movement (thus, Chenu) but rather in terms of concentric circles, each manifesting its own degree of necessity. These circles variously encompass the blessed Trinity, created natures, and the incarnation. Each center, then, requires different necessities which, in turn, import different causalities.

Thus, we can see in *Summa Theologiae* Ia qq. 2-43 one cycle, an entirely intra-Trinitarian coming-forth in the Word and, at the same time, a springing-back in Personal Love. Here the movement enjoys a certain necessity—i.e., that God cannot be other than a Father speaking a Word and together with that Word breathing forth the personal Bond of Love. The blessed Trinity remains the highest cause for everything that happens in the world; so we are not surprised to discover that Aquinas places this treatise at the very beginning of his *Summa*.

Broadly speaking, we should consider the material in the remainder of the *prima pars* and in the *secunda pars* under the aspect of nature. The necessity here remains hypothetical, i.e., given that God has freely chosen to create as he has. Nevertheless, once the divine will to create, there exists a certain intelligibility and consistency, certain intrinsic requirements, to the natures that have been freely posited. Since God has freely willed to create men and women for beatific communion, mankind cannot be other than human.[23] This represents Didymus the Blind's first conception, the one from human bodies in flesh and blood.

The final scheme of coming-forth and return occurs in the *tertia pars*, which recognizes the content of concrete history. Jesus comes forth and returns as the perfect and consummate historical agent; he realizes human nature in its historically unsurpassable concrete shape; he enacts human nature as a perfect history. And this event, the birth, life, sufferings, death and resurrection of the incarnate Word makes possible the other conception of which Didymus speaks, namely, the spiritual re-birth of all who are "born not of blood nor of the will of flesh, nor of the will of man, but of God."

The necessity here remains even more tenuous, in one respect; for there is no inner necessity that God accomplish the consummation of human destiny and human salvation from sin by the incarnation of the Son. Nevertheless, God's election of this mode of accomplishing his loving design for human history and the excellence of a human history that composes hypostatically that of the second Person of the blessed Trinity confers the necessity of an unsurpassable exemplar and final causality upon salvation-history as lived out in the personal history of Jesus of Nazareth. These necessities—that of salvation history, that of natures as constituted by God, and that of the divine triune reality itself—remain interlocking. In their consistency and intelligibility, the former two variously disclose to the world the divine "necessity" that God be a Father uttering a Word with whom he breathes forth the force of a loving Spirit. In this sense, God remains all in all.

Aquinas, then, and with him the tradition of the Church, remains convinced that Christian revelation can furnish grounds for speculation concerning the purposes and works of God. Of course, the *sacra doctrina* possesses a sacred scripture that serves as the written record of that revelation. But as a master of the *sacra doctrina*, Aquinas aims to combine into a single discipline both a study of salvation history itself and a speculative investigation of what that sacred history embodies.[24] Of course, the Incarnation remains an event of salvation history and therefore a contingent and gratuitous revelation of the merciful God. Yet it can enter into the pattern of the "exitus-reditus" even as a free act of God. Thomas envisioned nothing untoward in describing the diverse ontological relations that do or can exist between elements of the created universe (including Christ's human nature, the human person, and the Eucharistic species) and God prior to a direct reference to the actual way in which God chose to unfold historically his plan of salvation. On the contrary, he judged such a procedure both "a sound educational method" and an aid to teaching and understanding biblical revelation.

Thomas therefore makes no apology for talking about the life of man uplifted in grace in the *secunda pars* before he presents Christ, the one mediator of that grace, in the *tertia pars*. He announces that man's destiny points to something infinitely above what our natural powers can achieve, nothing less than union with the triune God. Therefore, he argues that the creature requires a *gratia elevans* in order that human capacities can reach out for God. This *gratia elevans* remains the reality that Aquinas properly designates as the grace of the new law:

> We say that God exists in any creature in two ways. First of all, by way of an agent cause, and in this way he exists in everything he creates. . . . Secondly, God exists in a special fashion in the rational creature who knows and loves him. . . . God is said to exist in this way in the saint by grace.[25]

Finally, we should mention what Aquinas cannot directly treat in the *secunda pars*, namely, the satisfaction of Christ. Why? Satisfaction remains indisputably linked to the contingent, historical fact of Christ's passion and death on the cross. "The incarnation was not absolutely necessary for the restoration of human nature," writes Thomas at the start of the *tertia pars*, "since by his infinite power God had many other ways to accomplish this end" (IIIa, q. 1, a. 2).[26] Thomas's metaphysical abilities and his penetration of the *Posterior Analytics*, in particular, helped him both to grasp and to articulate the utter gratuity of the divine dispensation. O'Meara, of course, recognizes this principal tenet of Christian doctrine. But the personal call to beatific fellowship that Christ issues to every person finds its specific graciousness and gratuity measured against an horizon of fallen natures and broken worlds. This world of created natures, including human nature, enjoys its own integrity even as it obeys its own dynamics. And such constitutes our first nature, to which divine grace, as Aquinas understands the term, does not properly belong. If St. Thomas had wanted to speak loosely, he could have, but precision in language remains characteristic of the medieval schoolmen. As Cajetan reminds us, "*Sanctus Thomas semper loquitur formaliter.*"

In the final analysis, however, the saints teach us most about divine truth; Aquinas, in fact, refers to theology as the wisdom of the saints.[27] In *The Book of Her Life*, St. Teresa of Avila explains how she came to learn the difference between God's creative presence to the world "according to essence, presence, and power" and his sanctifying presence in grace which terminates in proper relationships with the indwelling Trinity. She writes: "Those who had no learning told me that He was present only by grace. I couldn't believe this, because, as I say, it seemed to me He was present, and so I was troubled."[28] Her Dominican confessor explained the different modes of presence to her. "He told me that God was indeed present and described how he communicated himself to us, which brought me very great comfort."[29] This task remains incumbent on all those who seek to interpret the doctrine of Aquinas on grace and, *a fortiori*, to discover the threads that hold together his *Summa Theologiae*.

NOTES

1. For instance, see F. van Steenberghen, "Comment être thomiste aujourd'hui?," *Revue Philosophique de Louvain* 85 (1987): 171—197.

2. For historical information on this development, see Gerald A. McCool, S.J., *Nineteenth-Century Scholasticism: The Search for a Unitary Method* [originally published as *Catholic Theology in the Nineteenth Century*, New York: Fordham University Press 1977] and his new study *From Unity to Pluralism: The Internal Evolution of Thomism* (New York: Fordham University Press, 1989). While the heirs of ressourcement theology, i.e., those who depend on the work of theologians such as Jean Daniélou, Hans Urs von Balthasar and Henri de Lubac, show less enthusiasm for aligning themselves directly with the Thomist tradition, it is interesting to note that de Lubac's early interest in Maurice Blondel, Pierre Rousselot, and Joseph Maréchal earned him the reputation of being a "Thomist." See Joseph A. Komonchak, "Theology and Culture at Mid-Century: The Example of Henri de Lubac," *Theological Studies* 51 (1990): 581.

3. For example, see a recent article by Thomas F. O'Meara, "Karl Rahner: Some audiences and sources for his theology," *Communio* 18 (1991): 237—251. But also see J. A. DiNoia, O.P., "Karl Rahner" in *The Modern Theologians. An Introduction to Christian Theology in the Twentieth Century*, vol. 1, ed David F. Ford (Oxford: Basil Blackwell, 1989): 183—204, who notes the hesitations that some experience about the validity of the transcendental reading of Aquinas espoused by Rahner and others.

4. Ibid., 239.

5. The reasons for my serious misgivings about the adequacy of Rahnerian categories to explain fully the Thomist doctrine of grace can be found in William J. Hill, O.P., "Uncreated Grace—A Critique of Karl Rahner," *The Thomist* 27 (1963): 333-356. Although Father Hill has subsequently modified his estimate of Rahner's overall contribution to twentieth-century theology, this article still offers a penetrating critique of the argument that only a divine action exclusively in the line of formal causality, i.e., a "quasi-formal"

cause, can adequately account for the fully personal nature of the relationship between God and the human person. For another approach to personalist categories at the service of the theology of nature and grace that also takes exception to Rahner's proposal, see Robert L. Faricy, S.J., "The Trinitarian Indwelling," *The Thomist* 35 (1971): 369—404.

6. Thomas F. O'Meara, O.P., "Grace as a Theological Structure in the *Summa Theologiae* of Thomas Aquinas," *Recherches de théologie ancienne et médiévale* 55 (1988): 130—153.

7. *On the Trinity* Bk II, c. 12 (*PG* 39:670). Didymus the Blind (c. 313—98) took charge of the Catechetical School at Alexandria, where he formed some of the leading theologians of the fourth-century. His writings exhibit the fundamental tensions of Alexandrian theology, namely, between the orthodoxy of Athanasius and the idiosyncrasy of Origen. The latter, however, predominated with the result that II Constantinople (553) condemned Didymus's Origenist leanings.

8. M.D. Chenu, *Towards Understanding St. Thomas*, trans. A.-M. Landre, O.P. and D. Hughes, O.P., (Chicago: Henry Regnery Company, 1964): 309. This translation is from the French original, *Introduction à l'étude de saint Thomas d'Aquin* (Paris, 1950). In fact, O'Meara claims that M.D. Chenu is the first one to propose a "philosophico-theological form" for the *Summa Theologiae*. The author further asserts that subsequent critics pursued the search for the key to the structural unity of the *Summa Theologiae* "[b]ecause of Chenu's work" (131). In particular, O'Meara names six such theologians: A. Hayen, E. Persson, G. Lafont, E. Schillebeeckx, M. Seckler, and O. Pesch.

9. Chenu, of course, reacts principally to the efforts of French scholastics to make the thought of Aquinas fit the *denkformen* created by Continental rationalists. Thus, he cites the work of the seventeenth-century French Dominican, Antoninus Reginald (1605-1676), *Doctrinae D. Thomae Aquinatis tria principia cum suis consequentiis* (Toulouse, 1670, Paris, 1878) as a splendid example of this sort of Thomistic exegesis. Undoubtedly inspired by Descartes' *Discourse on Method* (1637), Père Reginald reduced Aquinas's theology to three clear and distinct ideas: (1) Being is transcendent, (2) God alone is pure act; (3) Absolute beings are specified by themselves, relative beings, by reference to others. Given our current theological perspectives, this sort of metaphysical grid clearly seems to distort the theological purposes Aquinas sets forth at the very start of his *Summa*. On the other hand, the methodology chosen by Père Reginald in the seventeenth century can put one in mind of certain twentieth-century theologians whose own methods betray an equally strong influence from the Parisian intellectual milieu, including, for instance, the prevalent school of French structuralism. To tell the truth, a literary analytical approach to the texts of Aquinas can bring its own distortions to his meaning, even if the contemporary intellectual world remains less sensitive to these sorts of deformations than to those caused by a heavy-handed metaphysics. See Claude Geffré, *Le Christianisme au risque de l'interprétation* (Paris: Editions du Cerf, 1983) for a non-metaphysical approach to theology that relies heavily on structural hermeneutics, especially as inspired by the work of Paul Ricoeur. But for the larger question of the real risks involved in attempts to reconcile a realist metaphysics with idealist presuppositions, see Etienne Gilson, *Réalisme thomiste et critique de la connaissance* (Paris: J. Vrin, 1983), English translation: *Thomist Realism & the Critique of Knowledge*, trans. Mark A. Wauck (San Francisco: Ignatius Press, 1986).

10. In fact, O'Meara makes this the first major conclusion of his study: "Grace under various terms is present in the entire *Summa Theologiae*, and not just in its allotted segment, qq. 109-114 of the I-II" (O'Meara, 148). See note 6 above.

11. Recently the Dutch Thomist Jan A. Aertsen has recalled this important feature of Aquinas's work. See his "The Circulation-motive and Man in the Thought of Thomas

Aquinas," in *L'homme et son Univers au Moyen Age I*, éd Christian Wenin, (Louvain-La-Neuve: Editions de l'Institut Supérieur de Philosophie, 1986): 432—39.

12. See note 20.

13. Aquinas discusses this important topic in *Summa Theologiae* IIIa, q. 3, a. 4: "Tres enim personae fecerunt ut humana natura uniretur uni personae Filii." If the whole Trinity does not cause the assumption of Christ's human nature, then the incarnation, which the Christian tradition celebrates as the greatest of the divine works *ad extra*, would violate a cardinal norm of Trinitarian theology, namely, the three divine Persons are a single principle of operation in their action *ad extra* (see *DS* 800—801). At the same time, if the assumed human nature does not terminate, i.e., possess its principle of subsistence, in the Logos/Son, then Jesus Christ is someone other than who the Council of Chalcedon confesses him to be (see *DS* 302).

14. See *Summa Theologiae* Ia, q. 8, a. 3. In the reply to the fourth argument, Aquinas refers to the distinct causality for which he reserves the term "gratia." In fact, the argument asserts that each divine perfection that changes a person's life should be given a special designation. But Aquinas replies: "Grace is the only perfection added to the substance of things which makes God exist in them as a known and loved object; grace alone then makes God exist in things in a unique way (*singularem modum*)." Aquinas then acknowledges the special case of the incarnation: "There is, however, another unique way in which God exists in a man, by union, and we will deal with this in its proper place" (ad 4). For an expert discussion of the distinguishing causality involved in divine grace, see William Hill, O.P., *Proper Relations to the Indwelling Persons* (Washington: Thomist Press, 1955).

15. In *Summa Theologiae* Ia, q. 6, a. 4, Aquinas relates the goodness of any creature to the divine goodness: "Sic ergo unumquodque dicitur bonum bonitate divina sicut primo principio exemplari, effectivo et finali totius bonitatis. Nihilominus tamen unumquodque dicitur bonum similitudine divinae bonitatis sibi inhaerente quae est formaliter sua bonitas denominans ipsum." But in the preceding line, Aquinas himself recalls the general principle concerning the way any creature can share in a divine perfection. Elsewhere Aquinas clearly enunciates this principle. "Creatures," he states in *Summa Theologiae* Ia, q. 4, a. 3, "are said to resemble God, not by sharing a form of the same specific or generic type, but only analogically, inasmuch as God exists by nature, and other things partake existence."

16. See George Vandervelde, "The Grammar of Grace: Karl Rahner as a Watershed in Contemporary Theology," *Theological Studies* 49 (1988): 445—459. The author's clear exposition gives some indication that O'Meara's hypothesis on how Aquinas employs "grace" in the *Summa Theologiae* owes a great deal to Karl Rahner's theology of grace as God's self-communication.

17. Thus, James A. Weisheipl, O.P., *Friar Thomas D'Aquino* (New York: Doubleday, 1983): 235, writes: "The most important work William translated while living with Thomas at Viterbo was the *Elementatio theologica* of Proclus. It was completed on May 18, 1268. Through this translation Thomas came to realize the true Platonic source of *Liber de causis*, which he commented on later." But René A. Gauthier, "Quelques questions à propos du commentaire de S. Thomas sur le *De anima*," *Angelicum* 51 (1974): 419—472 argues that Aquinas was actually in Rome during this period.

18. The so-called "second entry" of Aristotle comprised the discovery and use of his *Prior* and *Posterior Analytics*, the *Topics*, and the *Sophistic Refutations*. This provided the medieval schoolmen with studies of the syllogism and methods of demonstration, of probable reasoning, and of the places or loci of reasoning. In short, this constituted a theory of knowledge and demonstration. As a result, by the latter part of the twelfth cen-

tury, theology, especially as developed by the summists, became more and more dialectical in method.

19. See Thomas Aquinas's own commentary, *In I Analytica Posteriora*, lect. 4, 5, for his explanation of this canon. For general background to Aquinas's contribution to the commentatorial tradition on Aristotle's *Posterior Analytics*, see William A. Wallace, *Causality and Scientific Explanation*, vol. 1, (Ann Arbor: The University of Michigan Press, 1972), especially, 71—88.

20. John of St-Thomas, *Cursus Theologicus* I (Paris: Ludovicus Vivés, 1883): 191: "Igitur Divus Thomas juxta hanc triplicem considerationem Dei causantis, scilicet ut principium effectivum, ut beatitudo finalizans, ut Salvator reparans, divisit totam doctrinam summae theologiae, ut patet in initio secundae quaestionis huius primae partis." O'Meara, however, dismisses this commentator's work as an example of Baroque Thomism's interest only in the formal order of the *Summa* (130).

21. Ibid., 190: "Ex aliis vero duabus causis, scilicet efficienti, et finali, quae Deo conveniunt, considerat Divus Thomas tres generales modos causandi, per quos totum theologiae ordinem partitur." In addition to material causality, John of St-Thomas also excludes the pertinence of formal causality in matters of divine agency ("in quantum causa creaturarum est") since a formal cause implies either dependence or inferiority with respect to that for which it is a cause. The perfection of the divine being, of course, allows neither relationship to creatures.

22. It remains significant that Aquinas, who had already explicitly referred to the "exitus-reditus" theme in his *Scriptum super libros Sententiarum* (Paris, 1252—56), no longer chose to include the actual phrase in the *Summa Theologiae*.

23. See St Thomas Aquinas, *Quaestiones disputatae de malo* q. 4, a. 2: ". . . rectitudo enim gratie non est sine rectitudine nature."

24. Thus Thomas C. O'Brien, "'*Sacra Doctrina*' Revisited: The Context of Medieval Education," *The Thomist* 41 (1977), 475-509 takes exception to the position of James A. Weisheipl, O.P., "The Meaning of *Sacra Doctrina* in the *Summa Theologiae* I, q.1," *The Thomist* 38 (1974): 49—80, who O'Brien claims, tends to depreciate the speculative aspect of the *sacra doctrina*.

25. See *Summa Theologiae* Ia, q. 8, a. 3.

26. This consideration explains why we find the majority of texts on both penitential and Christological satisfaction in the *tertia pars*. For further discussion of this important point, see Romanus Cessario, O.P., *The Godly Image: Christ and Salvation in Catholic Thought from Anselm to Aquinas, Studies in Historical Theology VI* (Petersham, MA: St Bede's Publications, 1990).

27. See *Summa Theologiae* IIa-IIae, q. 45, a. 3, where Aquinas argues that wisdom belongs to those who enjoy a certain "connaturality with divine things." In fact, Christian theology attains its scientific character precisely as a subordinated science, "for it flows from founts recognized in the light of a higher science, namely God's very own which he shares with the blessed" (*Summa Theologiae* Ia, q. 1, a. 2).

28. *The Book of Her Life* 18.15 in *The Collected Works of St. Teresa of Avila*, trans. Kieran Kavanaugh, O.C.D. and Otilio Rodriguez, O.C.D., (Washington: ICS Publications, 1976—85), vol. 1: 121.

29. E. Allison Peers supposes that the Holy Mother refers to the celebrated Domingo Bañez, O.P. (1528-1604), but also acknowledges that other authors suggest a certain Padre Barron. See his *The Complete Works of Saint Teresa of Jesus* vol. 1 (New York: Sheed & Ward, 1946): 111. Bañez, of course, would have understood very well Aquinas's doctrine.

Chapter Four

Analogy, Necessity, and an Editor's Anxiety

John F. Boyle, Ph. D.

I am honored and grateful to have been invited to speak to you at the beginning of this conference on *Fides et Ratio*. For those of us engaged in the intellectual life of the Church, the relationship of faith and reason is ever at play. As the encyclical makes clear, the questions and implications of this relationship may well be the most pressing that face us, if only by reason of their reach and scope. The very speculative breadth of the encyclical reminds us of the speculative enormity of the reality it presents.

I would like to speak to a lesser corner of the encyclical. I say lesser but only in the sense of word count. The encyclical is, in great part, about philosophy and I would not presume to speak on matters philosophical. I shall turn my attention to theology, that is to say, to the systematic or scientific consideration of revealed truth known by faith. I have, by the adjective "scientific," tipped my hand to a scholastic bias, and I freely admit to a yet more specific Thomistic bias, for I wish to speak to a particular aspect of the relationship between reason in its stricter philosophical dimension and theology as science. As concrete particulars are helpful I would like to share with you a concrete problem.

I have titled this talk "Analogy, Necessity, and an Editor's Anxiety." I am that sub-species of historian, an editor, and I am the editor of my title. It has been my privilege to serve as co-editor with the late Father Leonard Boyle, O.P., of St. Thomas' long lost second commentary on Peter Lombard's *Book of Sentences*.[1]

This itself is a story. Tolomeo of Lucca, St. Thomas' friend and biographer, had reported in 1317 (forty years after St. Thomas' death) that St. Thomas had commented not once but twice on Book I of Lombard's *Sentences*. Tolomeo insists that in addition to a first commentary written while a bachelor in Paris, St. Thomas wrote a second commentary while a master in Rome. Tolomeo is alone among the early biographers of St. Thomas to speak of this second commentary. Perhaps his claim was already being questioned in the early fourteenth century, as Tolomeo reports that he even saw a manuscript of it. It was a tantalizer.

In the course of his work, Fr. Antoine Dondaine, O.P., of the Leonine Commission consulted a manuscript, now in Lincoln College, Oxford, that contained a copy of St. Thomas' first Parisian commentary. Fr. Dondaine found in the front flyleaves and margins of the manuscript what amounted to another second commentary on Lombard. It has no heading or colophon identifying it or its author. The hand is of an anonymous scribe of the late thirteenth century. But at several points in the text one finds reference to an "alia lectura fratris Thome," that is, to another lecture of brother Thomas. This raised the question: could this anonymous commentary be the second Roman Commentary of St. Thomas reported by Tolomeo of Lucca?

Fr. Hyacinth Dondaine, O.P., the brother of Fr. Antoine and also of the Leonine Commission, undertook to answer the question. He concluded that this was not the second commentary of St. Thomas. It was, instead, the work of a brilliant student of St. Thomas with an uncanny grasp of the master's thought and writings such that he was able to cut and paste from other works of the master and, in some cases, express the master's thought in ways yet more precise and more clear than the master himself.[2]

Enter Leonard Boyle, O.P. Fr. Boyle argued, against Dondaine, that this was indeed a work of St. Thomas and was none other than the lost Roman Commentary. The many textual and manuscript concerns of Fr. Dondaine were tidily laid to rest by Fr. Boyle.[3] Indeed, Fr. Dondaine came to agree with Fr. Boyle.

Although Fr. Boyle won the day, one of Fr. Dondaine's concerns remained. This one was a matter of speculative substance.

Fr. Dondaine said there was to be found in this commentary, and here he pointed specifically to two articles, a climate of rationalism in the treatment of the Trinity. In the Parisian commentary St. Thomas was always most careful to articulate the clear limits of reason in approaching the central mystery of the faith. Such caution was thrown to the wind in the *Roman Commentary* in which one finds not the carefully delineated limits of reason, but the repeated language of necessity. One finds a chain of arguments from reason for the Trinity. Fr. Dondaine said that we might well have in this commentary a new theological method not seen before in commentaries on the *Sentences*. Fr. Jean-Pierre Torrell, O.P., has more recently expressed the same concern about the text.[4]

Here at last is my editor's anxiety. If we have such a radical rationalism in this text, then we do not have a text of St. Thomas, or we have a copy of the text seriously corrupted and compromised.

And so I set to work. What precisely was the concern of Frs. Dondaine and Torrell?

The first and principal of the two offending articles is found in distinction 2 and asks, "Whether there can be a plurality of persons in the highest good."

The very opening sentence of the response had troubled Fr. Dondaine. It reads: "It is to be said that as faith proposes, so also reason, although never perfectly, can consider the divine Trinity of persons in unity of essence."[5] Dondaine took the form "as faith/so reason" (*sicut fides/ita ratio*) as disjunctive, that faith and reason work separately. One need not so take it; one could understand it as complementary, reason dependent upon faith. The response need be saying no more than simply what faith proposes, reason is able to consider imperfectly.

Fr. Dondaine noted that in the Parisian Commentary at this point, St. Thomas simply says that human reason cannot argue its way to the Trinity. Period.

Fr. Torrell turned to a parallel article in St. Thomas' disputed questions *De Potentia* (also of the Roman Period) and thus exactly contemporaneous with Tolomeo's reported second commentary on the *Sentences*. In this article, St. Thomas first articulates the limitations of reason's investigation of the Trinity. He states unequivocally that reason cannot demonstrate the Trinity.

Thus the question arises: is there any indication in the *Roman Commentary* of the limitations of reason before the mystery of the Trinity? Just such a consideration is in the next distinction when St. Thomas asks, "Whether one can come to knowledge of the divine Trinity of persons by natural reasons."[6] The response is clear: "It is to be said that one can never come to knowledge of the divine Trinity of persons through natural reasons." The explanation given is the one St. Thomas always gives: our natural reason comes to God through his effects, and all that pertains to God in his causality is essential. This is unambiguously Thomistic. The limitations are in place, if not in the exact place Frs. Dondaine and Torrell would want them.

Let us now turn to the argument itself in the *Roman Commentary*, for it was this, with its chains of necessity, that Frs. Dondaine and Torrell found unsettling. The response is a lengthy one; permit me to summarize. In it, St. Thomas gives an analogical account of the Trinity in two parts. In the first, St. Thomas argues from analogy by way of divine knowing and willing; in the second, he articulates a critical difference in the analogy between God and creatures.

Let us look to the first part in which St. Thomas lays out the analogy. He begins with divine perfection. Since the principal perfections among things are to know and to will (*intelligere* and *velle*), these cannot be lacking in God because God is perfect. St. Thomas then states what properly proceeds from knowing in the created order, that is, a word, and what properly proceeds from willing (that is, from loving) in the created order, that is, spirit. Since God is perfect, he must know and will; since word and spirit are proper to knowing and willing, there must be in God a divine word and spirit. Only after making this argument from analogy does St. Thomas turn to the proper names of the divine persons and apply them to what he has shown analogically, saying, we call the principle "Father," the word "Son," and the love "Holy Spirit." So the first part of the response.

In the second part of the response, St. Thomas states that there is a difference between created knowing and willing on the one hand and divine knowing and willing on the other, namely that what is accidental and intentional in us is essential in God. This is a statement of philosophical fact. He concludes this second part with the application of this fact by way of fittingness to what he has already said of the divine persons: "But because all of these are one in God which pertain to essence, thus it is fittingly said that Father, Son, and Holy Spirit are one God."

In the course of laying this out, St. Thomas uses language of necessity four times; this frequency was noted by Fr. Torrell as a matter of concern. But let us see where this language is to be found. In the argument from analogy it appears twice. First, in considering the natural analog of created love, St. Thomas says that it is necessary that the beloved be intrinsic to the lover. This is a claim on the natural order. The second instance is found in the move from the natural analog to God, namely, that since God knows and loves Himself perfectly, what proceeds by way of knowing and by way of loving must be in God. This is a claim for divine operation from divine perfection. The language of necessity is thus found in establishing the natural analog and in the relationship of divine perfection to divine operation analogically considered. At the critical point in the argument when St. Thomas applies this to the Trinity of divine persons, we find no language of necessity; rather, we have what we might call the implications of fittingness.

Two more instances of the language of necessity are found in the second part of the response which considers the difference between God and creatures. First, because God's *esse* is his *intelligere*, the word that proceeds from divine *intelligere* must be of the same essence and nature as God. The second instance is much like the first with regard to both word and spirit, namely, that since only what is subsisting is in the divine nature, both word and spirit must be *subsistens esse*. These are philosophical points. When St. Thomas makes the move to the divine persons proper, his language shifts from necessity to fittingness.

Such is what we find in the *Roman Commentary*. Is this line of argument and its use of necessity in argument compatible with St. Thomas?

We turn to the parallel article of the indubitably authentic *De Potentia* 9.5, with its more circumspect opening already noted by Fr. Torrell. In this article, St. Thomas asks whether there is a number of persons in the divine. We find here the same argument from analogy as in the *Roman Commentary*; or rather half of it. Here is the argument from knowing, developed more fully and technically, without the argument from willing. The distinction between created and divine knowing then follows. Likewise, we find the language of intellectual necessity at the critical point of the application of the analogy to God on the basis of his perfection. St. Thomas says it is necessary to posit knowing in God, and then because there is knowing in God, it is necessary to posit a word in God. In their respective arguments, the articles of the *De Potentia* and the *Roman Commentary* are the same.

I should note briefly the parallel chapters in St. Thomas' later *Compendium Theologiae*. In the *Compendium* we find, yet again, the same line of analogical argument from the operation of knowing and willing in creatures, to their operation in God, to their ultimate application to the divine persons, with the note on the significant difference that God is His operations. The argument is again the same; and no wonder, for much of the response in the *Roman Commentary* article is found verbatim in the *Compendium*.

We have, in short, a fine bit of Thomistic reasoning here in the *Roman Commentary*. St. Thomas looks to divine perfection and considers what, of necessity, this means we must say of God. Most perfect among created things are intellectual beings. He asks, what is proper to intellectual beings precisely as intellectual beings, that is, what must one have to have an intellectual being? Given the answer to that question, one knows what must be posited analogically of God. We see here the remarkable interplay in St. Thomas' thought between analogy and necessity. This takes him to truths about God. It even gets him close to the Trinity; that is, for those who have had the Trinity revealed to them, they can see that these truths of God are fitting to the revealed Triune God.

And then, as with any analogies applied to God, there are elements in the primary created analog that do not apply to God (hence this is analogy not univocity). In this case, it is the essential identity of divine essence and operations. Thus, to know and to love in God are different from how they are in any other intellectual being. Remarkably, that precise point of analogical difference is itself particularly fitting to the persons of the Trinity.

As an editor, I had put my anxieties about the charge of rationalism to rest.[7] Now, however, I was puzzled by the charge in the first place. Fr. Dondaine was one of the grand Dominicans of the Leonine Commission. Fr. Torrell needs no introduction to contemporary students of St. Thomas. These are not men to pose speculative concerns lightly. And yet, the problem was not the *Roman Commentary*. Dare I think the problem was St. Thomas himself? I will not presume to read the mind of Frs. Dondaine and Torrell, but something had spooked them.

Do we perhaps see here the theological consequences of some of the philosophical problems described in *Fides et Ratio*? Two of John Paul II's affirmations seem especially relevant: first, the importance of metaphysics understood as the science of things in their being and essence; and, second, that the human mind can know the truth. These two go together. That we know the truth means more than recognizing a formally valid argument. We know things, and we know them truly—albeit incompletely—in their being and their essence.

But philosophers are now hesitant before metaphysical claims of reality—or perhaps most claims of reality. How many philosophers think arguments can be given for the existence of God? And of those, how many think any of St. Thomas' five ways would be one of them? Or, to pick the subject closer to hand, how many philosophers would find St. Thomas' argument for divine intellection from divine perfection anything but formally valid? Dare we ask how many would give a moment's notice to St. Thomas' description of the production of a "word" in the act of intellection? I ask "how many" merely rhetorically. Choosing a sugarless gum may be a matter of three out of four dentists surveyed, but truth surely is not a matter of three out of four philosophers surveyed. Still, as John Paul II so keenly realized, these matters are also cultural matters. Three out of four philosophers do matter, if not for determining the truth, then for what a culture takes to be the truth.

So it is we would really rather not have St. Thomas quite so committed to particular truths of reason, since so many of those he seemed so committed to, are, well, the subject of ridicule in the hands of modern philosophers. Sir Anthony Kenney has recently argued that St. Thomas' very concept of being is wrong. And so it is, if Frege is your starting point. Worse than wrong, St. Thomas may be ridiculous.

I recall the visit to our University not long after the publication of *Fides et Ratio*, of a philosopher prelate, student and friend of Karol Wojtyla. I asked him informally about the role of St. Thomas Aquinas in the life of the Catholic intellectual in general and in *Fides et Ratio* in particular. He answered that St. Thomas is principally a model of method, not a teacher of content. St. Thomas shows us how to be open to reason, to new thinkers, to different ideas. This is certainly an inadequate summation of *Fides et Ratio*. It is, however, as Dr. David Berger noted in a lecture on the idea of Thomism, a typically German understanding of the importance of St. Thomas; for example, the editor of Josef Pieper's collected works insists that Pieper is not a Thomist, for he does not want Pieper identified with philosophically ridiculous ideas. Such a limit to St. Thomas' importance is found among non-German speakers, too. It admits of a personal piety towards St. Thomas without his embarrassing philosophical content.

Just such potentially embarrassing metaphysical reasoning is, however, at work in the *Roman Commentary*. What is the nature of beings with intellects? The difficult work is to get at what is proper to those things, what is essential to them, such that without it, one does not have such things. It is just such intellectual work that seems now so tentative, so questionable. Many philosophers have lost their nerve precisely at this point. A kind of timidity has overtaken philosophy, and even to philosophers, John Paul II has had to proclaim, "Be not afraid."

All of this has profound implications for theology. This is perhaps most obvious in those places where theology and philosophy so clearly overlap, such as the existence of God. We have a kind of withdrawal from metaphysical rigor or, perhaps better, from speculative rigor. By this I mean precisely the demands of necessity either by way of formal argument or, even more, by way of nature, property, and definition. If philosophers are timid, then theologians tend to follow suit. Thus, St. Thomas' regular and frequent appeal to just this kind of necessity strikes a modern ear as perhaps over-confident and unfounded. The theologian retreats to the certitudes of faith from the ever increasingly assaulted certitudes of reason. The certitudes of faith are indeed certain and are sufficient for heaven. They are not, however, sufficient for theology if it is to be a true science.

The theological implications of the metaphysical crisis are also found in those areas that are strictly a matter of revealed truth. Here, we work, with St. Thomas, by way of fittingness. But arguments from fittingness are load bearing only in proportion to the solidity of the philosophical work that undergirds them. It is fitting to speak of the second person of the Blessed Trinity as a word, and the third person as a spirit. But the strength of that fittingness is directly dependent upon the reality of intellectual beings as beings that know and love. Precisely because such beings must have certain properties or they would not be such beings, it is all the more fitting that these properties be attributed to the divine persons. And that argument from fittingness is even more powerful if, as St. Thomas argues, precinding from any consideration of divine persons, the very properties must necessarily be posited in God.

Let us return to our friend analogy, at the heart of the contentious article of the *Roman Commentary*. My impression is that much current theological reflection is interested in analogy, perhaps in part because it seems like a way around the attacks on reason. Trinitarian analogies seem to be particularly abundant. Many of them are rather moving and have a kind of insightfulness, of, if I may say, a literary kind. Like poetry, one might not want to push them too hard speculatively. One acknowledges, of course, that there are limitations to an analogy but the precise locus of limitation does not seem to be vigorously pursued, no more than one might vigorously pursue the ways in which my love is and is not like a rose. Do not get me wrong, I have no brief against poetry. No Thomist possibly can in the face of a master who composed *Lauda, Sion, Salvatorem*; but theology is not poetry or limited to poetry.

Analogy presupposes the very conditions that John Paul II has articulated. If two things are to be considered in their analogical relation, then one must be as clear as possible about the property that is the basis for the analogy in the primary analog. The truer one is to the essential properties of the thing itself, then the more profound and compelling the analogy. Likewise, the precise points of difference need to be discovered and articulated. Such is true for philosophy and any number of human sciences that make use of analogy, that is to say, all of them. It is most pressing for theology, which necessarily must speak analogically of God. What one sees so clearly in St. Thomas is how advancement in theology as a science dependent upon analogy, is utterly dependent upon the health of philosophy.

What strikes me about the work of St. Thomas is how a world that was metaphysically robust was vigorous and serious in its pursuit and critique of analogies. St. Thomas (and his predecessors and contemporaries) sought precision in the primary analog in created things. St. Thomas' move to intellectual procession as an analogy for the Trinity, presented so exquisitely in the *Summa Theologiae*, is, in its way, a radical precision of the Augustinian psychological analogies. For St. Thomas the goal is always the better understanding of the thing in front of him and this is the work of reason. Precision in understanding of the created order provides precision in theological analysis. This was impressed upon me afresh on a recent visit to the reading room of the John Ireland Library at The Saint Paul Seminary.

In an issue of *Communio*, Professor Adrian Walker of the John Paul II Institute in Washington posited an analogy between being and the Trinity. Something in the very nature of being is an outwardly directed excess and thereby relational. Thus, individual beings stand in some kind of necessary relation one to another and in that are analogous to the relationship between the persons of the Trinity. The essay has a poetic drama about it, but I must confess I can make little metaphysical sense of it. It looks like a category error. It might not be; but Professor Walker has not made the philosophical arguments for the primary natural analog in being itself. He is, I think, too eager to get to the Trinity and too confident that the revealed truth of the Trinity will fill in whatever gaps and slips are at work in the supposedly natural primary analog. I could have Professor Walker wrong. He is smart. I know; I taught him logic many years ago when he was an undergraduate at the University of San Francisco. I no longer teach logic.

On that same trip to the reading room, I found an essay in the most recent issue of *Mediaeval Studies* on the topic of excess (*excessus*) in St. Thomas by Professor Peter Kwasniewksi of the International Theological Institute in Gaming, Austria. Professor Kwasniewski traced this humble idea from its primary home in the category of quantity, through St. Thomas' many analogical uses of it in both philosophy and theology (including its use to describe a certain way of speaking about God). It stood in contrast to Professor Walker's essay which had dealt too with the theme of excess. Professor Kwasniewski's essay was perhaps a bit short on drama, but was nonetheless a model of the philosophical and metaphysical work that needs to be done to make analogies speculatively useful. Unfortunately, I cannot claim to have taught logic to Professor Kwasniewski.

I do not need to tell those gathered here this evening that *Fides et Ratio* is a remarkable document. John Paul II has set before us a noble and daunting task. There is much labor needed in this harvest. I am, however, increasingly convinced that our labor will be made lighter and richer by the study of St. Thomas who so ably tended the field before us.

NOTES

1. Thomas Aquinas, *Lectura romana in primum Sententiarum Petri Lombardi*, ed. Leonard E. Boyle, O.P. and John F. Boyle (Toronto: Pontifical Institute of Mediaeval Studies, 2006).

2. H.F. Dondaine, "'*Alia lectura fratris Thome? (Super I Sent.)*'", *Mediaeval Studies* 42 (1980): 308—36.

3. Leonard E. Boyle, "'*Alia lectura fratris Thome,*'" *Mediaeval Studies* 45 (1983): 418—29; reprinted with minor corrections in *Lectura romana*, 58—69.

4. Dondaine, 320; J.P. Torrell in his introduction to Leonard E. Boyle, *Facing History: A Different Thomas Aquinas* (Louvain-La-Neauve: Fédération Internationale des Instituts d'Études Médiévales, 2000), xxiii—xxiv.

5. Aquinas, *Lectura romana*, 2.2.4.resp.

6. Ibid., 3.1.3.

7. I have addressed this more fully in John F. Boyle, "Aquinas' Roman Commentary on Peter Lombard," *Anuario Filosofico* 39 (2006): 477—96 at 489—96.

Chapter Five

From Scholasticism to Personalism

Avery Cardinal Dulles, S.J. († 2008)

Pope John Paul II is generally, and I think correctly, characterized as a Thomist of the personalist school. St. Thomas Aquinas epitomizes the Scholasticism of the high Middle Ages. On the eve of Vatican II there was a revolt against Scholasticism on the part of personalists such as Henri de Lubac. Karol Wojtyla, the future John Paul II, was certainly close to de Lubac and other leaders of this revolt, but I do not find in his work any general criticism of Scholasticism. He shows no signs of being in rebellion against the Scholasticism of his professors. He wrote his Roman doctoral dissertation under the direction of Réginald Garrigou-Lagrange, O.P., who was the epitome of twentieth-century neoscholasticism and perhaps the most outspoken critic of de Lubac and the *nouvelle théologie*. It is very difficult, therefore, to say whether Karol Wojtyla should be characterized as a Scholastic. Perhaps we can say that he wanted to retrieve Scholasticism in a personalist key. That, at least, would be one way of reading the encyclical *Fides et Ratio (FR)*.

To characterize Scholasticism in general terms, we may say that it works by preference with universal concepts rather than individual perceptions. It uses history and experience as raw material from which to abstract universal concepts, including analogous concepts that are applicable to being as a whole in all its modalities. But it leaves aside the accidentals of individual cases and concentrates on the essential, known by the process of abstraction.

In the realm of philosophical anthropology, Scholasticism fixes its attention on human nature and on the properties and faculties that flow from nature. It recognizes that nature exists in individual persons, each of whom lives in particular circumstances which are capable of being described but evade precise definition. Human nature, like any other nature, has an inbuilt finality, which is described as the beatitude proportioned to human nature.

Scholastic theologians hold that human nature can be elevated by sanctifying grace, which imparts supernatural life. The supernatural is a gift that lies beyond the capacities and exigencies of nature, but one that nature is capable of receiving. The picture is therefore painted of a two-storey building, the lower storey being nature and the upper storey grace. Grace can be given or lost without intrinsically changing human nature.

Personalism does not necessarily reject this Scholastic view, but it prefers to take a concrete or existential approach. The human person, it insists, is not reducible to human nature. Nature is something that we *have*, but we *are* persons, subjects. Nature does not make decisions, but persons do. The person is inalienably individual and ineffable. No one can translate my individuality into a nature or a set of characteristics.

Personalists are not content to speak of sanctifying grace as a created entity, an entitative habit, as Scholastics do. They understand grace in interpersonal terms, as an inter-subjective relationship with God. The presence of God in the human spirit is not just a superstructure, they assert, but a matter of personal indwelling, an encounter with the divine as it freely gives itself in love. In place of created grace they speak by preference of uncreated grace, the grace that is inseparable from the very person of the one who gives it. In grace, they tell us, the divine persons give us not something but themselves.

A controversy arose in the 1940's about the supernatural. De Lubac insisted that it was not just a superadded gift standing on top of nature, so that nature without it could be complete and attain its own connatural end. Human persons were by nature ordained to a supernatural end, to the vision of God, and could not be satisfied with anything less. For de Lubac, the effort of modern Scholasticism to characterize the operations and finality of pure nature was misconceived. But the neoscholastics replied that if the supernatural is an undeserved gift, there must be such a thing as pure nature to receive it. To know what the supernatural contributes one must have some idea of what nature would be without it.

Scholastics do not deny that human nature does not and never has existed in a pure state. From the beginning it was constituted with an ordination to a supernatural end and was elevated by grace. After the Fall, nature was wounded by the loss of supernatural gifts, and with the Redemption it was recalled to supernatural life in Christ and the Holy Spirit. But the history of salvation does nothing to impugn the concept of pure nature.

Karl Rahner tried to build a bridge between Scholasticism and personalism by distinguishing between abstract human nature and concrete human nature. Nature has always existed in a supernatural order and is necessarily affected by the call to the supernatural vision of God. This call, he held, impresses on human nature a permanent mark which he called, in Heideggerian terminology, a supernatural existential; but it leaves nature in its essence intact.

In *Fides et Ratio* John Paul II does not involve himself in disputes about whether human nature exists or could exist in a pure state. But as a personalist he opts to speak of the actual order, in which every human person is made for God and cannot find rest except in God. The opening line of Augustine's *Confessions* is never far from the pope's thoughts. "In the far reaches of the human heart," he writes, "there is a seed of desire and nostalgia for God" (*FR,* §24). Human existence is a journey that necessarily unfolds within the horizon of self-consciousness.

The anthropology of *Fides et Ratio* is unmistakably Christian. Jesus Christ, it states, contains the fullness of truth, and is the key to understanding our human world (*FR,* §34; 81-82). Quoting from what is probably his favorite text from Vatican II, the pope asserts that Christ the Lord, "in revealing the mystery of the Father and his love, fully reveals man to himself and makes clear his supreme calling" which, the pope adds, is "to share in the divine mystery of the life of the Trinity" (*FR*, §13, cf. *Gaudium et Spes*, §22).

Pope John Paul II is interested chiefly in the life of the mind. Christ is for him the paragon and source of wisdom. Human blessedness for him is a matter of knowing God rather than having one's sins forgiven, as it might be for someone in the Lutheran or Evangelical tradition. At least in this encyclical one does not find much emphasis on sin, the cross, and redemption.

Scholasticism and personalism differ from each other in their conceptions of philosophy and theology. Scholasticism takes a highly objective approach to philosophy, which it defines as the study of ultimate principles or ultimate causes. Metaphysics for the Scholastic operates at the highest degree of abstraction, elucidating the nature and properties of being as such. Personalism cultivates a different type of philosophy or wisdom, is tied up with our existence as persons.

John Paul II, as I understand him, tries to do justice to both points of view. Early in the encyclical he seems to affirm that there is such a thing as "perennial philosophy." He says,

> Although times change and knowledge increases it is possible to discern a core of philosophical insight within the history of thought as a whole. Consider, for example, the principles of non-contradiction, finality and causality, as well as the concept of the person as a free and intelligent subject with the capacity to know God, truth, and goodness (*FR*, §4).

On guard against historical relativism, John Paul II notes with disapproval that "there are signs of a widespread distrust of universal and absolute statements" (*FR*, §56). He joins Pius XII in maintaining that the basic concepts of dogma retain their universal epistemological value and thus retain the truth of the propositions in which they are expressed (*FR* 96). Several times in the course of his encyclical the Pope affirms the importance of metaphysics, a term associated with Aristotle and the Scholastic tradition.

All of this would warm the heart of a Neo-Scholastic like Garrigou-Lagrange, but there is another side to Wojtyla. He likes to define philosophy more existentially as a discipline that throws light on the ultimate purposes of our existence as persons and on the path of life that leads to ultimate fulfillment (*FR*, §15). Philosophy begins with wonder, and seeks to carry out the precept, "Know thyself," inscribed on the temple portal at Delphi (*FR*, §1).

Metaphysics, for John Paul II, is not something abstract and impersonal. "Metaphysics," he writes, "should not be seen as an alternative to anthropology, since it is metaphysics which makes it possible to ground the concept of the person's dignity in virtue of the person's spiritual nature" (*FR*, §83). For John Paul II the experience of interiority is a privileged starting point for metaphysics which seeks to penetrate to the ultimate core of spiritual experience and to identify the grounds from which it arises (Ibid.).

Scholasticism leans toward using strictly rational and even deductive methods in philosophy, working as far as possible from self-evident and indubitable principles. It sees the individual thinker as self-sufficient, having within his own mind the evidence for what he holds. Personalism, however, emphasizes the fiducial component, as Michael Polanyi contends in his classic, *Personal Knowledge*. Within the individual psyche are tacit elements that we can never articulate, even to ourselves. But they weigh heavily in influencing our convictions about what is true. The individual, moreover, is never an isolated atom. He or she operates in a community with its traditions.

John Paul II in *Fides et Ratio* shows himself to have a decidedly personalist approach to philosophical method. Belief, he says,

> Is often humanly richer than mere evidence, because it involves an interpersonal relationship and brings into play not only a person's capacity to know but also the deeper capacity to entrust oneself to others, to enter into a relationship with them which is intimate and enduring. . . . In the act of believing, men and women entrust themselves to the truth which the other declares to them (*FR*, §32).

It is generally acknowledged that tradition plays an important part in theology because revelation is handed down in tradition. *Fides et Ratio*, however, holds that tradition is pervasive in human relations.

> Human beings are not made to live alone; they are born into a family and in a family they grow. . . . From birth, therefore, they are immersed in traditions which give them not only a language and a cultural formation but also a range of truths in which they believe almost instinctively (*FR*, §31).

Following Pius XII, John Paul II warns against neglect of the philosophical tradition (*FR*, §55). Philosophy, he contends, need to develop in continuity with the great tradition that begins with the ancients, passes through the fathers and the masters of Scholasticism. Because we belong to this tradition, it possesses us, and we are not in a position to dispose of it at will (*FR*, §85).

Just as personalism favors tacit knowledge and tradition, so too it calls for dialogue. Philosophical reason, says the Pope, needs to be sustained in all its searching by trusting dialogue and sincere friendship. Because the same principle holds to an even greater degree in theology, the gulf between the two disciplines is not as wide as some suppose. Theology cannot find its way apart from Tradition which works together with Sacred Scripture and the Magisterium to provide its source and guide (*FR*, §55).

Turning to theological method, John Paul II makes use of the distinction between the hearing of faith, which grounds positive theology, and the understanding of faith, which is the objective of speculative theology. In each of these two phases, theology relies upon the attitude of faith which must now be explored.

Faith itself is differently conceived in Scholasticism and personalism. Scholasticism sees it primarily as an intellectual assent to propositional truth based on the authority of a witness. Divine faith is an assent to the testimony of God the revealer. The act of faith is both reasonable and supernatural. It is reasonable because the fact of revelation is evident thanks to the proofs that are available. It is supernatural because only an assent given with the help of divine grace can be conductive to salvation.

According to Scholastic theologians, the Christian faith was given in its fullness in apostolic times and has been handed down since then as a deposit. It is accessible through Scripture and tradition.

Personalism has a different perspective on faith. It describes faith as an act of the whole person, whereby one entrusts oneself to God as he discloses himself in historical events. God's self-disclosure is seen to be an act of love and an invitation to communion. In *Fides et Ratio* §13 John Paul II, building on *Dei Verbum* §5, combines the Scholastic and the personalist visions of faith, with greater emphasis on the latter.

The Council teaches that "the obedience of faith must be given to God who reveals Himself." This brief but dense statement points to a fundamental truth of Christianity. Faith is said first to be an obedient response to God. This implies that God be acknowledged in His divinity, transcendence and supreme freedom. By the authority of His absolute transcendence, God who makes Himself known is also the source of the credibility of who He reveals. By faith, men and women give their assent to this divine testimony. This means that they acknowledge fully and integrally the truth of what is revealed, because it is God Himself who is the guarantor of that truth. They can make no claim upon the truth that comes to them as gift and which, set within the context of interpersonal communication, urges reason to be open to it and to embrace its profound meaning. This is why the Church has always considered the act of entrusting oneself to God to be a moment of fundamental decision which engages the whole person. In that act, the intellect and the will display their spiritual nature, enabling the subject to act in a way which realizes personal freedom to the full.

This text preserves the Scholastic idea of faith as assent to truth based on the authority of God the revealer, but combines it with several themes from personalism: namely that God reveals Himself, that His revelation is a free and loving gift, that faith establishes a relationship of mutual communication, that faith is an act of obedience, and that in faith the believer entrusts himself or herself entirely to God by a fully free, personal decision.

As opposed to Scholasticism, personalism is inclined to look upon revelation as an act occurring today. Its content may be the same as what was revealed to our ancestors, but God is active in disclosing Himself here and now. In Vatican II and *Fides et Ratio* the emphasis is on the revelation made in the past, handed down in Scripture and Tradition. In this respect, there has been no departure from Scholasticism.

In traditional Scholasticism it was common to say that faith is above reason, which is obviously the case if it means that faith grasps certain truths that lie beyond the reach of unaided human reason. *Fides et Ratio* approvingly quotes Vatican I as having said that there are two orders of knowledge, faith and reason, and that faith is superior to reason (*FR*, §53). But John Paul II also asserts that faith and reason are correlative; that they mutually support one another (*FR*, §100), and that faith itself is an exercise of reason in the sense that it is an act of intelligence (*FR*, §43). At one point the pope even says that faith and reason contain each other (*FR*, §17). In explaining the relationship between philosophy and theology, he states that it is best construed as a circle (*FR*, §73)—a statement that seems accurate enough if it refers to the use of reason in dogmatic theology. In general the pope seems to shy away from the metaphor of a building with different stories and to prefer circular or cyclical metaphors that are less hierarchical and Scholastic in tone.

In conclusion, I should like to say a few words about apologetics. In Scholasticism apologetics took on very great importance as a means of demonstrating that the assent of faith, while going beyond reason, was not irrational. It had to be shown that there were objective grounds of certitude that God had indeed spoken and that His word was true. Vatican I, written in this climate, took pains to point out that the existence of God as creator and last end could be proved by unaided reason, and that the fact of revelation in the case of Christianity was evidently credible. The divine origin of the Christian religion could be proved by the miracles and prophecies testifying in its favor.

With Vatican II a very different mentality prevailed. The Council's interest seemed to focus not on how the believer can be sure of his faith but rather on how God goes about making Himself known to persons such as ourselves. Miracles came to be viewed not as proofs but rather as divine signs or meaningful gestures, analogous to human speech.

In *Fides et Ratio* John Paul II shows more awareness of the apologetic question than Vatican II, but his suggested apologetics is more personalistic than that of Vatican I. As already noted, he makes much of the nostalgia for God that he finds rooted in the human heart. It is in the nature of the human being to seek for absolute truth (*FR*, §33). At one point he remarks, "It is unthinkable that a search so deeply rooted in human nature would be completely vain and useless" (*FR*, §29). Thus his proof for the existence of God seems to be based primarily on the natural desire to find God—a desire that nothing other than God himself could satisfy. The more ardently we love and desire God, the better disposed are we to find him (*FR*, §42).

The pope takes note, to be sure, of the natural knowledge of God that can be gained from the study of nature, but he treats this less as a proof than as the first stage in the process of revelation (*FR*, §§19, 22). God attests to Himself through the order of nature, and His testimony is credible. The fullness of revelation is given in Jesus Christ, "who in his testimony before Pontius Pilate made the good confession" (1 Tim 6:13). It is in faithful self-giving, says the pope, that a person finds the fullness of certainty and security. The martyrs, he maintains, are the most authentic witnesses to the truth about existence. They "stir in us a profound trust because they give voice to what we already feel and they declare what we would like to have the strength to express"(*FR*, §32). This sentence, even when read in context, does not contain a full apologetics of testimony but it seems to point in that direction.

To conclude, I would judge that *Fides et Ratio* represents a retrieval of Scholasticism in the light of modern personalism. This is a very promising direction for fundamental theology but it leaves some open questions. The genre of an encyclical cannot be expected to settle the theoretical questions that can be raised, but it is not difficult to see that the pope is treading a very narrow line.

He is clearly inclined toward personalism but develops it in a way that avoids contradicting the traditional theses of Scholasticism.

SECTION TWO

QUESTIONS ON THE NATURE AND
IMPORTANCE OF TRUTH FOR
THE CATHOLIC INTELLECTUAL

CHAPTER SIX

THE NATURAL KNOWLEDGE OF GOD IN *FIDES ET RATIO*

Guy Mansini, O.S.B.

Fides et Ratio affirms the capacity of human reason to know God. This is not a new teaching of the Roman Church. What is new is the careful consideration of the conditions of the exercise of this capacity. Faith and reason are the two wings of man, on which he rises to the knowledge of truth. And what the encyclical implies, if it does not assert it in so many words, is that just as there is no flight of bird or bat with but one wing, so reason does not succeed in rising to even the natural knowledge of God outside of the context of supernatural faith. It is my purpose to show this implication. This is not some Milbankian conflation of reason and faith, but the thesis that reason needs faith to attain to the knowledge of God of which reason is naturally capable.[1] Moreover, I mean to say that the need that reason has for faith in order to attain to the knowledge of God of which it is capable is a peculiarly modern need. That is, it is modern or contemporary reason that will not attain to the natural knowledge of God except within the precincts of religion.

Previous receptions of the encyclical have noted the confidence in reason the pope expresses, and the challenge to reason, to philosophical reason, that he issues to go beyond the limits of scientism and positivism, to shake off the lethargy of relativism and historicism, and re-possess itself of the metaphysical richness bequeathed to it from the Greeks.[2] This challenge, however, is accompanied by a finely tuned perception of the weakness and fragility of reason in fallen and unredeemed man.

I. THE CAPACITY TO KNOW GOD AND ITS EXERCISE

Fides et Ratio several times affirms the capacity of reason to know God. The Holy Father asserts that the import of the Letter to the Romans at 1:19-20 "is to concede to human reason a capacity which seems almost to surpass its natural limitations," in that "reason can reach the cause which lies at the origins of all perceptible reality," that is, God (II, 22a).[3] Such capacity is asserted also in discussing the Book of Wisdom, on which Romans draws (II, 19a). The encyclical invokes the teaching of the First Vatican Council, itself based on Romans, on the natural knowability of God (V, 53). This Council, it will be recalled, strictly affirms only a capacity. To say something is naturally knowable is not the same thing as to say it is naturally known. As it were, the Council asserts the natural knowledge of God *de jure*. But it does not assert it *de facto*, or tell us how the natural capacity to know God may be exercised beyond what we can read in Romans. *Fides et Ratio* asserts this capacity also apropos of Acts 17, speaking of "reason's capacity to rise beyond what is contingent and set out towards the infinite" (III, 24b).[4]

Capacities, however, are known from their exercises; possibilities are known from actualities. And there are affirmations of the exercise of the capacity to know God, too. First, when the discussion relies on Wisdom and Romans, it is clear that the Holy Father is assuming these texts to assert, not just a possibility, but an actuality: God has really and truly been known from the things that have been made (II, 19I, 22a).[5]

In IV, 36a, a natural knowledge of God is asserted, where the encyclical speaks of how Christians from the beginning appealed to it in preaching the gospel. And just after this, we have a very generous statement of how ancient pagan philosophy cleansed pagan religion of many unworthy elements (IV, 36b, and see IV, 41a).[6]

The natural knowledge of God achieved in "Christian Philosophy" is very clearly asserted in Chapter VI, 76c. At the same time, however, this paragraph seems to make a very important observation as to what reason in fact did *not* achieve apart from revelation, although it could have.

Revelation clearly proposes certain truths that might never have been discovered by reason unaided, although they are not of themselves inaccessible to reason. Among these truths is the notion of a free and personal God who is the Creator of the world.[7]

The implication is that the existence of God as Creator was a truth not in fact discovered by reason, not in fact seen by the natural light, until after the supernatural light had dawned on us.

If we let this statement of VI, 76c control our reading, as I think we should, then we will understand that the natural knowledge of God that the Letter to the Romans and the Book of Wisdom assert man has cannot be so full, and will likely not be unmixed with error, compared to the natural knowledge of God attained in Christian philosophy.[8] That is what the Holy Father implies when, just after appeal to Romans 1:20 in II, 22a, he speaks of sin making for a "diminished access to God" via reason (22b). In this context, it is only "the coming of Christ ... which redeemed reason from its weakness" (22c).

II. CONDITIONS OF THE EXERCISE OF THE CAPACITY TO KNOW GOD

Evidently, there are conditions on the exercise of the natural capacity of reason to know God. *Fides et Ratio*, moreover and as Cardinal Dulles points out, is distinctive among magisterial statements in how carefully it considers these conditions.[9]

This is after all nothing except to advert to the history of reason. Indeed, why is there an historical chapter in *Fides et Ratio*? Why is Chapter IV there? Because it is not only faith that has a history, but reason. The history of faith depends on the history of revelation, which Chapter I deals with (see especially 11). But reason, too has a history (see V, 51, especially), because reason works only under conditions, and the conditions vary; moreover, the knowledge of the conditions varies, and this itself enters into the history of reason. After all, we should expect reason, "discursive reason," temporally extended knowing, to have a history.

I will argue that, according to the encyclical, the exact condition under which post-lapsarian reason comes to the knowledge of God is faith.

If such be the case, we may well ask how such a truth itself comes to be known. Is the knowledge of this condition of the successful exercise of natural reason something known by reason itself or by faith? The conditions of the exercise of reason, since they have a history, are known historically. Also, one of the principal sources of our knowledge of these conditions, the decisive source, and the most important source of our knowledge of these conditions is revelation. In this way, the history of reason is something to be known only by faith.

The conditions are known only by faith, for the most encompassing human history is the history of salvation. Therefore only faith can say what reason is, insofar as knowledge of the concrete context of its deployment is a part of knowing it. Of course, reason says something about itself, its conditions and their history, but it cannot tell the full story. Only faith knows the full story, for only faith knows both faith and reason.

This is nothing but the deployment of a familiar argument that to know a limit as a limit requires being beyond the limit and the same kind of argument can be deployed with reference to history. We know a nature by knowing its powers, powers by knowing the operations, the operations by knowing the objects of the operations. But the objects to which human reason may extend are known fully only by faith; therefore, etc. At least, they are known more perfectly, as to what nature grasps, and to what nature aided by grace, reason illumined by faith, extends. Therefore, reason is known more perfectly through faith than through itself.[10]

So, Chapter I presents revelation as the foundation of the encyclical's considerations of faith and reason, as the Holy Father has already indicated he would do in the Introduction (6a-b).

To return to history: if there is a fuller history of reason than reason can know, then the knowledge of that fuller history, by faith, renders a better, more complete knowledge of reason than reason has of itself. Now, the history in Chapter IV is the history of faith and post-lapsarian reason. It therefore presupposes the fuller history that includes the fall. An allusion to this is found in IV, 21: the ready access to God reason enjoyed before the fall is diminished by sin. To be sure, it is the nature of post-lapasarian reason, its scope or extent, with which this essay is concerned.

III. THAT THE EXERCISE OF REASON IN ATTAINING TO GOD IS SUCCESSFUL ONLY UNDER FAITH

Fides et Ratio implies that reason attains to God successfully, where success means knowing God as Creator, only under the condition of faith. This reading of the encyclical is founded in both Chapter II and Chapter III. In Chapter II, *Credo ut intellegam*, there is as it were a theological assertion of the conditionedness of reason, such that it will attain to God only under faith. In Chapter III, *Intelligo ut credam*, there is a more philosophical manifestation of this conditionedness. Chapter III suggests *why* reason's attainment of God depends on faith. But also—*Fides et Ratio* is a very complex text—Chapter II provides a theological statement of how it is Christ enables reason to attain to God. Christ addresses the weakness of reason, the weakness induced by sin. Chapter III, on the other hand, lays out a sort of philosophical preparation for meeting the truth about man, addressing what the Holy Father calls "ultimate questions," in Christ. Both chapters end with Christ and are therefore true to the teaching of *Gaudium et Spes*, 22, that the truth about man is found completely only in Christ, whether our questioning begins theologically or philosophically.[11] Let us turn more closely to Chapters II and III.

In Chapter II, where faith precedes understanding, the Holy Father repeats the teaching of the Book of Wisdom that reason can come to know God from nature (19). Further: "Making his own the thought of Greek philosophy, to which he seems to refer in the context, the author affirms that, in reasoning about nature, the human being can rise to God." And then he quotes 13:5: "From the greatness and beauty of created things comes a corresponding perception of their Creator." This does not say exactly what the author took from the Greeks or that the Greeks knew God as creator from nature. According to its title, moreover, this chapter regards reason functioning under the guardianship of faith. What that guardianship consists of is spelled out in 18. The affirmation in 19, that according to the Book of Wisdom reason can come to know God, seems to be made with the understanding that reason does not abandon the "rules" listed just before in 18a. These rules are as follows: that reason realize the unfinished nature of its journey; that it realize the necessity of humility; and that it recognize the "transcendent sovereignty and provident love" of God. Thus, given the knowledge of faith, the knowledge that rests on accepting the word of God, reason can see also, from nature, that God exists. Abandoning these rules renders one a "fool," i.e. one who says there is no God (18b; Ps 14:1).

The discussion of Romans 1 also takes place in this chapter (22). John Paul II reports St. Paul as saying that reason can know God. Romans 1:20 "concede[s] to human reason a capacity which seems almost to surpass its natural limitations . . . reason can reach the cause that lies at the origin of all perceptible reality." However, while in the "original plan" of God, reason would have "ready access" to God, this access is diminished by Adam's sin (21). The coming of Christ, however—which is to say the fullness of revelation—frees reason "from the shackles in which it had imprisoned itself." This occurs, moreover, within the conviction of human wisdom as folly (1 Cor 1:20), and accords with St. Paul's observation that "when I am weak, then I am strong" (2 Cor 12:10). Christ redeems the weakness of reason, the weakness induced by sin, not as by the restoration of some praeternatural gift, but in the submission and obedience of faith. That is, given faith, reason can once more see relatively easily the power and divinity of God from the things that have been made.

It is true that subsequently in Chapter IV, 36b, the Holy Father will say that pre-Christian philosophical knowledge of the divine transcendence worked to "purify human notions of God of mythological elements." And in 70c, the various human cultures "point to the manifestation of God in nature, as we saw earlier in considering the wisdom literature and the teaching of St. Paul." However, the extent of this purification in 36b is not delimited, and the "pointing" of 70c may occur only "implicitly." The clear assertion of 76c that unaided human reason did not in fact know the Creator prior to revelation, although, to be sure, there is some sense in which it *could* have, must be remembered.

Chapter III is perhaps the most speculatively remarkable of the chapters of the encyclical, containing as it does a sort of deduction of the necessity of Christ. Just as St. Anselm showed the necessity of Christ in the order of love, Chapter III is a sort of *Cur Deus Homo* in the order of truth. St. Anselm showed that love's need to satisfy for past offence requires one who can offer perfect sacrifice. John Paul II makes a like deduction. The human desire for truth wants to meet both an absolute truth (24—30), a truth disclosing the meaning of man's existence (26—29), and at the same time in greeting this truth, it wants to embrace another *person* to whom we can entrust ourselves in and for this truth (31—34). In other words, precisely as seekers of truth, we seek Christ. "This unity of truth, natural and revealed, is embodied in a living and personal way in Christ, as the Apostle reminds us: 'Truth is in Jesus' (cf. Eph 4:21; Col 1:15-20)." In Christ, the Truth is loveable also in that it imparts itself to us as another person in friendship.

Chapter III is perhaps the most important chapter of the encyclical for fundamental theology. First, it shows the theological necessity of asserting the natural capacity to know God, for that is simply an expression of man essentially—according to his essence—in search for a final and absolute truth about himself, a search whose term is granted to it supernaturally by God in Christ. "One may define the human being ... as the one who seeks the truth" (§28). Could he not know God according to his "definition," therefore, which is to say, could he not know God "naturally," man could not naturally seek for the absolute truth. For this truth, in the end is divine, and the natural capacity to know God is nothing but man's openness to the supernatural fulfillment of his desire. Without the natural capacity to know God, supernatural revelation would not be anything for us, and could not engage us.

What of the exercise of this capacity? Paragraph 29 seems almost to present an argument for God's existence from the desire for truth. On the other hand, it is just here that Chapter III also contains an argument for the incapacity of natural reason to know God unless aided by faith. The paragraph begins by saying that the desire for truth is "so deeply rooted in human nature" that "it is unthinkable" that it be "completely vain and useless." Furthermore, just as no one asks a limited, scientific question without supposing an answer to be possible, "the same must be equally true of the search for truth when it comes to the ultimate questions." The *de facto* failure to find a satisfactory answer does not mean one cannot be found. It means that the search must continue. What, however, are these "ultimate questions?" They seem to be those articulated in 26: "Does life have a meaning? Where is it going?" These questions are asked against the knowledge of the inevitability of death. The ultimate questions therefore concern the meaning of human life and the hope for immortality. They are the "fundamental questions" of the beginning of the encyclical: "Who am I? Where have I come from and where am I going? Why is there evil? What is there after this life?" These are the questions that unite philosophy and theology (15b).

Furthermore, 27a says, the answer we give to these questions "will determine whether or not we think it possible to attain universal and absolute truth." A hopeful answer to the ultimate questions lets us think it possible to attain universal and absolute truth; an answer of despair, on the other hand, will prevent that. The truth in question, this same paragraph explains, is not just a meaning, but is also a "ground" of things, indeed, of *all* things. Such a truth would be difficult to distinguish from God. And therefore, the Holy Father is saying that the knowledge of God is necessarily conditioned by, necessarily determined by, the answer we give to the "ultimate questions." In this there is surely concealed an argument for the dependence of the natural knowledge of God on faith. If the ultimate questions are not answered hopefully, there will be no successful exercise of the natural capacity to know God. And how are they answered hopefully? Not apart from faith.

It is hard to hold fast to the world as created without a hopeful answer to the ultimate questions. Knowledge of creation brings with it knowledge of the goodness of God, but this knowledge is contradicted by human misery. More precisely, human misery both moral and physical, and in the absence of some explanation of its origin, contradicts the goodness of God. Death contradicts the goodness of God. This contradiction is of course removed by the knowledge of sin and grace, by the offer of forgiveness and the hope of divine help. And for this knowledge, faith is required. So, faith is required for the knowledge of creation, for the knowledge of the Creator. It is needed, not as bearing on the very argument that leads from the things of our experience to God, but it is needed as providing an unconflicted moral space, a hopeful space, in which reason can operate.

The claim is not that reason is natively incapable of rising to the divinity and power of God from the things that have been made outside of this space, but that it will be difficult. For the most part it will not, which is to say most human beings today will not so rise to the knowledge of God. If death is annihilation, then what is God to me? Let us eat and drink etc. (1 Cor 15). And again, if there is no personal communion with God, what could existence after death be like, and what could it be for? Supposing there is the continuance of life in some way after death, asserted on the basis of our properly intellectual nature and therefore of our properly intellectual desire, how could an indeterminate, infinite desire for the intelligible, the true, the good be anything except excruciating if there is not some communion with God? The perplexity expressed by Qoheleth in terms of eternity would be eternal: "God has put eternity into man's mind, yet so that he cannot find out what God has done from the beginning to the end" (3:11). This is a perplexity already striking in that it indicates an epistemic situation in which one can speak of God, yet without hope.

The unity of the knowledge of God and the knowledge of man is a theme of the encyclical, expressed in its opening lines. Part of this theme is the sort of dependence of the natural knowledge of God on faith that I have tried to pick out, which is a sort of unity even of the knowledge of the existence of God and of the existence of a human spirituality transcending matter.

IV. ANTECEDENTS

The sort of argument suggested by Chapter III has good antecedents. The Book of Wisdom asserts the natural capacity to know God from the things that have been made. Also, it shows the tightness of the connection between the knowledge of God and anthropology: in Chapter II, the dumb and hopeless materialism of those who live in practical atheism is brought vividly to light. The Book of Wisdom knows of the immortality of the soul; but it knows it only as a gift of God (3:1-4; 5:15; 15:3). Here, too, therefore, the hopeful answer to the "ultimate questions" is organically united to the knowledge of God from the things that have been made.

Second, there is Justin Martyr. Some take Justin to assert the natural capacity of the human mind to know God on the ground that it is a created participation of the Logos.[12] Arthur Droge, however, argues that this is misleading. That the mind be a participation of the Logos gives a capacity to know God, but the exercise of the capacity depends on revelation.[13] For Justin, the original and true philosophy was that delivered to Moses by Christ the Logos,[14] whence it came to Plato.[15]

The philosophic knowledge of God was thus not independent of revelation, and that we exercise the mind according to the natural light so as to know God happens only under supernatural conditions, of revelation and faith.

Let us turn finally to St. Thomas. Let us suppose that one held with him the following propositions. First, phantasms drawn from sensible things are the natural object of human understanding, without which there is no act of understanding.[16]

Second, since the act of understanding, just as such, is immaterial, this provides a strong ground upon which to assert that the formal cause of the human being, the human soul, is itself immaterial and so incorruptible.[17]

Next, on the ground of the motion, being, and finalities of things, the first principle of the world must be very like a mind that, transcendent to the world, and in a way very like efficient causation, causes the world to be.

Fourth, the idea of a substance that does not operate, that never enjoys its typical and defining operation, is self-contradictory.[18]

The above four assertions are not in formal conflict with one another, but they become difficult to hold together once we contemplate death. Death works as a kind of solvent on their hanging together. For if we hold to the first one, thinking's dependence on phantasm and so the body, then the state of the soul after death becomes problematic. Under the pressure of the first and fourth together, and unable to imagine an operation for the separated soul, we might perhaps think that, after all, the soul is not incorruptible and is not immaterial. A wise creator will not provide for the existence of substances with no operation. On the other hand, the immateriality of our own cognitive operation is what is first and most patent to us in the order of immaterial things. If we lose our grip on it, we should begin to lose our grip on our ability to conceive of an immaterial principle transcendent to the world. In other words, St. Thomas's anthropology is such that death makes it hard to hold on to the existence of the creator in the face of death.

St. Thomas himself, of course, does not seem to have experienced any difficulty entertaining all four propositions. But then, he also has well-developed answers to what the Holy Father refers to as the "ultimate questions." Moreover, the best of the pagan philosophical sources he used supposed the providence of God and an itinerary for the soul ending in God. That is, Christianity was not the only shop where "ultimate questions" were answered, and answered hopefully.

Even so, it is important for us to see that St. Thomas's "ultimate answers" are closely entwined with the knowledge of God. So, for instance, in the *Summa Contra Gentiles*, III, 48, St. Thomas argues from the natural desire for happiness that, since happiness is not attainable in this life, it must be attainable in the next, for a natural desire cannot be in vain. This consideration of ultimate things is completely controlled by the knowledge of God. First, it has already been established that man's happiness consists in the knowledge of God "in some way" (chapter 25). Chapter 48 therefore concludes that our happiness "will be in the knowledge of God which the human mind will have, in the way in which separate substances know him." But in the third place, how do we know that a natural desire cannot be in vain? What tends to another does so either in virtue of its own knowledge of what it tends to, or by knowledge of another, as when an archer directs the arrow to the target.[19] For natural desires, the relevant knowledge is the divine wisdom, according to which the nature and its natural appetites are created. This is the crux of the Fourth Way, after all.[20]

The point here is that, even when in considering ultimate questions his answers do not expressly appeal to revelation, they are not independent of the knowledge of God, his goodness and wisdom. We may well suppose that the separated substances and even the first principle of the world itself would come to the separated soul's aid.[21] This is nakedly to trust in the goodness of God, His good will for what He has created, the good order of what He has created.[22]

The foregoing way of meeting the demand that every substance have its operation does not deal with all the questions raised by death, however. The human soul would still not be operating really and truly in accord with its nature. Even if we could trust the goodness of God as naturally known to provide some solution to the problem raised by death, moreover, what of death itself? It remains for all we can see an evil. That the soul be without a body is, St. Thomas says, both *per accidens* and contrary to nature, and such a thing cannot be thought to endure forever; therefore, he concludes: "if the resurrection of the body be denied, it is not easy, rather, it will be hard to maintain the immortality of the soul."[23] We are back to square one. Evidently, the relation of God to the evil of death requires some word: is this an evil that God cannot or does not want to deal with?

Of course, given the manifest proof of the goodness of God in the economy of redemption, crowned as it is by the death of God's Son for us and for our salvation, given the knowledge of our death as the wages of sin and the promise of the forgiveness of sin and the resurrection of the body, then whatever calculations we make about the separated soul occur in a much more well-lighted space, a space where the air is, as it were sweet, and we are buoyed up with confidence and hope. But the hope, confidence, sweetness of the air and light are all supernatural.

The conclusion to be drawn from the encyclical, therefore, is that as we do not first come to an adequate knowledge of God the creator except through revelation (VI, 76c), so we will not in this day in the West continue to know Him even by reason except we also keep faith (III, 26—27). As the first thing, so the second thing is a matter of fact. As there is a sort of phenomenological necessity to the first thing, so there is a sort of anthropological or existential necessity to the second.[24]

NOTES

1. In "The Programme of Radical Orthodoxy," in *Radical Orthodoxy? A Catholic Enquiry*, ed. Laurence Paul Hemming (Aldershot: Ashgate, 2000), 33—45, Milbank says at 36 that *Fides et Ratio* "at times seems to come close to a Radically Orthodox perspective." Milbank argues extensively for the conflation in "Intensities," *Modern Theology* 15(1999): 445—497.

2. For example, Joseph Koterski, S.J., "The Challenge to Metaphysics in *Fides et Ratio*," in *The Two Wings of Catholic Thought: Essays on Fides et Ratio*, ed. David Ruel Foster and Joseph Koterski, S.J. (Washington, D.C.: The Catholic University of America Press, 2003), 22—35.

3. I cite the encyclical by chapter, section number, and paragraph (a, b, etc.) within the section.

4. See also V, 60a, referring to *Gaudium et Spes*, and VI, 67a, with reference again to Romans and Vatican I.

5. See as well VI, 70a, which speaks of the "manifestation of God in nature" apropos of Wisdom and Romans. For the assertion of the fact Romans makes, see Heinrich Schlier, "Kerygma und Sophia," in *Die Zeit der Kirche: Exegetische Aufsätze und Vorträge*, 4th ed. (Freiburg: Herder, 1966), I, 212.

6. And in IV, 41b, the meeting of creature and Creator is the "goal towards which it [reason] unwittingly tended."

7. This is the official translation and can be found on the Vatican web page. The Latin text reads: "... lucide quasdam exhibit veritates Revelatio, quas tametsi attingere potest ratio, nunquam tamen easdem repperisset si suis unis viribus innixa essent. Hoc in rerum prospectu quaestiones ponuntur, veluti notio Dei personalis, liberi et creatoris ..." It is rendered a little differently by Anthony Meredith and Laurence Paul Hemming, in *Restoring Faith in Reason: A New Translation of the Encyclical Letter Faith and Reason of Pope John Paul II: Together with a Commentary and Discussion*, ed. Laurence Paul Hemming and

Susan Frank Parsons (Notre Dame, Ind.: University of Notre Dame Press, 2002), 124: "Revelation brings into clear focus certain truths, which, though available to reason, would never have been discovered by it were it left to its own resources. In this general area certain questions are asked about the concept of a personal God who is both free and creator. . . ." On the issue, see in the same volume Robert Sokolowski, "The Autonomy of Philosophy in *Fides et Ratio*," 22, and more at length, *The God of Faith and Reason* (Notre Dame, Ind.: University of Notre Dame Press, 1982), 12—19.

8. See *Summa Theologiae* I, q. 1, a. 1, c.

9. Avery Cardinal Dulles, "Faith and Reason: From Vatican I to John Paul II," in *The Two Wings of Catholic Thought*, 199.

10. For the role of the redeemed will in the knowledge of self in faith, see Reinhard Hütter, "The Directedness of Reason(ing) and the Metaphysics of Creation," in *Reason and the Reasons of Faith*, ed. Paul J. Griffiths and Reinhard Hütter (London/New York: T & T Clark International, 2005).

11. The Christocentricity of *Fides et Ratio* is noted by Cardinal Dulles in, "Faith and Reason: From Vatican I to John Paul II," 202.

12. *Second Apology*, 13, *Dialogue with Trypho*, 4, in *Writings of Saint Justin Martyr*, trans. Thomas B. Falls, *The Fathers of the Church*, 6 (New York: Christian Heritage, 1948).

13. Arthur J. Droge, *Homer or Moses? Early Christian Interpretations of the History of Culture*. Hermeneutische Untersuchungen zur Theologie, 26 (Tübingen: J. C. B. Mohr [Paul Siebeck] Verlag, 1989), 72: "Like Numenius [of Apamea, 2nd c. AD, *On the Divergence of the Academics from Plato*], Justin traces Platonic philosophy back to an ancient oriental theology, but whereas Numenius allows that this primitive theological tradition was handed down by the 'most famous nations,' Justin contends that Moses was the exclusive source. What then is the original philosophy which 'was sent down to men?' It is nothing other than the revelation of the *logos* to Moses and the prophets contained in scripture. Christianity therefore is not one, or even the best, philosophy among many; it is the *only* philosophy insofar as it is the reconstitution of the original, primordial philosophy."

14. *First Apology*, 63.

15. *First Apology*, 44.

16. *Summa Theologiae* I, q. 84, a. 7.

17. *Summa Theologiae* I, q. 75, aa. 2 & 6.

18. See the *De anima* I, 1 (403a10—12), apropos of which St. Thomas says, *Quaestiones disputatae de Veritate*, Q. 19, a. 1, c: *si nulla operatio ipsius animae est ei propria, ut scilicet not posset eam sine corpore habere, impossibile est ipsam animam separari a corpore. Operatio enim cuislibet rei est quasi finis eius, cum sit optimum in ipsa.* But then he appeals to faith: *Unde, sicut firmiter secundum fidem catholicam sustinemus quod anima post mortem remaneat a corpore separata, ita sustinere necesse quod sine corpore existens intelligere posit.* See also *De ente et essentia*, I: *nomen naturae . . . videtur significare essentiam rei secundum quod habet ordinem ad propriam operationem rei, cum nulla res propria operatione destituatur.*

19. *Commentaria in octo libros Physicorum,* I, lect. 15, 138.

20. This should be kept in mind in considering the argument from natural desire for the immortality of the soul as in, say, *Contra Gentiles* II, 79.

21. *Summa Theologiae* I, q. 89, a. 1.

22. I omit from consideration here the possibility that the separated soul might depend for its operation on previously acquired habits of knowledge, and apart from sensation and imagination. See *Summa Theologiae* I, Q. 89, a. 6. Our ability to say how this could be seems unsatisfactory, and even so, this supposition does not address the more vexing problem of infant mortality.

23. *In I ad Cor.*, 924. For, St. Thomas explains, that the soul be without a body is both *per accidens* and contrary to nature, and such a thing cannot be thought to perdure infinitely.

24. For the necessity of the first thing, see the suggestive remarks in the last chapter of Robert Sokolowski, *Presence and Absence: A Philosophical Investigation of Language and Being* (Bloomington: Indiana University Press, 1978).

CHAPTER SEVEN

REDEEMED REASON, NATURAL LAW AND THE COMPETENCY OF THE MAGISTERIUM

Lawrence J. Welch, Ph. D.

In the opening sections of *Fides et Ratio* Pope John Paul II lays out his reasons for writing the encyclical. We read that one of the reasons is because modern philosophy has neglected the search for ultimate truth and has instead preferred to accentuate, even exaggerate, the limits of the human ability to know the truth.[1] A number of commentators on *Fides et Ratio* have noted the irony of a papal encyclical that defends reason in the face of the unreason of post modernism.[2] The encyclical insists upon reason's ability to recognize and grasp transcendent and metaphysical truth. The pope states that he writes his reflections because, together with his brother bishops, he has the task of proclaiming the truth openly. He hopes that in reaffirming the truth of faith there might be a restoration of a genuine trust in the human capacity to know. Philosophy also might be prodded to "recover and develop its full dignity." It is also significant that the pope recalls his observation in *Veritatis Splendor,* that there are "certain fundamental truths of Catholic doctrine which, in the present circumstances, risk being distorted or denied."[3] The pope declares that this subject is a further reason for the encyclical and states his intention of pursuing it "by concentrating on the theme of truth itself and on its foundation in relation to faith."[4] It is certainly true that throughout the encyclical the pope upholds the simultaneity of faith and reason and is careful not to speak of either of them in isolation from one another, but the pope also affirms with Vatican I the superiority of faith to reason.[5] This affirmation is not limited to his direct quotation in the fifth chapter of the encyclical but is present in an important way in the earlier chapters, and its presence is felt throughout the entire encyclical.[6]

Pope John Paul II lays particular stress on how faith assists fallen reason and how faith directs and perfects reason. In the course of his comments on the "enduring quality of the thought of St. Thomas Aquinas" the pope writes in *Fides et Ratio* (§43):

> [J]ust as grace builds upon nature and brings it to fulfillment, so faith builds upon and perfects reason. Illumined by faith, reason is set free from the fragility and limitations deriving from the disobedience of sin and finds the strength required to rise to the knowledge of the Triune God.

The pope is quite insistent in *Fides et Ratio* (§22) that owing to the sin of Adam and Eve human reason is damaged in its capacity to know the truth and the path to truth is "strewn with obstacles." "The eyes of the mind were no longer able to see clearly" with the consequence that reason's "ready access to God the Creator [was] diminished." Thus it was difficult for human reason to know the truths that it was created by God to reach by its native capability. The pope argues that Christ liberates and redeems reason from this condition. "The coming of Christ was the saving event which redeemed reason from its weakness, setting it free from the shackles in which it had imprisoned itself." The unity of truth, both natural and revealed, is proclaimed as being found in a living and personal way in the Lord Jesus Christ himself (*FR*, §34).

It is true that the pope is not pre-occupied as previous popes were with defending faith against reason. It is also true that the pope wants to defend the ability of reason to know the truth, but he does not do so in way that somehow undermines the superiority of faith to reason. This should not surprise us. The pope is certainly mindful of the teaching of Vatican I and he thinks about man historically as well. In all of his writings the human person is never abstracted from the historical drama of creation, sin and salvation in Christ by the power of the Holy Spirit. The pope presents an impressive display of the wealth and wisdom of the Church's doctrine about the superiority of faith to reason situating it as he does in a Christological context. Given the attention the pope gives to this topic, it seems reasonable to think that it is one of those fundamental truths of Catholic doctrine identified in *Veritatis Splendor* that is in danger of being distorted today, which the pope intends to address at greater length in *Fides et Ratio*. The pope's intention is a positive one, and he refrains from harsh condemnations. The superiority of faith to reason, especially its Christological context, has not always been well grasped or integrated by theology, particularly in the latter decades of the twentieth century. One place in theology where there has been a failure to uphold the superiority of faith over reason is in the relationship of the moral life to the Church's magisterium. This failure is still felt today. For instance, the ability of the magisterium to teach infallibly concrete moral norms, particularly those of the natural moral law, has been disputed at least from the time of *Humanae Vitae* and throughout the pontificate of John Paul II. How one understands the relationship of faith and reason will largely determine how one understands the magisterium's competence to teach moral norms of the natural law irreformably. More broadly and more importantly, how one understands the competence of the magisterium in the moral life is bound up with whether Christ is understood as empowering us to enter into him and the moral pattern that he lived. It is bound up with whether we understand that Christ is really revealed to us as the full revelation of the true identity of the rational creature that is man, or whether we conceive of a Christ who can be the truth and life, but who cannot be the way for man and his reason.

BEYOND ITS COMPETENCE?

In his widely read and influential book, *Magisterium*, Francis Sullivan claimed that while some basic principles of the natural moral law are formally revealed and may be the proper matter for infallible church teachings, concrete moral norms of the natural law are not.[7] Sullivan concurred with those theologians—which he claimed at the time were most Catholic theologians—who concluded that particular norms of the natural law are not the proper matter of irreformable teaching and thus have never been and never could be infallibly taught by the magisterium.[8] Sullivan claimed that man today faces moral problems that are very complex and that while the Gospel sheds light on them, it does not provide ready-made answers or solutions. He explained,

> It is now generally agreed that the process by which we arrive at the knowledge of the concrete norms of the natural law is through shared reflection on human experience; it is an inductive one rather than a deductive one.[9]

Sullivan argued, "it must be admitted that there are elements in this process which militate against the possibility of reaching an absolutely irreversible determination of a concrete norm of the natural law."[10] Permanency ought not to be attributed to concrete norms of the natural moral law because of the futurity of human experience and the fact that human nature is not a static closed reality but a dynamic one that exists in history and is subject to change. According to Sullivan, the difficult search for answers to complex and concrete norms of the natural moral law is not something limited only to Christians but shared with other persons of good will. This search depends on bringing human intelligence to bear on common human experience. Although the Church's magisterium has much to contribute, it does not have a monopoly in this endeavor.

This line of reasoning would seem to mean that the magisterium cannot teach irreversibly and infallibly negative moral precepts that admit of no exception, at least insofar as such norms belong to the natural moral law. In an article written for *Theological Studies* entitled "Medicaid and Abortion," which appeared shortly after Sullivan's *Magisterium* was published, Richard McCormick claimed that the Church's teaching on direct abortion was not and could not be taught infallibly by the magisterium.[11] McCormick argued against Germain Grisez who insisted that the Church's moral teaching on the grave immorality of direct abortion is infallibly taught by the magisterium. McCormick argued that particular norms of the moral law cannot be the object of infallibility.[12] He cited Sullivan's claim that this was the common opinion of Catholic moral theologians.[13]

For a number of years McCormick argued that while the magisterium has the competence to teach concrete moral norms, including those of the natural moral law, it could not teach them infallibly.[14] McCormick interpreted (erroneously) the Second Vatican Council to exclude from infallibility those moral questions that are not revealed.[15] Rejecting the claim that concrete moral norms can be taught infallibly because they belong in some way to our supernatural end, McCormick drew on a distinction constructed by Joseph Fuchs that distinguished between two levels of moral truths: those having to do with personal moral goodness and badness and those having to do with moral rightness or wrongness of human conduct.[16] Summing up his thought in 1989 McCormick wrote: "salvation (as in 'truths of salvation'), does not have a *direct* relationship to right behavior, but to personal moral goodness. Concrete moral norms, therefore, are truths of salvation only in an analogous sense." For McCormick, this distinction, together with the fact that concrete norms of the natural law are not revealed, explains why the magisterium possesses only a limited competence to teach them and in any event does not have the competence to teach them infallibly.[17]

NATURAL LAW AS GROUNDED IN DIVINE PROVIDENCE AND THE TRINITARIAN REVELATION

One way, of course, to respond to these objections is to point out that they all rest upon a faulty notion of the natural moral law. For one thing, after *Veritatis Splendor* it seems hard for Catholic moral theology to escape the conclusion that the entire moral law is contained in revelation or pertains to it.[18] Sullivan admits, in an article written after *Magisterium,* that there are good reasons to think that *Veritatis Splendor* teaches "that all traditional Catholic moral doctrine is, in the final analysis, the Church's interpretation of the contents of the Ten Commandments as reaffirmed and further specified in the New Testament."[19] Sullivan also admits, if somewhat reluctantly:

> This would insert all moral issues into the primary object of infallibility and make it much easier to claim that many traditional Catholic moral doctrines have been taught by the ordinary universal magisterium infallibly.[20]

Nevertheless he has not, to my knowledge, retracted his claim that the magisterium cannot teach infallibly concrete norms of the natural law.

There are other, no less important, foundational issues as well. Recently, Russell Hittinger has shown the need for theologians to attend to the theological foundations of the natural law. I agree, but I believe that the traditional understanding of the natural law is even more theological, especially for St. Thomas, than Hittinger may have had time to describe given the limited focus his study. I also believe that it is just as important for theologians to attend to the actual situation of man's reason as fallen and redeemed by Christ. Hittinger makes the observation that natural law can be understood as a theory of order in the human mind, in nature or in the mind of God. Modern readers and even some Catholic moral theologians have not focused on the order of priority of these three foci. This is important because without it either human nature or the human mind becomes the cause of the law itself. Without the careful distinction of what occurs first in the order of being and first in the order of knowing, divine providence becomes heteronomous. In order for God to govern, he must override, if not eliminate, the domain supposedly erected by human causality.

Hittinger believes that contemporary readers are apt to think that the human mind is first in the order of being or in the causal order because they perceive themselves as apprehending some rule of action. What is first in the order of discovery is confounded with what is first in the order of causality. It is all too easy to then, for example, to understand the natural law as the human capacity to make moral judgments reducing natural law to practical reason. Hittinger cites the late moralist Josef Füchs on this very score who, it seems, thought that human participation in the divine plan does not begin with the reception of a moral law but has to do with a moral reasoning that creatively uses the gift of nature, giving it order in conformity to practical judgments. These practical judgments do not flow from any kind of pre-existing law or moral norm external to the mind but from practical reason's interpretation and calculation of what action is required in the face of the totality of concrete circumstances.[21]

Hittinger argues, rightly, that traditional Catholic thought, together with St. Thomas, has understood the human mind and nature to be subordinate to the mind of God and to divine providence and so has understood a clear distinction between the mind's discovering or discerning a norm and the being or cause of the norm. For St. Thomas, natural law is defined on the basis of its causal origin, which makes it a law in the first place, rather than in a cognitive origin in the human mind which is of a secondary realm of causality. Natural law is a created, rational participation in the eternal law of God. This conception of natural law can be seen in what St. Thomas writes in question 91 in articles 1 and 2. In the former, St. Thomas argues that the existence of the eternal law follows from the truth that Divine Providence rules the cosmos:

> Law is nothing but a dictate of practical reason issued by a sovereign who governs a complete community. Granted that the world is ruled by Divine Providence, and this we have shown in the Prima Pars, it is evident that the whole community of the universe is governed by God's Reason. Therefore the ruling of things which exists in God as the effective sovereign of them all has the nature of a law.[22]

The next article, 91.2, defines the natural law as a created participation in the eternal law that is in Divine Providence. This text is worth quoting too:

> Since all things are regulated and measured by Eternal Law, as we have seen, it is evident that all somehow share in it, in that their tendencies to their own proper acts and ends are from its impression. Among them intelligent creatures are ranked under divine Providence the more nobly because they take part in Providence by their own providing for themselves and others. Thus they join and make their own the Eternal Reason through which they have their natural aptitudes for their activity and purpose. Now this sharing in the Eternal Law by intelligent creatures is what we call natural law. That is why Psalmist after bidding us, *Offer the sacrifice of justice* and, as though anticipating those who ask what are the works of justice, and adding, *There be many who say, Who will us any good?* makes reply, *The light of thy countenance, O Lord, is signed upon us,* implying that the light of natural reason by which we discern what is good and what evil is nothing but the impression of divine light on us.[23]

Divine Providence is central to St. Thomas's understanding of natural law, thus making it thoroughly theological.[24] There is another important way in which the natural law is theological for St. Thomas that Hittinger does not discuss: it is Trinitarian. In *ST* I-II, q. 93, a.1, St. Thomas takes up the question of whether the eternal law is the supreme exemplar existing in the mind of God. The Angelic Doctor answers in the affirmative. Just as there pre-exists an exemplar (*ratio*) in the mind of the artist of things that are to be made by his art, so too in the mind of a governor there must pre-exist an exemplar (*ratio ordinis*) of the activity to be done by those agents subject to the governor. This exemplar takes on the character of law. Now it is, of course, through Divine Wisdom that God is the creator of all things and stands in relation to them like an artist and governor. The exemplar of Divine Wisdom moves all things to their due ends and bears the nature of law. Accordingly, the eternal law is nothing less than the exemplar of Divine Wisdom as directing all actions and movements.

Thomas answers the second objection in question 93, article 1 on the basis of what God discloses about himself in revelation as well. The objection runs as follows: if it is essential to the law to be promulgated by a word, the eternal law cannot be a divine exemplar because the Word of God is a personal name in God whereas exemplar refers to essence. Thomas replies whatever is in the Father's knowledge is expressed by His Word and this includes the eternal law. He claims that the eternal law can be appropriated to the Son because of the association between exemplar and word:

> Whatsoever the word you can consider first, the word itself, and secondly, what it expresses. A spoken word is something uttered by the mouth of man, and expresses what it is meant to signify. The same applies to man's mental word, which is nothing other than a concept of mind expressing what he is thinking about. So it is in the life of God; the Word itself, conceived by the Father's mind, is a personal term. As it appears from Augustine, whatsoever is in the Father's knowledge, whether it refers to the divine nature or to the divine persons or to the works of God, is expressed by this Word. Included in what is there expressed is the Eternal Law. All the same it does not follow that the Eternal Law is used as a personal term in our vocabulary about divine things, though in fact it is specially attributed to the Son on account of the close agreement exemplar has with word.[25]

Thomas conceives of the eternal law in Trinitarian terms. So, the natural law which is a human, rational participation in the eternal law of God is at the same time something of a created participation in the Son, the Wisdom and Word of God.[26] There can be, then, no natural law that is independent from or immune from either Divine Providence or an eternal law defined in reference to the Trinitarian revelation.[27]

FIDES ET RATIO: UNDERSTANDING REASON HISTORICALLY

Hittinger seems to recognize, even if he does not develop the idea, that the normative meaning of the natural law cannot be had completely and adequately apart from revelation as mediated through the authoritative interpretation by the magisterium. Now to see how this includes the competency of the magisterium to teach concrete moral norms of the natural law we must attend to the relations between reason, revelation and our apprehension of the natural law. Let it be noted that the natural law is treated independently for various reasons: whether it is claimed that human historical reasoning is complex and has many elements that are changeable for which the Church possesses no special competence (Sullivan); or whether it is asserted that concrete moral norms of the natural law are not revealed, are not truths of salvation and therefore are excluded from the charism of infallibility (McCormick); or whether natural law is conceived as the human power and ability to make moral judgments (Josef Fuchs and McCormick following him). In each of these cases, the rationality that is supposed to deliberate about concrete moral norms of the natural law is conceived to be somehow on the periphery or outside the history of creation, the fall and redemption in Christ. There is a failure to understand the relation between reason, grace, sin, and revelation and our apprehension of the natural law as creatures that are fallen and redeemed in Christ.

At the beginning of this paper I noted that *Fides et Ratio* maintains the superiority of faith to reason and that faith redeems and liberates reason from the weakness and limitations caused by the disobedience of sin. *Fides et Ratio* conceives of reason as thoroughly historical, caught up in the drama of creation, the fall and redemption in Christ. This emphasis is quite explicit in *Fides et Ratio* (§22). After stating that Adam and Eve diminished their "ready access to God" because they chose a relationship of absolute autonomy in relation to the Creator, Pope John II wrote:

> This is the human condition vividly described by the Book of Genesis when it tells us that God placed the human being in the Garden of Eden, in the middle of which there stood "the tree of knowledge of good and evil" (2:17). The symbol is clear: man was in no position to discern and decide for himself what was good and what was evil, but was constrained to appeal to a higher source. The blindness of pride deceived our first parents into thinking themselves sovereign and autonomous, and into thinking that they could ignore the knowledge which comes from God. All men and women were caught up in this primal disobedience, which so wounded reason that from then on its path to full truth would be strewn with obstacles. *From that time onwards the human capacity to know the truth was impaired by an aversion to the One who is the source and origin of truth. It is again the Apostle who reveals just how far human thinking, because of sin, became "empty", and human reasoning became distorted and inclined to falsehood* (cf. *Rom* 1:21-22). The eyes of the mind were no longer able to see clearly: reason became more and more a prisoner to itself. *The coming of Christ was the saving event which redeemed reason from its weakness, setting it free from the shackles in which it had imprisoned itself.*[28]

Fides et Ratio reminds us that reason is not abstract and ahistorical but is something always embedded in the historical drama of the Fall of the first couple whose descendants are children of concupiscence, wounded in their rationality by sin, but redeemed in Christ in mind, soul and body. Christ redeems reason by reversing the disobedience which wounded it. As reason is illumined by faith and freed from the aversion that impaired its capacity to know the truth, it is strengthened in its understanding of the natural law.

The position of St. Thomas is helpful for showing the wisdom of *Fides et*

Ratio's understanding of reason as conditioned by sin and grace. Hittinger has noticed that St. Thomas in one of his late Lenten conferences went so far as to say that the "law of nature was destroyed by the law of concupiscence" and that man needed the written law in order "to be brought back to the works of virtue and to be drawn away from vice." St. Thomas does not mean, of course, that natural law as law is destroyed in the Divine Mind which establishes it in the first place. The immutability of the natural law remains. What St. Thomas means is that the natural law can be said to be "in" human nature in the sense that there is an ordering of the human inclinations of reason and will which move human beings toward a common good. It is the effect of this law in man that is bent and misdirected. Hittinger is certainly correct in his reading of St. Thomas but, as he undoubtedly knows, there is more to the Angelic Doctor's position than just this one text. Denis J. M. Bradley has recently addressed the question of whether, for St. Thomas, we need revelation to strengthen our grip on the natural law. After noting that the love of neighbor is a primary and self-evident principle of the natural law for St. Thomas, he reports his position on how evident the Ten Commandments are:

> It should be . . . apparent that killing, committing adultery, bearing false witness, and stealing are not beneficent acts to one's neighbor. These acts clearly violate the first-order principle that one should not harm or do evil to any person. Yet ordinary men, because of passions and evil habits, can ignore what is obviously just and what is obviously unjust.[29]

This is an accurate summary. Can the natural law be removed from the heart of man according to St. Thomas? In the abstract, the first principles of the natural law cannot *not* be known; they cannot be expunged from the human heart, St. Thomas says.[30] Concretely, even they can, as it were, be suspended by passion. These principles of the law, such things as that life is to be preserved, remain always in the habit of *synderesis,* which can be styled a natural habit, which is to say a natural faculty of the intellect whereby we understand and assent to the truth of these principles. Since the first principles are correlative to the fundamental inclinations of human nature, and human nature is wounded but not destroyed by sin, they must always be able to be formulated. These are but seeds, however; to get a crop requires more. The first principles must grow into prudence and the moral virtues and are themselves as insufficient for human action.

What about the secondary principles, such as are to be found in the Decalogue? They are even more fragile. St. Thomas says

> [A]s for its other and secondary precepts, natural law can be erased from the human heart, either by evil persuasions, just as in speculative matters errors occur in respect to necessary conclusions; or by perverse customs and corrupt habits; for instance robbery, was not reputed to wrong among some people, nor even, as Apostle mentions [Rom 1:24], some unnatural sins.[31]

Therefore, St. Thomas expressly remarks the "fittingness" of the assistance provided by revelation for our apprehension of the secondary principles of the natural law, conclusions from the first principles. Reason can err, and sinful habits corrupt our purchase on these principles. Hence, he concludes, "there was need for the authority of the divine law to rescue man from both these defects."[32] St. Thomas believed that the condition and orientation of our will affects what we can see. The deformation of our appetite and the wounding of our will are known to be conditioned by sin both original and actual, and by the absence of original justice. There is something of a vicious circle. Due to the sin of our first parents our will is bent and our reason cannot grasp the secondary principles of the natural law as it should. The more we actually sin, the more reason is darkened and the harder it is to see secondary principles. The harder it is to see them the harder it is for the will to live in accordance with them.

In *ST* I-II, q. 85, a.3 St. Thomas describes this situation of man. He states that as a result of the sin of our first parents, the powers of the soul lost the order that was proper to them, that is their natural order to virtue. There is a fourfold wounding of nature. There is the wound of ignorance in so far as reason is deprived of its ordering to the true. There is the wound of malice in so far as the will is lacking in its order toward the good. Because the irascible appetite is deprived of its power to face what is strenuous, there is the wound of weakness. To the extent that the concupiscible appetite is unable to moderate the pleasurable, there is the wound of concupiscence. These wounds afflict every human person. Actual sins further distort our reason and will. St. Thomas argues:

> In this way, therefore, these four are the wounds inflicted upon all human nature by reason of the sin of our first parents. But these four result also from other sins so that the inclination towards virtuous action is lessened in everyone because of actual sin, as is evident from what has been said. Because of sin the reason, especially with regard to moral decision, is blunted, the will becomes hardened against the true good; sustained virtuous activity becomes increasingly difficult; concupiscence grows in ardor.

For St. Thomas, that the wounding of our reason harms our moral reasoning is an undeniable fact of our historical existence. There are no human creatures whose reason is somehow unscathed by this wounding. Our natural knowledge of the good must be strengthened by the knowledge of faith. Thomas makes this point for example in *ST* I-II q.93, a.6. He says that while the affairs of the human creature are subject to the eternal law because man as a rational creature has some knowledge of the Eternal Law and because man has a natural inclination to that which is in accordance with the eternal law, nevertheless these two ways are imperfect. St. Thomas argues:

> Both manners of sharing in the Eternal Law are imperfect and, as it were, decayed in the wicked; their natural instinct for virtue is spoilt by vice and their natural knowledge of what is right is darkened by the passions and habits of sin. In the good, however, the Eternal Law is more fully possessed, and on both counts, for above the natural bent to good there is added the interior moving power of grace and the virtues, and above the natural knowledge of what is right there is added knowledge by faith and wisdom.

St Thomas helps us to see the context, both cognitive and affective, in which we both act morally and think about our moral action. It is awareness of this context, however, the context of sin and grace, that in part constitutes Catholic moral theology as Catholic. The grace that St. Thomas speaks of in the passage above is, of course, the grace of Christ. Now, just as Christ is the author of grace, so is he the fullness of revelation and perfects it in both word and deed, in the personal history that leads from cradle to cross and from death to risen life. Just as we should not expect to keep the moral law apart from his grace, so we should not expect to know it in its fullness and in any detail apart from His light. The kind of rationality that grasps the fullness of the natural law is that which is redeemed from its fallenness and perfected by Christ.[33]

To speak of Christ as redeeming rationality and revealing the full meaning of the natural law is in no way to deny that the whole natural law is in principle knowable by reason or worse to absorb human nature into grace. To say that our knowledge of the natural law is limited and partial is only to think historically about the nature of man wounded by sin but redeemed by Christ. If Christ fully reveals the truth about the human person to us, then He must reveal to us the full and complete meaning of the natural law, and if we exist in Him we cannot but strengthen our grasp of it. If grace perfects human nature then there is no part of human existence that is not touched and elevated by it.

Related to the fact that Christ redeems rationality is the issue of where the unity of truth is found. It is found in Him who is truth and who became incarnate for our sakes. *Fides et Ratio* (§34) sums up this point:

> This unity of truth, natural and revealed, is embodied in a living and personal way in Christ, as the Apostle reminds us: "Truth is in Jesus" (cf. Eph 4:21; Col 1:15-20). He is the eternal Word in whom all things were created, and He is the incarnate Word who in His entire person reveals the Father (cf. Jn 1:14, 18). What human reason seeks "without knowing it" (cf. Acts 17:23) can be found only through Christ: what is revealed in Him is "the full truth" (cf. Jn 1:14-16) of everything which was created in Him and through Him and which therefore in Him finds its fulfillment (cf. Col 1:17).

The above passage might be compared profitably with the following one from *Veritatis Splendor* (§45):

> Even if moral-theological reflection usually distinguishes between the positive or revealed law of God and the natural law, and, within the economy of salvation, between the "old" and the "new" law, it must not be forgotten that these and other useful distinctions always refer to that law whose author is the one and the same God and which is always meant for man. The different ways in which God, acting in history, cares for the world and for mankind are not mutually exclusive on the contrary, they support each other and intersect. They have their origin and goal in the eternal, wise and loving counsel whereby God predestines men and women "to be conformed to the image of his Son" (Rom 8:29).

It is not to exaggerate to say that Christ is the cornerstone of the theological foundation of the natural law. If we take the unity of truth seriously, we should not imagine the natural law to be autonomous or apart from Christ. The truth of the natural law does not, so speak, work without Him because He, as the eternal law, is the source of its truth and as the incarnate Word reveals the full meaning of it to fallen man. The meaning of the natural law cannot lie somehow outside of Christ otherwise He would only be a partial answer as to who the human person is.

CONCLUSION

What is the import of these theological foundations of the natural law for the question of whether the magisterium can teach infallibly the concrete norms of the natural law? If we understand that the reason that deliberates about natural law is wounded by sin and illumined and liberated by grace, and if we understand the moral law as being one in Christ then it follows that the Church's authority in moral matters, including those of the natural moral law, rests upon its authority to interpret the revelation entrusted to it by Christ. If this be the case, it would follow that the magisterium could, in principle, speak even definitively with regard to concrete norms of the natural moral law.[34] If Christ is, as *Gaudium et spes* 22 proclaims, the full revelation of the human person then there are no moral issues that somehow lie outside of Him or apart from Him. There are no great moral questions that Christ does not in some way answer nor can we answer fully without his light and guidance. Again, in the words, of *Veritatis Splendor* Christ's reply to our moral questions today "is a reply that possesses a light and a power capable of answering even the most controversial and complex questions."[35] This reply of Christ which comes to us today is authoritatively interpreted and discerned not by some mechanism or structure of the Church's creation but by an office instituted by Christ that we believe mediates his authority by the power of the Holy Spirit.

What about Sullivan's objection that questions pertaining to the natural moral law have to do with matters that are very complex, that the Gospel does not explicitly address, and that can only be answered through a shared process of human intelligence reflecting on human experience—something not limited to Christians. First, there is a failure here to address the theological, especially the Christological foundation, of the natural law. The kind of rationality that grasps the integral meaning of the natural law and thinks out its implications for complex moral problems is the kind that is redeemed by Christ. If we are really to uphold the theological foundations of the natural law then we must not imagine Christians sizing up complex moral problems by way of a reason independent from the history of sin and grace, that is to say, independent from something that is central to man's historical existence. If we have a clear understanding of the natural law's theological-Christological foundations, then we will understand that the process of working out answers to complex moral problems will draw on a concept of natural law that is fully grasped on the basis of revelation which in turn is understood as mediated by way of an authoritative interpretation of the magisterium. Does this mean that we can find somehow in revelation a ready-made answer to every complex moral problem or that the magisterium will always possess answers on the spot? By no means. It does mean that some moral truths including those of the natural moral law, like dogmatic truths of the deposit of faith, blossom forth down through history unchanged in their substance but specified and determined in light of the historical circumstances.[36]

For example, take the problem of in-vitro fertilization. Let us say that a woman wants to conceive a child through this method and that the donated sperm is obtained from a married man who is not her husband. Obviously, the morality of human conception outside the womb is not explicitly addressed in Scripture or in prior Church teaching. Nevertheless, the Church now teaches that such a procedure is immoral because it is contrary to the divine plan and design for human conception, is offensive and injurious to the unitive dimension of the sexual act, and, at least in the case described, is unfaithful to the marital covenant. Here we have the magisterium making a specific moral judgment based on moral truths unchanged in their substance but applied to new historical circumstances and which arguably sheds new light and a new perspective on those truths. Can the Church teach such a matter infallibly? Yes; once the magisterium determines that such a new and specific moral judgment pertains or belongs, indirectly or directly to the deposit of faith. Sullivan recognized something like this process of judgment and discernment, instanced above, occurred with regard to other doctrines of the Church such as the dogma of the Assumption. He claims that the deposit of faith is more than a certain number of revealed truths but:

> [T]hat insights which are the fruit of such ecclesial contemplation can bring to light truths which are really contained in the total Christ-event, and therefore really are contained in the Gospel, even though they are not found explicitly in Scripture or explicitly in the early record of explicit Christian belief.[37]

If dogmatic truths are capable of being as discerned, as belonging or pertaining to the deposit of faith and capable of being taught infallibly, so are moral norms of the natural moral law.

What about the objection that moral norms, including concrete norms of the natural law, cannot be taught irreformably because of the fact that future human experience, unable to be imagined now, might put a moral problem in a new context that would require a revision of the moral norm?[38] While this may be true of some moral norms of the natural law—it is mistaken to think this applies to *every* concrete norm of the natural law, especially the negative precepts of the natural law. One might reply to this objection pointing out the obvious historicism that is behind it as well as the fact that *Veritatis Splendor* teaches that the negative precepts of the natural law are universally valid.[39] But it is also important to see that there is a faulty Christology at work. If there cannot be a concrete absolute norm of the natural law that applies to every possibility and answers all questions put to it, then neither can there be a Christ who is both a concrete historical figure and unequivocally moral absolute demanding our total conversion, firm attachment and absolute fidelity. Christ as the concrete historical absolute continues to require our love and fidelity through the Church, His Bride with whom He is one flesh. Also, the objection about the futurity of historical experience makes meaningless Christ's discourse on marriage and divorce where the historical, social, and cultural context—human experience—has distorted and disfigured the meaning of moral norms intended by the Father from the "Beginning."[40]

This paper began with the observation that one of the stated reasons for *Fides et Ratio* was to pursue a reflection on a matter first identified in *Veritatis Splendor*: certain fundamental truths that are in danger today of being denied or distorted. One of these truths within these reflections is the superiority of faith to reason. The pope's approach is a positive one centered as it is on Christ who redeems human reason. The unity of truth, both natural and revealed, is to be found in a living and personal way in Christ. Lorenzo Albacete has commented:

> Thinking in accordance with the natural law is thinking within creative Wisdom, but creative Wisdom is a very concrete person. It is Jesus of Nazareth. Thinking in accordance with the natural law is thinking with Jesus Christ; it is "co-judging" reality with Christ. It is therefore being taken up into His concrete personal presence.[41]

In the end the question of the magisterium's competence to teach concrete norms of the natural moral law depends on Christology and ecclesiology. If we co-judge reality with Christ who is the way, who is capable of answering our most complex moral problems, we must also assert straight away, that this is something done within the Church: where the concrete personal presence of Christ is found and where redeemed rationality reflecting on the moral law, natural or divine, is interpreted by the authority of Christ as sacramentally mediated in the apostolic office founded by him. Just as the baptized need to have surety about the articles of faith in the creed and just as they must be certain that grace is communicated *ex opere operato* in the sacraments, so the baptized must have a surety about the moral pattern of full humanity in Christ. Radical doubting and uncertainty about the Church's ability to teach irreversible universal concrete moral norms, including those of the natural moral law, impairs the moral revival that life in Christ entails. For if there is not surety about universal concrete moral norms, negative universal moral precepts, then conversion is made much more difficult. A person may affirm a moral norm in general but in the face of attraction to some apparent good he will be enticed to ask if the norm really applies to him in his case.[42] None of this means that prudence is eliminated in the moral life but such uncertainty cannot be part of the adventure of our freedom in Christ.

NOTES

1. *Fides et Ratio*, §5.
2. For example, Joseph Koterski, S.J., "The Challenge to Metaphysics in *Fides et ratio*," in *The Two Wings of Catholic Thought*, ed. David Ruel Foster and Joseph Koterski, S.J. (Washington, D.C.: Catholic University Press, 2003).
3. *Fides et Ratio*, §6.
4. Ibid.

5. Avery Cardinal Dulles, "From Vatican I to John Paul II," in *The Two Wings of Catholic Thought*, 201.

6. *Fides et Ratio*, §53.

7. Francis Sullivan, *Magisterium: Teaching Authority in the Catholic Church* (New York: Paulist Press, 1983).

8. Ibid., 152. In n. 46 Sullivan gives a long list of theologians whom he judges to hold this view: Franz Bockle, Charles E. Curran, J. David, Klaus Demmer, Josef Fuchs, Louis Janssens, Daniel Maguire, Richard McCormick, Bruno Schuller, Gregory Baum, John P. Boyle, P. Chirico, Joseph A. Komonchak, J.P. Mackey, Karl Rahner, Gustave Thils and William Levada.

9. Ibid., 150.

10. Ibid., 151.

11. Richard McCormick, "Medicaid and Abortion," *Theological Studies* (December, 1984): 715—721. The occasion of the debate with Grisez was over the case of Sr. Agnes Mary Mansour, Director of the Michigan Department of Social Services, who approved of Medicaid funding of abortions. Grisez argued that for a Catholic government official to advocate or support public funding of abortion amounted to formal cooperation with an act that the magisterium infallibly taught is gravely immoral. McCormick went on to say that while he believed there should not be Medicaid funding of abortions, the Church's teaching on abortion, which is not infallible, did not rule out dissent on the matter of the public funding of abortion. The reader, though, is lead to the obvious unstated conclusion: if dissent is possible for government officials on the issue of public funding of abortion because the Church teaching against direct abortion is not taught infallibly, then presumably dissent from the Church teaching against abortion itself is possible as well.

12. Ibid., 720.They [theologians] simply disagree—as most would and should—with Grisez that the immorality of direct abortion is infallibly taught by the ordinary magisterium. More generally, they deny that such particular norms are the proper object of infallibility.

13. Ibid.

14. For example, see "Notes on Moral Theology," *Theological Studies* 29 (1968): 709; "Notes on Moral Theology," *Theological Studies*, 30 (1969): 660; *Theological Studies* (December 1984): 715-721, *The Critical Calling* (Georgetown University Press, 1989): 98f. For an overview of McCormick's position see Richard R. Gaillardetz, "Richard McCormick and the Moral Magisterium," *Louvain Studies*, 25 (2000): 356—361.

15. See Richard McCormick, *The Critical Calling*, 98: "On the other hand, Vatican II states that the charism of infallibility is coextensive with the 'treasure of divine revelation'(what Vatican I called the *depositum fidei*). [Footnote omitted] This would exclude from infallibility those moral questions that are not revealed. Competence, therefore, is a very analogous concept. One can be competent without being infallibly competent. As we shall see, that is the case in concrete moral questions." McCormick cites Fuchs in this passage: Josef Fuchs, S.J., "Moral Truths—Truth of Salvation?" *Christian Ethics in a Secular Arena* (Washington: Georgetown University Press, 1984), 48-67. McCormick's position is based on a mis-interpretation of *Lumen Gentium*, §25, which did not limit the infallibility of magisterium to what has been revealed. The object of infallibility extends not only to the deposit of faith but includes all those things which directly pertain to it or those things without which the deposit of faith cannot be explained and defended. See the discussion on this point in Sullivan, *Magisterium*, 131—134.

16. Ibid. "Moral goodness refers to the person as such, to the person's being open to and decided for the self-giving love of God. It is the vertical dimension of our being. It is salvation. Therefore what we can say about moral goodness of the person is a truth of salvation." The rightness or wrongness of human acts are only moral in an analogous sense insofar as they are related to the moral goodness of being decided for the self-giving love of God. Moral goodness, for McCormick resides in persons not in acts and is concerned with inclinations, attitudes and intentions that the Gospel transforms with its law of love and call to conversion.

17. McCormick allowed that the Gospel's law of love, its demand for unlimited forgiveness, the command not to judge and the like were capable of being infallibly taught but not concrete moral norms. See the discussion summarizing McCormick's position in Gaillardetz, "Richard McCormick and the Moral Magisterium," 356—361.

18. For example see *Veritatis Splendor*, §§36, 44, 45, 70, 81. The present article is largely indebted to *Veritatis Splendor* on this point. See my "Christ, the Moral Law, and the Teaching Authority of the Magisterium," *Irish Theological Quarterly*, 64 (1999): 16—28.

19. Sullivan, "Infallible Teaching on Moral Issues? Reflections on *Veritatis splendor* and *Evangelium Vitae*," in *Choosing Life: A Dialogue on Evangelium Vitae*, ed. Kevin Wm. Wildes, S.J. and Alan C. Mitchell, (Washington, D.C.: Georgetown University, 1997), 77—89.

20. Ibid. It is clear now in, especially the light of the *motu proprio Ad Tuendam Fidem*, that while the pope in *Veritatis Splendor* considered a great deal of the moral law to be contained in revelation (first object of infallibility) he also supposed that other precepts of the natural moral law pertain to revelation (secondary object of infallibility).

21. For example see Josef Fuchs, tr. Brian McNeil, *Moral Demands and Personal Obligations*, (Washington, D.C.: Georgetown University Press, 1993): 33, 39.

22. *Summa Theologiae* I-II, q. 91, art. 1 and 2. Unless otherwise noted, all citations in English are taken from the New Blackfriars, *Summa Theologiae* 60 vols. (London: Eyre & Spottiswoode, 1963).

23. *ST* I-II, q. 93, a. 1.

24. Ernest Fortin has observed that we can see in his discussion of the relationship between the natural law and the precepts of the Decalogue how St. Thomas the regarded natural law as being only fully coherent and intelligible within the context of revelation. In sum, the argument runs as follows: the second table of the Decalogue which is in principle knowable by reason alone depends for its efficacy upon the first table as willed by a law giver, which orders us to the love and worship of God as willed by the law giver. The knowledge of the latter, St. Thomas tells us, is arrived at not by reason alone but human reason instructed by revelation and faith. Here again Divine Providence is the premise of the natural law where God, who is entitled to love and worship, enforces and upholds the precepts of the second table. To make the point another way: It is one thing to say that a man who avoids adultery and does not murder is virtuous; it is quite another to say that in the end only this kind of man will be happy because he is devoted to the design and will of God. See Ernest Fortin: "Augustine, Thomas Aquinas, and the Problem in the Natural Law," *Collected Essays, II: Classical Christianity and the Political Order*, ed. J. Brian Benestad (New York: Rowman & Littlefield, 1996), 199—22.

25. This coheres with *Catechism of the Catholic Church* #1701 which teaches that "It is in Christ, 'the image of the invisible God,' that man has been created 'in the image and likeness' of the Creator."

26. Pope John Paul II in his encyclical *Dominum et Vivificantem*, §33, notices this text from St. Thomas and comments: This Word is the same Word who was "in the beginning with God," who "was God," and without whom "nothing has been made of all that is," since "the world was made through him." He is the Word who is also the eternal law, the source of every law which regulates the world and especially human acts.

27. *Fides et Ratio*, §22. Emphasis mine. See also *Fides et Ratio*, §43: "Just as grace builds on nature and brings it to fulfillment., so faith builds upon and perfects reason. Illumined by faith, reason is set free from the fragility and limitations deriving from the disobedience of sin and finds the strength required to rise to the knowledge of the Triune God."

28. Denis J. M. Bradley, *Aquinas on the Twofold Human Good: Reason and Human Happiness in Aquinas's Moral Science* (Washington, D.C.: The Catholic University of America Press, 1997), 321.

29. *Summa Theologiae* I-II, q. 94, a. 6.

30. I have slightly re-worked the Blackfriars translation which does not translate *cordibus hominum*.

31. *Summa Theologiae* I-II, q. 99, a. 2, ad 2. See also q. 100, a. 5, ad 1. See for the same position St. Augustine, *The City of God*, Book 18 and Book 22.

32. Cf. *Veritatis Splendor*, §72: "The morality of acts is defined by the relationship of man's freedom with the authentic good. This good is established, as the eternal law, by Divine Wisdom which orders every being towards its end: this eternal law is known both by man's natural reason (hence it is "natural law"), and-in an integral and perfect way-by God's supernatural Revelation (hence it is called Divine law)."

33. For example, in *Evangelium Vitae*, §62 Pope John Paul II declared the teaching on the intrinsic evil of direct abortion to be unchangeable and that this doctrine of the Church was based upon the natural law and the written Word of God.

34. *Veritatis Splendor*, §30.

35. *Veritatis Splendor*, §53. There is room here, of course, for moral questions pertaining to the positive moral precepts that involve prudential judgments as to whether they apply in specific situations. In such cases the Magisterium would not be teaching irreversibly or infallibly. One example might be judgments about whether a certain war is just or unjust.

36. Sullivan, *Magisterium*, 130.

37. Sullivan limits the objection to concrete norms of the natural law, *Magisterium*, 150, but it not clear why he does not think it applies to all moral norms.

38. For example *Veritatis Splendor*, §§52—53.

39. *Veritatis Splendor*, §53.

40. Lorenzo Albacete, "The Relevance of Christ or the *sequela Christi*," *Communio*, 2 (1994): 258.

41. See the illuminating discussion on this point in John McDermott, S.J., "Metaphysical Conundrums at the Root of Moral Disagreement," *Irish Theological Quarterly* 71 (1990): 713—742, especially 739.

Chapter Eight

Figurative and Properly Literal Discourse in Scripture and Theology

Christopher J. Malloy, Ph.D.

Two crucial elements of the theological enterprise, according to *Fides et Ratio*, are clarity of discourse and truthfulness. Clarity of discourse is desirable insofar as it serves truthfulness, whereas truthfulness—which enables genuine freedom—is desirable of itself. This paper, focusing on clarity, will argue that clarity is achieved through precise and properly analogical expressions and not through imprecise or figurative expressions.

Granted, "There is a season" (Eccl 3:1) for every form of discourse: poetic, parabolic, ironic, prophetic, hyperbolic, etc. The theological lights of Melito, Ephrem, Dionysius, and others must not be placed under a bushel (Mt 5:15), for the theological enterprise includes many approaches and styles.[1] Significantly, the privileged locus of revelation, Sacred Scripture, abounds in the so-called "improper" literal sense (that sense which includes figures of speech).[2] Notwithstanding, the theological enterprise must include a time for judgment, for what I would call "the moment of truth," in which one asks, "Is this statement true?"[3] Now, in order to render an intelligent and informed answer to this question, the theologian must have recourse to proper and not merely "figurative" discourse.[4] Such recourse can be either explicit or implicit. In the former case, the theologian actually transposes figures of speech into precise statements, which may involve "proper analogies" but not metaphors or hyperboles, etc. In the latter case, the theologian performs an interpretive operation as it were "in the recesses of his mind," implicitly discerning what the proper *meaning* of the expression is. In either case, the transposition from figurative to precise discourse involves distinguishing the poetic from the properly literal. Such transposition does not replace the poetic; rather, it frees the poetic from the subversion of fundamentalist readings, since fundamentalism is the habit of interpreting figurative discourse as though it contains no figures of speech.[5] On the basis of explicit or implicit transposition to proper discourse (which will likely include proper analogies), the theologian is better able to *attempt* a competent answer to the question, "Is this claim true?"

This judgment, or the "moment of truth," concerns either *(a)* the meaning of a statement or *(b)* the truthfulness of a statement. Further, this "moment of truth" involves both theological investigation and interpretation of revelation. With respect to interpretation of revelation, only the former element *(a)* is the object of the judgment (at least, for those who accept revelation as conveying the truth about salvation without error).[6] With respect to theological investigation, both elements are at play, but the former *(a)* must precede the latter. We cannot judge the truth of a claim until we understand it.

I alight upon the theme of transposition to "proper" discourse—from the figurative to the analogical—in connection with several key points in *Fides et Ratio*.[7] The Holy Father suggests that philosophical inquiry—with its attempt at universally communicable discourse and conceptual language—can serve to purify the treasures native to different cultures.[8] He echoes this suggestion in calling for a theological discourse that, mindful of the precision demanded by intellectual rigor, reaches the level of concept and analogy.[9] In a key passage, he states, "Faith clearly presupposes that human language is capable of expressing divine and transcendent reality in a universal way—analogically, it is true, but no less meaningfully for that."[10]

As an attempt to respond to Pope John Paul II's call, this article is intended to foster discussion about the importance of attending to the meaning (*sententia*) of the scriptures and of theological works. What does the text of scripture mean? What does this or that theologian mean, and are his or her conclusions correct? Specifically, I seek to bring Thomas Aquinas's rigorous distinction between figurative and proper (analogical) discourse to bear upon two contemporary problems, one a matter of exegesis and the other a matter of theological discourse. Despite their attempts to avoid "fundamentalist" interpretations, some exegetes practicing "source criticism" exhibit a "fundamentalism of the sources." They neglect to distinguish the meaning of the text from the figurative way in which this meaning is expressed, concluding that the final text contains violent contradictions. To draw such a conclusion violates the Catholic teaching that "truth cannot contradict truth," definitively taught at Vatican I and reaffirmed by John Paul II.[11] In the realm of theology, a number of theologians, though in rightful pursuit of beauty, have at times wandered far from the "moment of truth" in their investigations, neglecting to submit to the discipline of precision. As a result, they exhibit a performative failure to distinguish between proper and improper discourse, leaving their readers with expressions inimical to the claims of reason and tradition. Perhaps their expressions are purely figurative; perhaps not. In any case, given the apparently erroneous character of some of their claims, it is desirable to achieve clarity about the meaning of the expressions. Foremost among these theologians is Hans Urs von Balthasar.

This article consists of three sections. First, I summarize Thomas's understanding of the distinction between figurative discourse (metaphor) and proper discourse (especially, analogy). Given this investigation, the second section examines cases of "source criticism" that judge merely apparent contradictions in a biblical text to be actual contradictions. The root of the problem appears to be a failure to discern the genuine meaning of a passage by transposing figures of speech into proper discourse. Third, I ask whether Hans Urs von Balthasar *employs* an adequate distinction between metaphor and proper analogy in notable sections of his otherwise invigorating theology. The question pertains also to the truthfulness of his claims.

METAPHOR VS. ANALOGY IN AQUINAS

Aquinas provides criteria by which to discern whether a statement is metaphorical (figurative) or analogical.[12] For Thomas, we name things in accordance with the way we know them. How we name reflects how we think we know. Analogous use of a word stands between univocal and purely equivocal uses of a word. A word is used univocally when it is said of different things but with the same meaning in each case: Fido is a dog; Rover is a dog. A word is used purely equivocally when it is said of different things but with no ostensible connection in meaning: Staples are dietary; staples are metallic and sharp.[13] Univocal naming suggests that we have the same concept for two different things. Purely equivocal naming suggests that we have ostensibly unrelated concepts for two different things while using one name.

The import of the distinction is vast, for one gains knowledge by univocal use of a name but not by equivocal use of a name. The reason for this is that we gain knowledge through reasoning, and reasoning, whether explicit or implicit, has a syllogistic character. Now, one can generate a syllogism from univocal use of a name but not from purely equivocal use of a name, since the latter yields the "fallacy of equivocation." Take the following example:

Staples sustain health.
Staples are metallic and sharp paper-binders.
Therefore, metallic and sharp paper-binders sustain health.

The argument does not follow, so we gain no knowledge. Thus, to gain knowledge one must avoid purely equivocal naming. This is true in any field, including theology.

However, it does not appear that we can use a name for creatures and for God univocally. Why? Since univocal naming involves the same concept in two cases, were we to use one name univocally of creatures and of God, we would imply that we really had a concept about God—one identical to our concept of some creature. Few contemporary theologians hold that we can name God from creatures univocally. On the other hand, those who hold that all our names for God are purely equivocal imply that we have no knowledge about God whatsoever. The logical result is that any name can be equally applied to God. Here, we end up with radically negative theology or agnosticism.[14] The fruit of the effort to defend God's transcendence in this way is a diminishment of his transcendence, for in practice, pragmatism discerns the benefits of this or that choice in this or that situation. Many seek to find a middle ground between univocity and pure equivocity. This middle ground is analogy, which involves different but related accounts (*rationes*) of a term.

The account thus far may well be agreeable for most contemporary theologians. Troubles arise when one distinguishes proper from improper analogy. Improper analogy is metaphor. The distinction between metaphor and (proper) analogy is crucial in the pivotal moment of the theological enterprise: the moment of truth. The distinction is crucial because metaphorical (or figurative) statements are literally falsifiable, but analogical statements are not literally falsifiable. One could argue that it was (in part) failure to distinguish metaphor and analogy that stayed the conversion of Augustine, who once spurned Genesis 1—2. Augustine could not be false to his intellect, which found the surface of the text repugnant. If *he* was helped by Ambrose's appeal to allegory, others have found greater merit in appeal to "metaphor," broadly construed.

For Aquinas, metaphorical statements always signify by way of comparison.[15] In literary terms, they carry meaning from one thing to another. The comparison is "alive" because the term properly signifies one thing, though it is said of another.[16] The meaning of the term is restricted in scope, and this restricted signification, in juxtaposition to another thing, can provide a tension that keeps the metaphor alive: "God is my fortress!" In this statement, I have in mind a mighty building, providing protection. I say this of God metaphorically, drawing attention to some fortress, affirming this of God only by comparison. A test for metaphor involves whether or not the signification runs through one thing to another thing—often evoking an image of the former to illuminate the latter. If this comparison is functioning in the very signification of the name, the statement or utterance is likely metaphorical: because metaphorical, literally falsifiable. That is, if the metaphorical statement is interpreted according to its bare letter—and hence, *against* the intention of the speaker or author—it is false.[17]

In contrast, analogical statements are not literally falsifiable. That they are not literally falsifiable rings true with the common sense of many persons. For example, when I say, "God is good," I do not need to negate the statement as literally falsifiable. I do not have to add, "No, he is not literally good." Still, *how* analogical statements are not literally falsifiable is a more difficult matter. Simply put, a word said of God analogically imports no defect in the perfection it designates. Yet, how?

As said above, analogous uses of a term involve different but related accounts (*rationes*) of the term. The accounts are not purely diverse—hence, the term is not used purely equivocally—because they involve one perfection (*res significata*) designated by the term. The accounts are not identical—hence, the term is not used univocally—because they involve diverse modes of signifying (*modi significandi* or *modi praedicandi*) that perfection.[18] The *res significata* of a term used analogically must be supple enough to be wedded to different *modi significandi*, since analogy demands a flexibility of signifying range. To recapitulate, a term can be said analogously of two things if the perfection it designates (*res significata*) has the flexibility to be signified in different ways (*modi significandi*), yielding different but related accounts of the same term said of different things.[19]

The flexibility of terms used analogically distinguishes them from the potentially fruitful inflexibility of terms used metaphorically. Take, for instance, the term "protection." The *res significata* of the term is "what shields from potential harm." The perfection signified is flexible, able to be said of rocks, a rightful army, parental guidance, and divine prevention. "Protection" is said of these in different ways (*modi significandi* or *modi praedicandi*) but designates each by the *res significata*, or note, "what shields from potential harm."

Let us apply these distinctions to words said of God. It is not just any kind of signifying flexibility that is required of names said analogously of God. For Thomas, a term that can be said of creatures and of God analogously must have a *res significata* that is flexible *and* that imports no imperfection.[20] A term whose *res significata* is necessarily restricted in scope can be said of God only metaphorically.[21] "File cabinet" clearly designates "metallic/wooden/plastic" and "shaped for storing in drawers." Obviously, this cannot be said of God in any way, let alone analogously. In contrast, "knows," which simply designates "aware of something" can be said of creatures and God, albeit not univocally. When said of God, the term "knows" designates the perfection "aware of something," a perfection that imports no limitation of itself. Still, just as no human has quidditative knowledge of God, no one can name God univocally. Therefore, in attributing "knows" to God, the human assigns the perfection, which he understands with respect creatures, to the uncreated God who must "have" this perfection in a totally superior way, without any defect. Despite the perfect character of the *res significata*, no created intellect can signify the *res significata* without also necessarily importing creaturely *modi significandi*. Thus, in the act of attribution, which American theologian Gregory Rocca rightly calls a "judgment," the human must "negate" the creaturely *modi significandi*. This negating judgment allows the human to establish non-conceptually a significance for this term as it is being attributed to God[22] so that the *res significata* is affirmed "as incomprehended and exceeding the significance of the name."[23]

Thomas's rigorous criteria for distinguishing figurative (metaphorical) and proper (analogical) discourse about God are at the service of the "moment of truth." They help render possible a judgment about *(a)* the meaning of biblical or theological statements and *(b)* the truth of theological statements. The distinction between metaphor and analogy enables one to perceive the roots of the problematic conclusions of certain examples of "source criticism."

FUNDAMENTALISM OF THE SOURCES

First, I will show that in ascertaining the "literal sense" of Scripture one must not interpret figurative language as though it were not figurative; one must avoid literalism or fundamentalism. Second, I will examine examples of "source criticism" that fail to interpret figurative language as figurative. In this section, the term "figurative" ought to be taken in a very wide sense, including any noteworthy literary device.

The Literal Sense. Catholic teaching has for centuries focused attention on the literal sense of Scripture.[24] Thomas Aquinas showed some sophistication in his understanding of the "literal" sense by his appeal to the divine author's intention, which is mediated through the agency of the human author. The literal sense may be defined as follows: The meaning the divine and human authors intend to convey by the use of language, which may include noteworthy literary devices.[25] Since the literal sense may include noteworthy literary devices, it is not always the bare words that constitute the literal sense. It is, however, always the intended meaning that constitutes the literal sense of Scripture.[26]

On this definition of the literal sense, failure to attend to noteworthy literary devices amounts to failure to read the text literally. Such a failure is fundamentalism. The fundamentalist neglects to follow the curve of the literary device(s) at hand—whether they apply to a word, a sentence, a unit, or an entire work. The fundamentalist thus crashes against the shoals of reason or genuine tradition or the canon of Scripture. On the other hand, due attention to literary devices enables one to defend the unicity of truth—no contradictions among the Scriptures and no contradictions between Scripture and reason—in a reasonable manner.

Let us take two test cases as examples. First, a clear test case. According to Ps 98:1, God's "right hand and his holy arm have gotten him victory." Few, if any, will suppose that the author meant that God has a hairy arm. Were that the meaning, God's perfection would be severely threatened. As it is, this passage involves a noteworthy literary device, a figure of speech called metaphor. Reading this verse metaphorically is so connatural to us that we effortlessly enter the movement of implicit comparison: God has power as a man has a strong arm. The fundamentalist—should there be one—would see a hairy arm.[27]

Second, a more profound example. The priestly account of creation (Gen 1:1—2:4a)—so majestic, orderly, and de-mythologizing—is quite different from the earthy narrative of the Yahwist account in Gen 2:4b—3:24. When taken in their literary light and with due regard for the content and unity of all Scripture and for the analogy of faith, these accounts are not contradictory.[28] The priestly version attends to God's transcendence and yet shows God "coming down" as it were by His making man and woman in His image. The Yahwist highlights God's intimacy with humans, giving space for human freedom through the use of anthropomorphisms. Though irreducibly different, these accounts work in synergy to convey variations on a rich theme: One God made humans the jewel of this world, sharing something of the divine, and calls for their loving cooperation.

Fundamentalist readings of Genesis 1 and 2 are enslaved to the bare words of the text, multiplying apparent conflicts and requiring mental gymnastics to explain away the conflicts. Many medievals were far from such gymnastics, schooled as they were in the perennial truths of Greek wisdom.[29] If (for some) the medievals may have glossed too quickly over textual differences, they merit praise for defending the harmony that must—according to Catholic faith—exist among the texts as well as between the texts and the legitimate findings of reason.

Some examples of fundamentalism are easily detected. One not easily discerned is that of "higher critics" themselves, who professedly take their roots in an understandable reaction against fundamentalism. Despite the many contributions of twentieth-century historical-critical methods, some practitioners of "source criticism" fall prey to "fundamentalism of the sources."

Source Criticism.[30] Source criticism is the discipline of trying to discover the original sources lying behind a final text.[31] The method arose as a way of handling a set of noteworthy phenomena. One of the more noteworthy of these is the presence of apparent inconsistencies within works traditionally held to be authored by one person or tradition.[32] Source critics analyze the final product into distinct units, each considered to be coherent within itself. Often, these units are drawn from "doublets" (single events twice told) or from "blended accounts" (a weaving of two accounts of one event). Sometimes, units stand by themselves. Having analyzed these units, critics recognize patterns. Many units can be grouped together on the basis of family resemblances. These patterns unite the members of each set while distinguishing the various sets of units. The patterns involve the following: writing style,[33] sequences of events,[34] numbers,[35] names for God,[36] and thematic and/or theological concerns.[37] Decades of source-critical research on the Pentateuch yielded various versions of the well-known "Documentary Hypothesis," a powerful explanatory hypothesis for the phenomena exhibited by the Torah (and by a number of books that follow).[38]

There are three chief steps of the process. First, critics break the text into its smallest coherent units (sometimes, bits). The word "coherent" is key, for it presupposes a judgment call by the critic, which is made on the basis of criteria. Of course, the criteria can differ according to perspective. British Scripture scholar John Barton writes, "The source critic must note each point where there is a break, inconsistency, or discontinuity in the text, and so establish for each chapter how many different pieces of underlying material are present."[39] Second, critics group these units together insofar as they share family resemblances. Third, critics identify the distinct messages of each group.

It is the competence of biblical scholars to debate about the different findings of their methodologies, including also form criticism and redaction criticism, which many rightly profess to be inter-dependent.[40] I do not propose to dispute these methods. I wish only to observe that, in the context of postmodernity—which highlights "difference" in a refreshing, yet excessive, way—some performances of biblical interpretation unwittingly mirror the "fundamentalism" that critics rightly shun.

Some source critics, perceiving an apparent contradiction between two or more texts, unfortunately wish not to resolve the contradiction by appeal to literary devices but rather to exploit the apparent contradiction as though it were a real contradiction between sources. To be sure, some of these critics wish to find a resolution at the level of "redaction criticism." This desire is praiseworthy and often leads to promising results. Still, others leave the reader with contradictions. For instance, of the Documentary Hypothesis generally, John Barton exclaims, "It is the unresolved clashes between the four mutually incompatible presentations that make the Pentateuch so bewildering to the casual reader."[41] Is this claim compatible with the unicity of truth?

A recent text is even more startling:

> The Old Testament gives us three *substantially irreconcilable* insights into creation (one: Gen 1:1—2:4a; two: Gen 2:4b—25; three: Isa 51:9—10; Job 7:12; 9:13; 26:12—13; Ps 74:12—17 etc., these last involving mythic combat). We might say that in principle there is hardly a faith position taken in the OT that is not open to the possibility of being contradicted by another faith position that might equally be taken in the Old Testament.[42]

Apparently, the Psalmist (and even *Second* Isaiah) drank from the well of Marduk! The foregoing are examples of historical critical claims that the sources (as well as different books) actually contradict one another. Given that the final redactor chose to weave these incompatible messages together, the reader is left to his own lights to determine what "the truth" is: "It seems that in the Bible, God does not dictate what we should think, but rather invites us to thought."[43] Further, to appeal to the intention of the redactor (or to the final author) as relevant to determining the meaning of the whole is "patently absurd."[44] My question is, does this clashing of symbols provide nourishment for the human person searching for truth?

Other critics actually seize upon *one* of the *non-final* strains of thought in a book to the neglect of any final redactional comments. They thus measure the truth of the whole by a non-final chord in the dissonance. Take, for instance, Stephen Harris's comparison between the message of one part of the Gilgamesh Epic—a part I do not consider final—and one part of Ecclesiastes. As Gilgamesh searches for immortality, a jealous goddess tells him that the search is fruitless and that he ought to rest content with food, sex, and family.[45] Harris implies that this is the basic message of the great epic. He then cites Eccles 9:7—9 and comments, "Ecclesiastes' counsel to console oneself with life's small pleasures reflects the Bible's agreement with ancient Mesopotamian beliefs about the gods' claims to exclusive rights to immortality."[46] Harris's implication that human immortality is not to be found in the Old Testament can certainly be criticized.[47] Moreover, he neglects to attend to sin in drawing this comparison. Most problematically, Harris does not attend to the closing remarks of the final redactor, remarks—by no means isolated in this text—that greatly affect the proper meaning of the text as expressive of revelation: "Fear God, and keep his commandments. . . . For God will bring every deed into judgment" (Eccles 12:13—14).

Is there not an unwitting "fundamentalism of the sources" in the above examples of biblical criticism? When source critics rest at the level of contradiction among units, they disallow resolution either at the level of literary form or at the level of final redaction. In fact, recognition of the final redaction ought to be an integral factor in determining the canonical sense of any part of the work. I would suggest that Catholic faith bids us consider all apparent contradictions to be either merely apparent, genuinely complementary, or even moments in dialogical processes of thought. I think of Psalm 22 as a fine example of dialogical process: The Psalmist debates with himself about his own misery and God's fidelity in general and, then, about his own misery and God's fidelity in particular. The Psalmist concludes with praise to God and a call for all peoples to praise Him. Similarly, one may read the final form of Ecclesiastes as expressive of a "dialogue of thought" within the redactor's mind.[48] If, however, we arrest the development of thought, or if we neglect the poetic as poetic, we end with something less than the final and genuine fruit. We thus misinterpret the sacred text.

Of course, many biblical scholars practice their methods in ways that are quite fruitful and do not exhibit the problems presented above. Increasingly, however, the discipline appears to be a breeding ground for post-modern idolatry of "differences," in disenchanting harmony with the skeptical horizons of its pioneers, Spinoza and Reimarus.

UNWITTING BLURRING OF METAPHOR AND ANALOGY

The question of the "moment of truth" in exegesis ought to be, "Is my reading on the mark?" The questions of the "moment of truth" in theology are, "What does the theologian mean" and, further, "Are his claims true?" In order to ask the latter question, we must ask the former. We hope that we can understand the sense of the theologian's expressions, whether they are literal (properly analogical) or figurative (metaphorical).

As may be evident from the first part of this presentation, working out the technical aspects of the distinction between metaphor and analogy is a delicate matter, not void of difficulties. One reason for difficulties is that the use of both metaphor and analogy presupposes similarity. So, both metaphorical and analogical statements about God rest upon the similarity of creatures to God. Catholics confess, with Lateran IV, that any similarity is exceeded by a greater dissimilarity.[49] Now, because similarity within an ever-greater difference is presupposed in both metaphor and analogy, describing analogy as "similarity within a greater difference" cannot be sufficient in distinguishing metaphorical from analogical discourse. Unfortunately, a number of theologians root their notions of "analogy" in Lateran IV, seemingly as though the council provides criteria sufficient for the purpose. Perhaps foremost among these is twentieth-century Swiss theologian Hans Urs von Balthasar. Now, if we recall that metaphors are literally falsifiable—"literally" here means "the signification of the bare words"— whereas analogies are not, we readily see that a vague distinction between analogy and metaphor can yield havoc.

In the second part of his great trilogy, Von Balthasar increasingly discusses the "becoming" of God, all the while shunning "process" theology. He suggests that there may be something like infinite "duration" and infinite "space" in God.[50] His methodological starting point for such claims is reflection on Jesus' kenosis (Phil 2:6—11). From this "economic"[51] starting point, he argues for an immanent Trinitarian ground of the economic kenosis.[52] He infers that, in order for the Son to be able "to become" incarnate, there must be some ground for this in the immanent Trinity; that is, there must be something like becoming in God, albeit in a perfect and *very* different way. Further, this immanent Trinitarian ground will also provide the condition for the possibility of sin—creaturely alienation from God. Balthasar thereby infers that the infinite distance between Father and Son grounds every other possible difference of creatures from God, including the abyss of sin and hell.[53] This infinite hypostatic distance grounds Balthasar's claim that there is in God "something like infinite 'duration' and infinite 'space'." This is a space not of indigence, but of the possibility of an ever-greater love: "so that the life of the *communio*, of fellowship, can develop."[54]

This economic starting point appears to necessitate a subversion of the "perennial philosophy," now judged pejoratively as the "wisdom of the world" (1

Cor 1:20): "The very thing that negative ('philosophical') theology prohibits seems to be demanded by the *oikonomia* in Christ."[55] Jesus manifests a temporal "becoming" of divine love, thereby disclosing an "eternal 'happening.'"[56] In short, "We must resolve to see these two apparently contradictory concepts as a unity: eternal or absolute Being—and "happening."[57]

With the words "something like," Balthasar is striving to affirm similarity within an ever-greater difference. He takes refuge in the "ever-greater" difference in order to avoid crass anthropomorphism. This "similarity within difference" is, for him, constitutive of analogy. German theologian Jan-Heiner Tück writes, "The distinctive characteristic of analogical discourse is that it affirms a likeness (*similitudo*), but, at the same time, notes an even greater unlikeness (*dissimilitudo*)."[58] Balthasar clearly wishes to avoid importing "defect" into God: "We cannot entertain any form of 'process theology.'"[59] Yet, American theologian Guy Mansini indicts Balthasar on the very charge of process theology, since by definition "becoming requires potency."[60] Mansini chastises Balthasar for seeking shelter from reason's rigor in the balm of revelation:

> To say that revelation, as read by Balthasar, trumps Aristotle here is not to preserve revelation and therefore the autonomy of theology; it is to say that grace does not complete but rather destroys nature, that faith kills and does not perfect reason.[61]

Matthew Levering queries cautiously, "Once 'analogy' ultimately overturns the principle of contradiction, one wonders whether the limits of human language about God have been overstepped."[62]

There grows, among Balthasarians and Thomists, the palpable sense of a looming debate. In adjudicating the positions, we can distinguish two issues. First, there is the question of truth. Second, there is the question of discourse. Mansini raises the question of truth; Levering alludes to the question of discourse. As I have contended, the two issues are ultimately related, although in this case they are not reducible to each other.

As to the issue of truth, we must ask whether one can truthfully affirm "being is becoming." The question is not sufficiently resolved by appeal to "revelation," since revelation has long been read as including figurative discourse and since reason has assisted in such readings. Among the teachings of faith is the belief that the principles of faith do not and must not violate the truths of reason. So, reason can aid in a discernment of figurative expressions in Scripture (e.g., Gen 6:6). Given the necessary harmony between reason and faith, we must not interpret the revealed data in a manner that violates the demonstrable truths of reason. We must avoid the pitfalls of recourse to "two truths" and of violation of the principle of non-contradiction.[63] With this wish as our guiding light, we must reckon with Mansini's contention that motion *necessarily* implies potency and imperfection. If these are the implications, how can we ascribe motion to God *analogously*? The very "thing signified" would include "imperfection." Granted, Balthasar professes to deny imperfection of God, but is he consistent? Is the perennial wisdom simply wordly wisdom? Must something like limitation or motion be affirmed of God, analogously, in order that interpersonal love may have room to develop?[64] Should we follow this latter route, would we not end up violating the reason by which we might know God (Rom 1; Wis 13:1—9) rather than scandalizing reason where it refuses a greater truth?

On the other hand, perhaps Balthasar has chosen a deliberately metaphorical style. If this is the case, if his appeals to "space" and "time" in the godhead are metaphorical, then they are literally falsifiable. Yet, on the supposition of metaphorical discourse, it would be a mistake to interpret Balthasar as properly affirming space and time of God. It would be as mistaken as suggesting that the Psalmist meant that God has a hairy arm. Yet, the metaphorical reading of von Balthasar on these points is not favored by those who favor his work. For instance, Tück writes,

> Only the qualification of a greater unlikeness marking the difference between the *eternal* kenotic event in God and the *temporal* kenosis of the Son enables us to do justice to the legitimate concern of negative theology, which warns us against applying anthropomorphic conceptions to God.[65]

Resting content with the appeal to Lateran IV, Tück does not distinguish analogy from metaphor in this article. Similarly, Indian theologian Joseph Palakeel contends

> [T]he essence of Balthasar's insight is that God is *semper major* not only for us, but also for God's own self.... This is possible only by virtue of Balthasar's dynamic concept of God as the most constant (as absolute Being) and the most dynamic (as event of love). The Trinity is eternal movement and event of love between Father and Son, the Spirit being the *ever greater love* in person.... This self-surrendering love always moves towards perfection and fullness of being (love) and brings everlasting surprises of mutual love.... Thus God is *semper major* both within the immanent and economic perspectives.[66]

If these and other notable commentators are reliable—and it seems they are—it is not in the least evident that Balthasar intended the above expressions in *Theo-Drama* to be taken metaphorically. It appears that we are left with the question of truth.

CONCLUSION

I suggest that, for the sake of clarity and truth, both von Balthasar's "Theodramatics" and some post-modern examples of biblical criticism ought to be baptized into the rigor of the distinction between figurative and proper discourse. If Balthasar unwittingly evades the distinction between metaphor and analogy, does he not risk obfuscating the truth? Rather, does he not risk violating basic rational principles and foundering upon the rocks of God-given reason? If biblical critics rest content with clashing, do they not imply (at best) a "multiple truth" theory in a way that has unwitting affinity with fundamentalism—only this time, "of the sources?" It may well be that, at the end of our enterprise, we must either return to the language of metaphor (Scripture and Hopkins rather than Aquinas) or surrender to silence before the adorable mystery (Mysticism). Yet, would not such apophaticism (of theological reason *or* of philosophical reason) be more "learn-ed" if it emerged from the baptismal "moment of truth," which is inextricably linked to the distinction between figurative and proper discourse?

NOTES

1. This enterprise is vast and multi-faceted. There are many theological styles within any one discipline of theology, and there are many disciplines. There are many sciences, including many philosophies, from which to choose and with which one may ground or correlate one's undertaking. Nevertheless, lest the array of choices so bewilder everyone and lead slowly to that false humility of relativism, which ends in the despair or the violence of nihilism, the many endeavors of the theological enterprise should strive to come together in some fashion. In what better way to come together, or at least to approach one another, than around the question of truth? Within the horizon of reference to truth, every theological affirmation from whatever field or approach ought to have the potential—as I read *Fides et Ratio*—of being related to any other affirmation, however arduous the task of relating them may be. Denial of this possibility or refusal to attempt such an undertaking, at least in some limited fashion, risks the problems that ultimately impinge upon man's ability to be set free by the truth.

2. See Francis Martin and Sean McEvenue, "Truth Told in the Bible: Biblical Poetics and the Question of Truth," *The International Bible Commentary: A Catholic and Ecumenical Commentary for the Twenty-First Century*, ed. William Farmer (Collegeville, MN: The Liturgical Press, 1998), 116—27 [hereafter, IBC].

3. I have also treated the theme of truth and analogical vs. metaphorical discourse in Christopher J. Malloy, "Participation and Theology: A Response to Schindler's 'What's the Difference?'" *The Saint Anselm Journal* 3.1 (Fall, 2005), www.anselm.edu/library/SAJ/SAJindex.html. A modified version of this article is forthcoming in *Nova et Vetera*. The present paper bears thematic resemblance to that article but is original in content.

4. The terms "figurative" and "metaphorical" should be construed very widely, as standing for any noteworthy literary device. Noteworthy literary devices include at least the following: a) those pertaining to words/phrases (metaphor proper, hyperbole, metonymy, synecdoche, symbol); b) those pertaining to small units within a work (parable, allegory, fable, law, song, etc.); and c) those pertaining to larger units or whole works (myth, psalm [of several genres], Gospel, epistle, and apocalyptic). These are to name only a few "devices." I have gathered these categories from various introductory sources, including the following: Lawrence Boadt, *Reading the Old Testament: An Introduction* (New York: Paulist Press, 1984); Stephen Harris, *Understanding the Bible* (Mountain View, CA: Mayfield Publishing Company, 2000), 5th edition; and John E. Steinmueller, *General Introduction to the Bible*, vol. 1, *A Companion to Scripture Studies* (New York: Joseph F. Wagner, Inc., 1941), esp. 226—28.

5. As the Holy Father hints, mythological language is privileged in terms of its primal nature and evocative power. But in order to be preserved from false interpretations—and, perhaps, from false teachings/views themselves—mythological *and* phenomenological accounts must undergo the purifying question of truth if they are to provide lasting fruit for intelligent man (see John Paul II, *Fides et Ratio*, §§36, 48, 61, 66, 69, 82, 83, 86, 87, and 92).

6. See Francis Martin, "Spirit and Flesh in the Doing of Theology," *Journal of Pentecostal Theology* 18 (2001): 5—31.

7. The late Avery Cardinal Dulles, S.J., observes the pope's critical use of reason in theology, a use that preserves faith from deterioration "into myth and superstition" (Avery Cardinal Dulles, "Faith and Reason: From Vatican I to John Paul II," *The Two Wings of Catholic Thought: Essays on Fides et Ratio*, ed. David Ruel Foster and Joseph W. Koterski, S.J. [Washington, D.C.: The Catholic University of America Press, 2003], 207).

8. See John Paul II, *Fides et Ratio*, §§3, 4, 36, 61, 75, 83, and 92.

9. See John Paul II, *Fides et Ratio*, §§48, 56, 65, 69, 77, 82, 84, 86, 87, 95, and 96.

10. John Paul II, *Fides et Ratio*, §84. Translation by www.vatican.va.

11. See *Dei Filius*, IV (DS 3017) and John Paul II, *Fides et Ratio*, §§4, 34, 43, and 53.

12. I am following in large part Ralph McInerny, *Aquinas and Analogy* (Washington, D.C.: The Catholic University of America Press, 1996). I am indebted to John Finley, Ph.D. candidate in philosophy at The University of Dallas, for helping me clarify the delicate connection and distinction between *modus significandi* and *res significata*. I have also benefited from discussion with John Mortensen, Ph.D. candidate at the Pontifical University of Santa Croce, and from reading a section of his dissertation in progress, "Understanding St. Thomas on Analogy" (Pontifical University of Santa Croce, Rome). Mortensen argues, with some force, against McInerny's thesis that the *res significata* remains one and the same when its term is said analogously.

13. Of course, one may raise the issue of whether "pure equivocation" is possible. In short, is a name partially constituted by intention, so that equivocals are not really equivocals but just happen to share the same letters and pronunciation? Perhaps equivocals are just orthographic versions of homonyms. And yet, even if there are no "genuinely pure equivocals," there are nonetheless functional equivocals that render arguments fallacious. Take, for instance, the English homonyms "Pole" and "pole." These terms function as oral equivocals and can yield an invalid argument: A pole is a metal rod with two ends; the former pope was a Pole; therefore the former pope was a metal rod with two ends. It is because of the fallacy of equivocation that the category "pure equivocation" is important.

14. Interestingly, Thomas Aquinas finds that those who reduce speech about God simply to affirmations of God as cause ultimately fall into the same difficulties that radically negative theology faces. For Thomas, God is known through His effects not simply as the cause without defect but also as the one who really has, in plenary and supereminent fashion, the perfections partially manifested among creatures (Thomas Aquinas, *ST* I, q. 13,a. 1, ad 2).

15. Thomas Aquinas, *Summa Contra Gentiles* I, 30, par. 2.

16. I take it that a dead metaphor may be a word univocally signifying something without comparison to that which it used to signify properly: I blew my chance! Or perhaps a dead metaphor is a word analogically signifying a range of things. Let me illustrate with two examples. First, "pen" said of a writing device has no ostensible connection to an enclosure for animals. Although it is an enclosure for ink, we do not think of pigs when we use the word. Thus, pen has become a univocal signifier of certain writing devices. When used of both the pig's home and these writing devices, it functions equivocally. Second, "light" sometimes serves, in philosophical discourse, to signify analogously the agent intellect as "that which makes manifest," although earlier in history it was only metaphorically said of the agent intellect, since its *res significata* was communally determined to physical light. See Aquinas's brief but attentive observations on this at two points in his career (Thomas Aquinas, *In II Sent*, dist. 13, art. 2 and *ST* I, q. 67, a. 1). It is evident that communal (and individual) praxis bears upon how names function.

17. "False," here means "against the speaker's intention." I take for granted that the speaker has uttered something "true" in the poetic sense.

18. There is, of course, an intra-Thomist debate about whether the *res significata* is the same through the various analogates. The import of this debate is not slight, but the various positions one may take within this debate do not directly affect the central contention in this article, namely, the distinction between properly analogical and figurative discourse. On McInerny's thesis, which for practical purposes I am following here (though I am not certain about its accuracy) the *res significata* is the same. The question arises, how are we to differentiate this account from secret univocity? American theologian David Tracy rightly warns, "If that power [i.e., the defamiliarizing and negating power of the event] is lost, analogical concepts become mere categories of easy likenesses, falling finally into the sterility of a relaxed univocity and a facilely affirmative harmony" (David Tracy, *The Analogical Imagination: Christian Theology and the Culture of Pluralism* [New York: Crossroad, 1981], 410). Yet, see Ralph McInerny, "Scotus and Univocity," *Being and Predication: Thomistic Interpretations*, vol. 16, Studies in Philosophy and the History of Philosophy (Washington: CUA Press, 1986), 159—64. Mortensen and others raise insightful objections to McInerny's reading. One objection is that McInerny cannot justify his claim by any text; another is that he may imply secret univocity. Of course, there are responses to the latter accusation. I gather that, presupposing McInerny's thesis, *modus significandi* must be taken in at least two ways. It may refer to a) the grammatical residue of an utterance (e.g., implying something *either* subsistent but concrete and therefore composite *or* abstract and thus, non-subsistent) or b) the qualifying ways in which the *res significata* is in fact signified in the *ratio* of the term (e.g., affirming "good" of God includes the addition, "is the substance of," etc.). It is the latter (b) that is most important for McInerny's account. Further, his account would suggest that we cannot neatly "separate" these *modi* (b) from the *res significata* in such a way as to "perceive" a pure, unadulterated *res significata*. Various *modi significandi* are wedded to the *res significata* in various utterances, but no utterance is devoid of any *modi significandi*. For perhaps the most profound recent treatment of analogy in Aquinas, see Gregory Rocca, *Speaking the Incomprehensible God: Thomas Aquinas on the Interplay of Positive and Negative Theology* (Washington, D.C.: 2004).

19. We must, of course, distinguish between the *res significata*—which is the perfection of something (that aspect under which we know and name it) and not a "thing"—and the concrete thing for which the word stands in a given utterance. This grammatically concrete thing is called a "suppositum."

20. Thomas Aquinas, *Summa Contra Gentiles* I, 30, par. 2.

21. Such names are restricted as follows: Their *res significatae* cannot be applied to all beings "above" a certain range. It is true that non-transcendentals, such as "to know" and "to will," can be said of God analogously even though, as non-transcendentals, their scope is limited. This "limitation," however, is rather a perfection than an imperfection, for it has limitless upward applicability.

22. See Gregory Rocca, "Analogy as Judgment and Faith in God's Incomprehensibility: A Study in the Theological Epistemology of Thomas Aquinas," (Ph.D. Dissertation: The Catholic University of America, 1989), 639—41.

23. *ST* I, q. 13, a. 5, resp.

24. This focus, due in part to Thomas Aquinas's work, does not preclude attention to the spiritual senses but provides a solid anchor for theological argument, since appeals to the spiritual senses—especially to allegory *as distinct* from typology—can lead to untamed and incredible readings.

25. See *ST* 1.1.10, ad 3. Similarly, the Pontifical Biblical Commission states, "It is not only legitimate, it is also absolutely necessary to seek to define the precise meaning of texts as produced by their authors—what is called the 'literal' meaning" (Joseph A. Fitzmeyer, *The Biblical Commission's Document "The Interpretation of the Bible in the Church": Text and Commentary*, no. 18, Subsidia Biblica [Rome: Editrice Pontificio Istituto Biblico, 1995], II.B.1, p. 119 [hereafter, PBC]). The basic claim here is sound. Notwithstanding, one may wish to make a qualification. Francis Martin rightly guards against the "romantic empathy" by which one is supposed to enter the recesses of some ancient mind. Martin also rightly cautions against limiting oneself to "explaining" the text (Ricoeur's phrase), which is merely to understand the interrelated structure of the text's symbolic world. He urges the reader to enter the dynamism of the text, that is, to "understand" it (again, Ricoeur), to appropriate it by entering into the mystery of the realities signified by the text (Martin, "Spirit," 24—26). I concur with Martin here, although I would identify this appropriation with adequate understanding of the literal sense. In a number of cases, such understanding cannot be had apart from faith. Such understanding is the reader's co-contemplation of the mysteries, hand in hand with the sacred author. Scripture is often a "riddle" until the Spirit opens it to us (Lk 18:34).

26. "When a text is metaphorical, its literal sense is not that which flows immediately from a word to word translation (e.g., 'Let your loins be girt': *Luke* 12:35), but that which corresponds to the metaphorical use of these terms ('Be ready for action')," in PBC, II.B.1, p. 120.

Of course, all language is literary, so every sentence teems with literary devices. I refer only to *noteworthy* literary devices, intending to call to mind expressions the original meaning of which is not readily discerned or which are patently figurative in some way. Literary devices can be of all sorts, as noted above (n. 4). Today, biblical and literary critics bring even greater hermeneutical sophistication, together with archeological and historical data relevant to interpretation. We are far beyond the praiseworthy, though limited, efforts of medievals at identifying the true meaning of texts. Contrast today's steadfast attention to literary form with the laudable fits and starts of those who resolved unpalatable readings by appeal to the spiritual senses (e.g., Hugh of Saint Victor, *Didascalicon*, V.2—3 and VI.3—5). The ancients and medievals indeed used reason critically in the service of the *truth* of faith, yet today we need not dismiss any "historical (literal)" sense at all, since we can appeal to literary forms. And this appeal resonates well with the text itself.

27. If, on the contrary, one accounts for the noteworthy literary device, one does not reduce the God who is "above all nations" and "above the heavens" (Ps 113:4) to a mere human being. In this way, without losing the teaching that man and woman are made in God's image and likeness (Gen 1:26), one is mindful that God cannot be likened to what He has made (Is 40:18).

28. *Dei Verbum*, art. 12.

29. Bonaventure, for one, was no fundamentalist. He observed apparent conflicts but was able to resolve them at the level of meaning (*sententia*) rather than at the level of detailed retelling of history: "Nor is there an opposition [in the accounts of the institution of the Eucharist], since the authors do not intend to relate the form of the words [Jesus used] precisely, but to weave together the history" (*Nec est contrarietas, quia scribentes non intendunt formam verborum praecise describere, sed historiam texere* [St. Bonaventure, *Commentarius in Evangelium S. Lucae*, vol. 7, *Opera Omnia* {Quaracchi, 1895}, 547b]). Bonaventure observes that while Matthew and Mark agree, there is no agreement between these and Luke and Paul and the Church! Yet it is the sense, not the bald letters, that constitutes the literal sense, and this literal sense is not in real conflict among the different texts (including that of the Mass). Nor is Bonaventure's judgment merely "me-

dieval." Hartmut Gese contends that study of the traditional roots of the Lord's Supper shows that the differences in form were not significant for the early community, in comparison to the significance the Supper must have had for all alike (see Hartmut Gese, "Die Herkunft des Herrenmahls," in *Zur biblischen Theologie: Alttestamentliche Vortrage* [Tubingen: J.C.B. Mohr, 1989], 107—08).

30. I am relying heavily on the following excellent articles: John Barton, "Source Criticism: OT," and Dietrich-Alex Koch, "Source Criticism: NT," in *Si—Z*, vol. 6, *Anchor Bible Dictionary*, ed. David Noel Freedman (New York: Doubleday, 1992), 162—171 (hereafter, ABD).

31. When ancient writers borrowed from other sources, they did not "footnote" the source. This practice was customary and not considered offensive. So, it is neither objectionable nor surprising that the biblical authors themselves do not "footnote" primary sources, written or oral, when they draw upon them.

32. By using the word "apparent," I mean simply to affirm that there certainly are appearances of inconsistencies.

33. "The variations within books such as these are wide enough to make it unlikely that a single author is responsible for all the material" (Barton, 163).

34. For example, man is formed after all other animals (Gen 1:26) or before all other animals (Gen 2:18—19).

35. For example, the number of pairs of animals taken onto the ark is (commonly understood to be one but in fact) not specified in Gen 6:19, while in Gen 7:2 the number of "pairs" is seven. Again, in Gen 7:17, the flood appears to last forty days while in Gen 7:24, it appears to last one hundred fifty days. For an attempt at reconciling these apparent discrepancies, see John E. Steinmueller, *Special Introduction to the Old Testament* 2, *A Companion to Scripture Studies* (New York: Joseph F. Wagner, Inc., 1942), 40.

36. Genesis 1 refers to God as "Elohim" (though it has clear signs of priestly redaction) and Genesis 2—3 refers to "Yahweh God."

37. Barton writes, "Thematic inconsistency arises when a text seems to give expression to two incompatible points of view" (Barton, 163). In 1 Sam 8—12, some accounts "regard Saul's election and anointing as reflecting a decision by God (e.g., 9:15—16; 10:1), while others present the people's insistence on selecting a king to be a sinful rejection of God (e.g., 8:1—22; 10:17—19)" (Barton, p. 163).

38. Some scholars argue that the "four sources" might have been in large part oral (see Stephen Harris, 89—92). Others reject as highly improbable the notion of relatively distinct oral traditions (see Richard Elliott Friedman, "Torah [Pentateuch]," in ABD, vol. 6, 605—622).

39. Barton, 163.

40. Boadt, for example, emphasizes the interdependence of form criticism and source criticism: "*Neither stands alone*" (Lawrence Boadt, 107).

41. Barton, 164.

42. Antony Campbell and Mark O'Brien, "1—2 Samuel," in IBC, 576a (italics mine).

43. Ibid., 576a/b.

44. Ibid., p. 576b. Perhaps the authors refer simply to the writer whose opinion occurs "last" in a sequence. Yet, if a redactor buried his own views in the middle of an argument (or series of contradictory positions), we might wonder at his rhetorical savvy.

45. Gilgamesh, 3.4.

46. Harris, 63.

47. The work is post-exilic, written between the third and second centuries B.C. (see Antoon Schoors, "Ecclesiastes," in IBC, 884). At that time, many Jews had adopted belief in the resurrection. Indeed, this is an important theme in Wisdom literature generally (Wisdom 3). See the following fine work: N.T. Wright, *The Resurrection of the Son of*

God (Minneapolis: Fortress Press, 2003).

48. One *need* not have recourse to the category of "implicit citation" in this case. The groaning in the first part is wholly human, given our situation. Yet, there is an answer: Nonetheless, obey God (for that is what the happy man does). On the other hand, there is a scholarly basis for appealing to implicit citations (see Schoors, 884a).

49. "Between the creator and the creature one cannot note a similarity without also noting a greater difference between them" (*Quia inter creatorem et creaturam non potest similitudo notary, quin inter eos maior sit dissimilitudo notanda* [DS 806 {432}]).

50. See Hans Urs von Balthasar, *Dramatis Personae: Man in God*, vol. 2, *Theo-Drama: Theological Dramatic Theory*, trans. Graham Harrison (San Francisco: Ignatius Press, 1990), 257.

51. "Economic" is a theological term coming from "economy," which signifies God's salvific action in the world.

52. He wishes to identify, in a non-tautological way, the immanent and economic Trinity (see Jan-Heiner Tück, "The Utmost: On the Possibilities and Limits of a Trinitarian Theology of the Cross," *Communio* 30 [2003]: 442).

53. Hans Urs von Balthasar, *The Action*, vol. 4, *Theo-Drama: Theological Dramatic Theory*, trans. Graham Harrison (San Francisco: Ignatius Press, 1994), 323—28.

54. Von Balthasar, *Man in God*, 257.

55. Von Balthasar, *The Action*, 324.

56. Von Balthasar, *The Last Act*, vol. 5, *Theo-Drama: Theological Dramatic Theory*, trans. Graham Harrison (San Francisco: Ignatius Press, 1998), 67.

57. Ibid., 67.

58. Tück, *The Utmost*, 440.

59. Von Balthasar, *The Action*, 324. See also *Man in God*, 261.

60. Guy Mansini, "Balthasar and the Theodramatic Enrichment of the Trinity," *The Thomist* 64 (2000): 517.

61. Ibid., 519.

62. Matthew Levering, *Scripture and Metaphysics: Aquinas and the Renewal of Trinitarian Theology* (Malden, MA: Blackwell Publishing, 2004), 132.

63. See John Paul II, *Fides et Ratio*, §§ 34, 43, 53, and 79. See also Etienne Gilson, *Reason and Revelation in the Middle Ages* (New York: Charles Scribner's Sons, 1938), esp. 78—85.

64. See D.C. Schindler, *Hans Urs von Balthasar and the Dramatic Structure of Truth: A Philosophical Investigation* (New York: Fordham University Press, 2004), 68—69.

65. Tück, *The Utmost*, 441—42.

66. See Joseph Palakeel, "The Use of Analogy in Theological Discourse: An Ecumenical Investigation," *Tesi Gregoriana Serie Teologia* 4 (Rome: Editrice Pontificia Università Gregoriana, 1995), 106. For analogy as similarity within an ever-greater difference, see 74.

CHAPTER NINE

FIDES ET RATIO AND THE ENGLISH CATHOLIC REVIVAL: CLASSIC APOLOGISTS ON FAITH AND REASON

David Paul Deavel

INTRODUCTION: THE INSPIRATION OF CONTEMPORARY AMERICAN APOLOGETICS

"Theological work in the church," Pope John Paul II tells us, "is first of all at the service of the proclamation of the faith in catechesis" (*FR*, §99). Apologetics and evangelization are two activities incorporating catechesis. The early- and mid-twentieth-century was not only a startling, flowering period of theology in the Catholic Church. England, despite producing little high-level Catholic theology (Anscar Vonier's *A Key to the Doctrine of the Eucharist* being a prominent counter-example) primarily experienced a flowering of popular apologetics at a high level, with figures like Robert Hugh Benson, Ronald Knox, and Frank Sheed and Maisie Ward gaining popular audiences for Catholic topics with their witty yet wise presentations of Catholic faith, as well as with their success in other genres. Knox wrote mysteries and Benson wrote popular novels. Sheed was the only "non-literary" character of the group, yet his wife Maisie Ward's biographies of people like Newman and Chesterton, as well as the publishing company he and she owned together, provided the two with a certain amount of comparable public exposure. (It did not hurt, either, that Benson was the convert son of an archbishop of Canterbury and Knox's father was the Anglican bishop of Manchester).

Despite the literary and popular quality of this movement, Cardinal Dulles characterized the mood of this apologetic movement as "at once rationalist and authoritarian" (*A History of Apologetics* [Philadelphia: Westminster, 1971], 219), contrasting their writings negatively with those of continental apologists like Louis Bouyer and Heinrich Schlier. Yet the Anglo-American movement of Catholic apologetics that revived after the Second Vatican Council still finds its most popular models in the former group. While two of Louis Bouyer's apologetics books have been reprinted recently,[1] Schlier is almost unknown in America and England. Robert Hugh Benson, though not prominent, is gaining popularity again.[2] Catholic Answers, the largest Catholic apologetics organization in North America, looks to Knox and Sheed especially for their examples, and their catalogue includes numerous books by both men, as well as the *Catholic Evidence Guild Training Outlines* compiled and introduced by Sheed and Ward. Karl Keating, the founder of Catholic Answers, has written the introduction to Ignatius Press's 2000 edition of *The Beliefs of Catholics* and refers to Sheed and Knox constantly on "Catholic Answers Live," the organization's daily call-in radio show.[3]

In short, the North American apologetics scene shows much more influence by the English Catholic revival authors than by the continental writers. These writers, claims Cardinal Dulles, shared a "rationalist and authoritarian" streak, that is, perhaps an imbalance in their understanding or presentation of the relationship between faith and reason. Being somewhat authoritarian, it is obvious that these writers, mostly converts, took their lead from authoritative teachings of the Church, most obviously from Vatican I's declaration *Dei Filius*. I want to examine more closely my selected apologists' treatments, both explicit and implicit, of the relationship between faith and reason. I will contend in this essay that these apologists, despite displaying at times the rationalist and authoritarian mode of presenting the faith in line with the mood of the Church after Vatican I, anticipated many of the emphases that John Paul II, no slouch at catechesis, made in his new and daring treatment of faith and reason in *Fides et Ratio*.

COMPARING VATICAN I AND JOHN PAUL II

What was new about John Paul II's treatment of faith and reason? Cardinal Dulles provides us with a complete analysis in his essay, "Faith and Reason: From Vatican I to John Paul II."[4] One could summarize his judgments under eight categories:

1. Context: Whereas Vatican I was responding to a dominant intellectual culture vacillating between fideism and rationalism, John Paul II faced an academic culture tending toward pessimism about the ability of reason to know at all.
2. Tone: Therefore John Paul II shows very little inclination to counsels of restraint regarding reason.[5] He sees himself more as "friend and ally" than as prophet demanding "submission to the God who reveals." He "adopts the posture of a physician helping a patient on the road to recovery." And he depicts the Church as a "partner" with humanity in its quest for truth.[6]
3. In this capacity he stresses the role of "testimony and dialogue" in contrast to Vatican I's emphasis on evidence and proofs as part of a "scientific apologetics." Faith, for John Paul II is conceived "not in terms of a faculty psychology as a submission of will and intellect," but instead as a "decision of the whole person."[7]
4. Universality and Particularity: In his consideration of the whole person, John Paul II avoids Vatican I's "scholastic and abstract" way of speaking in "an undifferentiated way of 'natural reason'." Instead, he pays "close attention to the concrete factors of history and culture," making clear not only that philosophy "is found in less abstract and technical forms in every great culture, from the ancient Near East to present-day

India and Japan," but that the Christian philosophical tradition could benefit from a dialogue with them, as well as African oral traditions.[8] While Vatican I (as well as Leo XIII and Pius XII) had no words of praise for any but scholastic philosophy, John Paul II approves in some sense of a "philosophical pluralism," giving unprecedented "concessions" to the valid points found in movements like historicism and postmodernism, while still giving honor to Thomas as "a master of thought and a model of the right way to do theology" (*FR*, §43).[9]

5. Apostolic Tradition and Development: Vatican I's "way of speaking suggests that tradition is something passively received and impervious to change or development," while John Paul II "asserts that the content of revelation has been progressively unfolded in the course of the centuries (§65) and that the faith has been differently handed on in different cultural contexts (§71)."[10]

6. Models for Relationship of Faith and Reason: Vatican I worked with a "two-stage schematism in which reason, with its natural powers, provided a firm platform upon which faith, as a supernatural gift, could be erected." John Paul II "softens this dualism of faith and reason," pointing both to the biblical Wisdom literature and the Christian tradition up to the time of St. Thomas for his models faith and reason as constant partners. Without denying the validity of Vatican I's models, John Paul uses circular and often dialectical images.[11] Indeed, he favors Maurice Blondel's model of "immanence," whereby one attempts to demonstrate "the aspiration to the transcendent that is inscribed in the human spirit."[12]

7. Trinitarian Focus: Vatican I's focus is theocentric while John Paul II highlights the "unity of all truth, natural and revealed, . . . found in a living and personal way in Christ himself (§34)."[13]

8. Higher Synthesis: Vatican I makes no reference to a higher synthesis of philosophical and theological wisdom, but John Paul II affirms in *Fides et Ratio*, §44 the possibility of a wisdom infused by the Holy Spirit enabling "the human mind to penetrate divine things through a kind of connaturality."[14]

This list provides a basic framework for evaluating how much the Catholic Revival apologists stood within their own age and how much their own approaches to faith and reason, both in their explicit delineations of their relationship, as well as what we can discern of it from their apologetic methods as evident in their work. I will present these authors in the order by which they anticipate John Paul II's vision.

KNOX: RATIONALISM—BASED ON TRUST

Although Benson was the older of the two clergy converts (and an influence on Knox[15]), Knox's work is perhaps closest to Dulles' characterization of a rationalistic apologetic. Knox is, if you will, the "straight-up" version of Vatican I insights about faith and reason, even if he rarely uses the language of the schoolmen to express himself. The best place to examine Knox's understanding of faith and reason is his 1927 classic *The Beliefs of Catholics*. While Knox did begin an attempt at a more "modern" apologetic book at the end of his life, it was never finished. No matter, it is the earlier book that is still around and in print.

The Beliefs of Catholics is in fact very light on the authority of the Catholic Church, much less authoritarian. Knox's own view of Catholic life of his day was that ordinary Catholics depended too much on taking things on faith, that is, on the authority of the Church and not enough on exploration of the theological issues at hand. In this he was following *Dei Filius*'s demand that believers give submission of both the will and the intellect. In his popular series of sermons, *The Creed in Slow Motion*, the first sermon spends much time explaining why "belief" means not just assent to a truth, but focusing the mind on that truth.[16] In approaching Catholic faith from the outside, Knox is no less intent on getting potential converts to think their way to the Church. He describes the typical English attitude to Catholic faith as a "grotesque illusion" that "Catholics base *all* their religious beliefs on the authority of the Church. . . . These people are Catholics, therefore any reason or no reason is good enough for them. They are a race apart, ogres, not men."[17] To counteract this belief in a Catholic over-reliance on authority, Knox lists six beliefs, "a list of certain leading doctrines which no Catholic, upon a moment's reflection, could accept on the authority of the Church and on that ground alone." The six beliefs are *(1)* the existence of God, *(2)* his revelation to the world made in Jesus Christ, *(3)* Christ's life, death, and resurrection, *(4)* Christ's foundation of a Church, *(5)* Christ's bestowal to the Church of his own teaching office, along with a guarantee against error in that office, and *(6)* the consequent intellectual duty of belief in what the Church believes.[18]

If Vatican I insisted on the ability of demonstrating God's existence with a reason unaided by the enlightenment of saving grace, Knox goes well beyond, declaring that many of the matters of religious controversy of his day (and ours, I might add) "are beliefs which meet us and have to be dealt with before we get on to the act of faith at all; they are the preambles of faith, the motives of credibility. And we have to deal with them by a reasoning process, which throws the responsibility for our own decision, not upon the authority of the Church, but upon our own private judgment."[19] And so it is that Knox presents in the next seven chapters, arguments designed to convince the reader of the truths of the enumerated list.

Knox's defense in these chapters stays strongly on the side of a scientific apologetics, taking account of the evidences given and demanding a verdict on them. Three areas call for attention, two in which his approach is dissimilar to John Paul II's and one in which it is similar.

First, with regard to the existence of God, Knox shows little patience for any methods of immanence in this regard, which he seems to consider Protestant and idealistic:

> Thus, you will seldom read any piece of non-Catholic apologetic without coming across some reference to man's sense of his need for God, or man's notion of holiness, a notion which can only be perfectly realized in God. The implica-

tion of all such language is that it is possible to argue directly from the existence of concepts in our own mind to the existence of real objects, to which those concepts correspond. The Catholic Church discountenances all such methods of approach to the subject; some of them, at the Vatican Council, she has actually condemned. She discountenances them, at least, if and in so far as they claim to be the sole or main argument for the existence of God. The main, if not the sole, argument for the existence of God—so she holds, and has always held—is the argument which proves the Unseen from the seen, the existence of the Creator from his visible effects in Creation.[20]

Thus Knox lumps in arguments from notions of holiness or our incompleteness with the Anselmian/Cartesian approach to the existence of God as gained from concepts in the mind. Of course, it is not clear that such arguments deserve to be categorized in this way. It would seem, says Knox, that all such arguments derive "their plausibility on a postulate which we do not grant, namely, that it would have been impossible for the human race to infer God's existence from his creatures."[21] It is not clear that such arguments depend for their plausibility on any such postulate. They depend instead on a different orientation toward the human being himself as locus of reason's connection to revelation. John Paul II's reference to a "path which begins with reason's capacity to rise beyond what is contingent and set out toward the infinite" (*FR*, §24) is, I believe, deliberately ambiguous. John Paul II acknowledges that to rise beyond the contingent may spring from different reflections—both those on the physical world and those on the contingent creature that is man.

The second main consideration of Knox's apologetic is his defense of the more specific claims of Christian faith, which he claims are accessible by reason alone. Knox's arguments here are "scientific" in that his main arguments concern the "evidences" of Christianity, by which he means a defense of the historicity of the Gospels and an examination of Jesus' conscious claims to Messiahship and divinity. He settles the matter of Christ's divinity, not by appealing to miracles (though he is concerned to show that whatever the miracles are, they are done in Christ's own name[22]) but by the coherence of the narratives about Christ. What is interesting about his approach is that the "narrative" includes not just the life of Christ, or even the life of Christ in the context of the Jewish prophecies, but the history of the world, as well. His chapter "The Seed-Ground of Revelation" makes the case for the miraculous phenomenon that was Jewish identity and worship, as well as the broader situation in which a true world religion had the means via the Roman Empire of spreading. And everywhere, Knox argues, there was a sense of expectation of something new.

Thus when he comes to the narratives of Christ's life, Knox has already planted their particularity in the soil of the universal readiness and desire for something new. But he must show that the newness that was expected was given in Christ. He gives three options for those who claim that Jesus was not the Messianic world-savior Christians claim him to be: "*(1)* Jesus Christ did not claim to be God; *(2)* Jesus Christ was a conscious Impostor; *(3)* Jesus Christ was a religious maniac."[23] In the chapter on whether Christ claimed to be God, Knox dispatches with any possibility of seeing Christ's less explicit claims as not meant to be understood as to their implicit meaning. Thus, like C. S. Lewis's "liar, lunatic, or Lord" argument, Knox's discussion of Christ's claims in the next chapter is meant to eliminate any rational possibility of accepting any answer but that Christ claimed to be God and was, beyond any reasonable doubt, God.

It is in this proof of Christ's claims that Knox appeals not merely to the facts of Christ's career but also to aspects of his "Personality," and his arguments become, if you will, more "personalist." In response to the possibility that Christ was "a conscious impostor" or liar, Knox responds that "[I]t is bad criticism to explain a career on a theory of conduct for which no motive can be assigned."[24] Of course, this is a somewhat human, but not scientific response. That one cannot ascertain why a historical figure would have lied is not to say that he might. Fiction may need plausibility to make it work, but real life does not. Knox's claim that such a deliberate deceit could not possibly "be consistent with all that we know about Jesus of Nazareth, his humility, his love of retirement, his hatred of shams and hypocrisies" is again a very human argument, but it is not scientific in the sense that it rests merely on logic.[25] Instead, it relies on the subjective analysis of a figure whom one knows through four accounts written, as he admits it, somewhat later by contemporaries and/or those who knew them. Similarly, Knox's reason for rejecting the claim that Christ was mad is that the "letters of lunatics—how inexpressibly *boring* they are, to say nothing of their other qualities!" And so Knox compares them with Swedenborg's "Heaven and Hell" and "The Book of Mormon," asking if the words of Jesus contained therein do not "provide *food for thought* beyond anything which the pale mystics of the East have ever achieved? Are they not, whatever they are, a permanent addition to the triumphs of the human genius?"[26] The rest of the chapter details Christ's life as a fulfillment of prophecy and the evident reality of the miracles, particularly the resurrection. Yet, Knox's argument here is always that these must be taken as evidence because it is impossible to believe that Christ could be an impostor or a madman.[27] Thus, Knox's "proof" of the truth of Christ's claims is primarily the witness of the personality of Christ in the Gospels. This is something not quite scientific or even quantifiable. Knox admits that historical evidence cannot produce "mathematical certainty," but that it can "exclude reasonable doubt."[28] It is not clear that Knox's arguments have really excluded reasonable doubt, unless you count part of the argument as Knox's evident reasonableness and clearheaded thinking and his own willingness to believe. It is Knox's friendly tone and his evident belief that causes one to take his arguments as convincing. Knox's appeal to the personality of Christ is primarily based on the testimony of Christ, the early Church, and Knox himself. It is here that the search for truth by reason is clearly seen as an appeal to the testimony of witnesses and not simply impersonal "evidences." And what one gains from faith is simply a greater certainty than one could get otherwise, because in the act of faith, God himself gives his own testimony as to the truth of what the convert has only been able to get to with rough certainty.

The final area to consider is Knox's view of the deposit of faith. Knox allows for no "development" other than "a growing rigidity of doctrinal definition."[29] This view is nuanced somewhat by his insistence that in former times people have been rather vague about their beliefs but that at some point a note of clarification might be introduced, but Knox does not hold as robust a view of development as Newman or John Paul II. In this, however, we may see again an anti-authoritarian streak. Knox explains why it is important to understand development as rigidity rather than unfolding:

> I have insisted upon this point, because it would be an obvious cause of additional distrust, calculated to make us ignore the appeal of the Catholic Church altogether, if we had to suppose that the act of submission to her involved drawing a blank cheque (as it were) upon your credulity; declaring your adhesion, not merely to those doctrines which the Church at present holds, but to all those doctrines of which she may contrive to persuade herself in or after your lifetime.[30]

If Knox is a rationalist at some levels, his rationalism proceeds out of an understanding of the Church as someone to be trusted with one's self, because she would be true to her deposit.

BENSON: THE MIDDLE STEP

Benson's career was cut short by his early death, but his views are plain enough from his works. If Knox stressed the rationality of Christian belief perhaps too much, Benson puts more stress on faith and faith's authority, showing it to be the essential "middle-step" in all human searches for truth, but also more emphasis on the abilities of reason after the object of faith is attained. His essential views are summed up in his sermon "Faith and Reason" found in his book, *The Paradoxes of Catholicism*.[31]

Benson's goal in this sermon is not so much to defend the reasonableness of Christian belief as to show how faith and reason are so integrally tied together that they cannot be pulled apart, as critics of Catholicism tend to do from either a fideist or a rationalist side. Benson's first move then is to show that the questions of faith and reason come not merely in matters of religion but in science as well—the scientific method can be said to be a rough analogue to pursuit of religious truth:

> A scientist, let us say, proposes to make observations upon the structure of a fly's leg. He catches his fly, dissects, prepares, places it in his microscope, observes, and records. Now here, it would seem, is Pure Science at its purest and Reason in its most reasonable aspect. Yet the acts of faith in this very simple process are, if we consider closely, simply numberless. The scientist must make acts of faith, certainly reasonable acts, yet none the less of faith, for all that: first, that his fly is not a freak of nature; next that his lens is symmetrically ground; then that his observation is adequate; then that his memory has not played him false between his observing and his recording that which he has seen. These acts are so reasonable that we forget that they are acts of faith. They are justified by reason before they are made, and they are usually, though not invariably, verified by reason afterwards. Yet they are, in their essence, faith and reason.[32]

Here Benson predates by some time the analyses of philosophers of science like Michael Polanyi (and John Paul II in *Fides et Ratio*) in noting the personal aspects to knowledge.[33] Yet his goal is not to downplay the rationality of science, but to show that faith itself is a part of any rational process, emphasizing that "[t]hese acts are so reasonable that we forget that they are acts of faith." The other example he gives is perhaps even more pertinent and connects us to Ronald Knox's own apologetic stance.

Benson asks us to consider a child learning a foreign language. Such a child makes at least four acts of faith: *(1)* that the teacher is competent, *(2)* that his grammar is correct, *(3)* that he sees, hears, and understands the information correctly, and *(4)* that such a language exists. Given an ordinary childhood, the child's assumption that all these acts of faith are worth taking is reasonable, yet only when the child visits the foreign country can he verify, within limits, the acts of faith he has already made by acts of reason. Of course, Benson does not mention it, but these verifications by reason will be subject to a need for many of the same acts of faith that were made originally in the foreign language course. "In a word, then," says Benson, "no acquirement of or progress in any branch of human knowledge is possible without the exercise of faith."[34]

Benson goes on to show that Jesus himself did not demand faith without giving reasons: "He presented his credentials, so to say; He fulfilled prophecy; He wrought miracles; He satisfied the moral sense."[35] Like Knox, he claims that Jesus gives evidence that demands a verdict from the private judgment of humans. Like Knox he claims that reason gives the person enough evidence for it to reasonably step aside and let faith and the authority of the Church which faith points to take over. But Benson's preceding explanation of how much faith is involved, even in the living of ordinary life, makes the understanding of faith and reason much more like John Paul II's image of the two wings that help the human ascend to truth. And the emphasis, particularly in Benson's example of the school child learning a foreign language, on the faith involved in trusting teachers, gives a much more satisfying understanding of faith's relationship to reason than does Knox's severely delineated journey of reason first, then faith.

Benson's presentation, much more than Knox's, also emphasizes much more the activity and interweaving of faith and reason after the gift of faith has been given. In a line very close to John Paul II's formulations, reason, when assisted by faith "has learned her limitations, and with that has come to understand her inviolable rights." Reason knows that it cannot contradict revelation and it has ceased to attempt to verify whether the revelation is true, but it is no less busy, "with incredible labours, in examining what follows from that fact, in sorting the new treasures that are opened to her with the dawn of Revelation in her eyes, in arranging, deducting, and understanding the details and structure of the astonishing Vision of Truth."[36] While it is not clear that Benson has in mind the sort of synthesis that John Paul II has in mind with regard to philosophical truths, Benson certainly sees reason sanctified by faith attaining to deeper theological truths as a possibility. And one can see the possibility of a higher synthesis of the sort John Paul II offers in the conclusion to Benson's sermon. The image of faith and reason on quest that together for the ultimate reality is God is presented in as stirring a vocabulary as John Paul can muster: "And so, little by little, vistas of truth will open about you and doctrines glow with an undreamed-of light. So Faith will be interpreted by Reason and Reason hold up the hands of Faith, until you come indeed to the unveiled vision of the Truth whose feet you already grasp in love and adoration; until you see, face to face in Heaven, Him Who is at once the Giver of Reason and the *Author of Faith*."[37]

SHEED: APOLOGETICS FROM PROOF TO TESTIMONY

Frank Sheed's and Maisie Ward's careers were longer than that of either Benson or Knox. They were also much more involved in direct apologetic speaking through leadership roles in the Catholic Evidence Guild. I want to examine their views on apologetics from the standpoint of the year 1934. The first publication of the famous *Catholic Evidence Training Outlines* was 1925, but after nine more years of speaking experience, the two saw that a new, though not completely different, method of apologetics was wanted. By the sixth addition they had added thirteen new lectures to the original book as well as an extensive introduction giving a new orientation to apologetics. A close look at this introduction, will show that Sheed and Ward had moved from a scholastic and abstract approach to apologetics to a more personal one, driven primarily by testimony.

Sheed and Ward begin their introduction by noting that the apologetic of the mid-twenties was primarily directed at two types of persons: those who felt the Catholic Church had placed Mary in God's position and those who thought the Church was anti-scientific, denying an evolutionary ancestry and thinking that the earth came to be in six days. After ten years it was not the case that new opponents of the Church had come to be; it was simply that people had ceased to care enough to oppose the Church actively. The challenge was not first of all to meet objections to Catholic teaching, but to interest people in Catholic teaching. In short, as Sheed and Ward put it, "proof has ceased to be the apologist's principal weapon." Or, more strongly: "Proof ... for the Catholic apologist, has gone into comparative eclipse. It will simply not do the work." To prove to a man that God exists or that Christ is God or that the pope is not the anti-Christ simply did not accomplish much, considering that people no longer had any real sense of what this meant for them. They explain that the two things needed for a proof to be effective are that the listener *(1)* "must understand quite clearly what the thing is that you are trying to prove"; and *(2)* "must realize that it is important—and important for *him*."[38] The connection between the doctrines of Christian faith and the identity of the human person had been severed. What Sheed and Ward had observed was the change from the context of Vatican I to the context of John Paul II's world. Reason had lost its confidence in its ability to attain to ultimate truth.

It is thus the second condition that points the way toward John Paul II's demand that philosophers and theologians make their central focus of study anthropology. Man, at least in the modern west, had forgotten—or doubted—his calling to use his reason to attain to Truth, capital "T." He retains interest in himself as a human being, but no longer feels able to move to the universal or to God. Thus, in order to ready the listener to hear evidence as the kind of thing that demands a verdict, Sheed and Ward recommend exposition of Catholic teaching as the most important method of the apologist. Whereas the implicit tone of a talk giving proof is that of an authority demanding submission to the truth, the tone of exposition is that of a friend and ally, one who is giving testimony to the truth. And this form of apologetic demands faith on the part of the apologist, because it puts the answers to the hearer, while assuming that the truths therein will spur him to ask the questions himself. This is a more difficult way:

> That this positive apologetic is in some ways, or even most ways, more difficult, scarcely needs stating. Consider this fact alone: the speaker can never tell how far he has succeeded. If his aim is to prove something he can know that he has proved it: if his aim is to win an argument, he can know that he has won it. But if his aim is to make the crowd *see* a doctrine, how can he know whether he has succeeded? The other method, then gives quick and obvious results: though they are less valuable. Any successes the new method may have are immeasurably worthwhile, but the speaker must go along without the stimulus of results immediately evident.[39]

Assuming what John Paul II assumes, that philosophy and theology begin from below, it is the Catholic teaching on the human person that is recommended as the opening subject matter. And this is the hook: "Now human beings find as such one thing interesting: they are interested in themselves." The goal is to go from the day-to-day interests of the crowd and proceed to what they point out about the nature of man. What Sheed and Ward suggest is that by "hammering away" at the very simple truth that *(1)* a man cannot "use himself intelligently until he knows what he is made for," and that *(2)* God knows what we are for, therefore *(3)* knowledge of his revelation is the first condition for intelligent living, the speaker can "bring them to an absolute horror of not knowing the purpose of their existence and a sheer fascination at the idea that God has enabled man to know." Thus the first step in apologetics is to rouse the desire to ask the questions that they should want to know "naturally." It is interesting to note that the third point suggested is that knowledge of God's revelation is a first condition for intelligent living. Instead of bringing the listeners simply a philosophical lecture, revelation is brought in as the answer and, indeed, starting point, to the real quest for truth about the human person. Thus they suggest three topics first: *(1)* what man is, *(2)* the meaning of man's life, under which topic is included the Church, the supernatural life, prayer, and the beatific vision, among others, and *(3)* God. Whereas Ronald Knox's apologetic began with a discussion of the proofs of God's existence and then moved on to what God is like, Sheed and Ward say that the goal is to show immediately what God is like, including immediately the fact of the Incarnation.[40]

This last point is important. Sheed and Ward's method is not to establish first the fact of God's existence, but to show them God's nature, more specifically Christ's Incarnate nature. They note that three specific topics above all are the most gripping: the divinity of Christ, the meaning of suffering, and the supernatural life and the beatific vision. Just as John Paul II moves from the theocentricity of Vatican I to the Christocentricity of Vatican II where it is affirmed (as John Paul II quotes in *FR,* §12) that "Only in the mystery of the incarnate

Word does the mystery of man take on light" (*GS*, §22), so the lesson of the early years of the Catholic Evidence Guild is the same. While humans have always had some means of seeing God through nature, "at best the knowledge of a being gained from what He has made must be remote, and will only in exceptional souls be vitalizing." But the fact that Christ is God tells much more about God because "it enables us to see God working not merely in his own nature but in ours also."[41]

To summarize, the new method of the Catholic Evidence Guild assumes that *(1)* the philosophy that proceeds from below must be provoked in the average person, and that doing so requires *(2)* an exposition of the Catholic view of the meaning of human life and *(3)* an exposition of the nature of God who is the one who gives this meaning to human life by *(4)* working in Christ. What this method thus assumes is something more like John Paul II's dialectical or circular understanding of the relationship of faith and reason.

CONCLUSION

These apologists, either explicitly or implicitly, came to many of the conclusions that were reached by Vatican II and, later, by John Paul II. Knox's emphasis on the powers of rationality seem to me overreaching, but the form of his arguments show the power of testimony in providing intellectual conviction in coming to faith. Benson's emphasis on the role of faith as trust even in ordinary reasoning helps avoid the tendency to overvalue reason, as his vision of faith being interpreted by reason and reason holding up the arms of faith in the journey toward the beatific vision offers a delightful biblical image to complement John Paul II's images of two wings of a dove and his other, more circular images. Sheed and Ward show the practical proof of John Paul II's Christocentricity by their claim that what has worked to make men and women become the practical philosophers they are is to present to them Christ himself (including the *totus Christus*) and often in the context of suffering (another key for John Paul II). Their insights make them still relevant for the New Evangelization for which John Paul II called.

NOTES

1. Louis Bouyer, *The Spirit and Forms of Protestantism* (Princeton, N.J.: Scepter Press, 2001; rpt. 1956) and Louis Bouyer, *Word, Church and Sacrament in Protestantism and Catholicism* (San Francisco: Ignatius Press, 2004).

2. Roman Catholic Publishers has reprinted Benson's *The Paradoxes of Catholicism* as well as *The Religion of the Plain Man* while St. Augustine's Press brought out a new edition of Benson's *The Lord of the World* (with an introduction by Ralph McInerny), an apocalyptic novel said to have influenced Alasdair MacIntyre.

3. For recent books on Knox, see Milton Walsh, *Ronald Knox ads Apologist: Wit, Laughter, and the Popish Creed* (San Francisco, Ignatius: 2007); idem, *Second Friends: C.S. Lewis and Ronald Knox in Conversation* (San Francisco: Ignatius, 2008); David Rooney, *The Wine of Certitude: A Literary Biography of Ronald Knox* (San Francisco: Ignatius, 2008).

4. In David Ruel Foster and Joseph W. Koterski, S.J., eds. *The Two Wings of Catholic Thought: Essays on* Fides et Ratio (Washington, D.C.: The Catholic University of American Press, 2003): 193—208.
5. Ibid., 196.
6. Ibid., 197.
7. Ibid., 198.
8. Ibid., 199—200.
9. Ibid., 202—3, 206.
10. Ibid., 200.
11. Ibid., 201.
12. Ibid., 204.
13. Ibid., 202.
14. Ibid.
15. For accounts of some of these near-perichoretic relationships see Joseph Pearce, *Literary Converts* (San Francisco: Ignatius, 2000).
16. Ronald Knox, *The Creed in Slow Motion* (New York: Sheed & Ward, 1949), 5—6. Knox's other books full of retreat sermons are similarly full of admonition to *think* about the faith.
17. Ronald Knox, *The Beliefs of Catholics* (San Francisco: Ignatius, 2000 [1927 orig.]), 30.
18. Ibid., 30—31.
19. Ibid., 34.
20. Ibid., 43.
21. Ibid., 44.
22. Ibid., 92—93.
23. Ibid., 100.
24. Ibid., 97.
25. Ibid., 98.
26. Ibid., 99.
27. Ibid, 103: "If we could pronounce him an Impostor, we might suppose that he had contrived to achieve this reputation by artificial means. If we could write him down as a Madman, we might suppose that he had been crazed by overmuch reading of apocalyptic literature, and had unconsciously come to live the part which his fancies suggested to him. As it is, are we not compelled to admit that there is a providential coincidence between Messianic prophecy and the actual career of him whom we worship as the Christ, significant enough to vindicate our belief in Divine Foreknowledge?" For a similar statement on the miracles, see 105.
28. Ibid., 110.
29. Ibid., 144—5.
30. Ibid., 146.
31. *The Paradoxes of Catholicism* (Fort Collins, Co.: Roman Catholic Books, 2000 [Repr. 1913]).
32. Ibid., 86—7.
33. Benson's sermon does have a clear predecessor in John Henry Newman's semon, "Religious Faith Rational," in *Plain and Parochial Sermons* I (Londaon: Longmans, Green, and Col, 1907): 190—202.
34. Ibid., 87.
35. Ibid., 88.
36. Ibid., 92.
37. Ibid., 93.
38. *Catholic Evidence Training Outlines* (New York: Sheed & Ward, 1934), 15.
39. Ibid., 18.

40. Ibid., 19—20.
41. Ibid., 22.

SECTION THREE

PERSON, FREEDOM AND THE GOOD IN CONTEMPORARY INTELLECTUAL CULTURE

CHAPTER TEN

LEST THE CROSS OF CHRIST BE EMPTIED OF ITS POWER: NEGATIVE MORAL NORMS IN THE MORAL LIFE

Christopher J. Thompson, Ph. D.

Those of us in Catholic formation often tend to emphasize in our teaching the more "positive" dimensions of living the moral life. We insist on the notion that morality is less about avoiding sin and more about fulfillment and promise. Any number of reasons can be invoked to defend why this might be the case. Pastorally, it's always more prudent to persuade one's hearers by an appeal to their hopes rather than their fears, to emphasize the promise of heaven rather than the threat of hell. Historically, Catholic scholars have observed that moral theology, especially in the decades leading up to the Second Vatican Council, placed an undue emphasis on the place of obligation, law and sin rather than the call to grow in perfection and holiness. As the more recent work of Servais Pinckaers, O. P., and others have reminded us, the Christian life of perfection is found not merely in avoiding sin, but in responding fully to the vocation to beatitude, to dwell eternally in the friendship of Christ.[1]

It is imperative, then, for anyone wishing to take time out for a consideration of morality in its "negative dimensions," i.e., a consideration of evil acts and the negative moral norms prohibiting such, to insist that this is done only in a self-conscious excision from the broader and more fundamental context of the call to perfection and beatitude.

With this essential caveat in mind, this essay is intended to draw our attention to those negative dimensions of the moral life, specifically what has been traditionally understood as the "negative moral precepts," those moral norms prohibiting certain kinds of behavior. The aim here is not to emphasize such dimensions in a manner that falls victim to a distortion of the Christian moral life, but precisely to draw out further the importance of the presence of negative moral norms in the Christian moral patrimony.

Giving due consideration to the significance of negative precepts— precisely as negative formulations of the moral law— sheds light on the overall vision of the place of the human person and the moral order. For negative precepts have a unique status in moral reasoning (and thus the moral life) and it is the aim of this paper to draw out that significance. It takes seriously the invitation offered to moral theologians at the close of *Veritatis Splendor*,

> [T]o develop a deeper understanding of the reasons underlying [the Church's] teachings and *to expound the validity and obligatory nature of the precepts it proposes*, demonstrating their connection with one another and their relationship with man's ultimate end." (*VS*, §110; emphasis added).

The precepts in question here whose obligatory nature moral theologians are called upon to expound, it needs to be noted, are the negative precepts of the moral law.

There are, of course, other facets to be noted in the document: the recognition of the natural moral law as having a divine origin and thus theological import;[2] the placement of the moral life within the *sequela Christi*;[3] the analysis of the interpenetration of freedom and truth; the use of scripture as the point of departure for contemporary moral reasoning.[4] But it is hardly overstated to say that what is primarily at stake in the overall document is defending the traditional notion concerning the absolute binding character of the negative moral precepts, especially as formulated in the decalogue.[5]

At the outset it needs to be stated that negative and affirmative precepts are not to be understood in simply a logical manner, the one taken to be the obverse of the other.[6] The distinction reflects much more than a logical one and it is the aim of this essay to bring some of these dimensions to light.

In the first place, positive and negative precepts, as further articulations of the natural law, bind individual consciences differently: the former bind at all times; the latter bind at all times *and in every instance*.[7] The distinction is perhaps subtle but very important in the moral life. The positive prescription to honor one's parents, for example, is binding at all times. At no time in one's moral life is the duty to honor parents abrogated. However, the obligation doesn't bind in every individual instance, in every particular circumstance. Granted that one ought to honor one's parents, just what is precisely demanded of the situation in each particular instance is left to the individual conscience to determine. Though universally binding in their general formulation, the fulfillment of such norms demands the prudential assessment of the overall situation to determine concretely: "X" ought to be done as an instance of honoring. As such, the positive injunction to honor one's parents lacks the specificity necessary to guide consciences in matters of particular choices; there remains the further specification provided by prudential reasoning in order to guide the acting subject from the general norm to the concrete demands of the situation. Speaking specifically about the positive precepts of the natural law, the Holy Father notes that, "These universal and permanent laws correspond to things known by the practical reason and are applied to particular acts through the judgment of conscience." (*VS*, §52) The particular judgment of conscience concerns the rightness or wrongness of the action proposed and is situated within the overall assessment of prudential reflection which, in light of the positive obligation to honor one's parents, determines the wisest course of action in the light of the particular circumstances. As in the enactment of all positive injunctions, "the acting subject personally assimilates the truth contained in the law. He appropriates this truth of his being and makes it his own by his acts and the corresponding virtues." (*VS*, §52) The situation not only permits but demands the exercise of a prudential judgment. The end of honoring one's parents is to be achieved through the deliberate means determined by a prudential judgment, issuing in a command: Do "X".

There is, then, in meeting the positive obligations of the moral life (most generally expressed in the command to love God and neighbor) a significant range of possibilities available to the well-ordered soul. Prudential reasoning in matters of positive obligation will not yield a universally valid conclusion concerning individual acts under consideration. Any number of individual actions may be rightly considered as appropriate responses on the part of the agent to love God and neighbor. It is with regard to this positive dimension that one can rightly say:

> This universality [of the natural law] does not ignore the individuality of human beings, nor is it opposed to the absolute uniqueness of each person. On the contrary, it embraces at its root each of the person's free acts, which are meant to bear witness to the universality of the true good. (*VS*, §51)

It is precisely in this positive dimension that one appreciates the famous dictum of St. Augustine: Love! And do what you will. It is the positive enactment of the good, the unfolding of the person in his or her personal perfection, that the moral life yields this abundant diversity of expression and development.

This is in marked contrast, however, to the negative injunctions which also bind universally, but now in every individual instance.

> They oblige each and every individual, always and in every circumstance. It is a matter of prohibitions which forbid a given action *semper et pro semper*, without exception, because the choice of this kind of behavior is in no case compatible with the goodness of the will of the acting person, with his vocation to life with God and to communion with his neighbor. It is prohibited—to everyone and in every case—to violate these precepts. They oblige everyone, regardless of the cost, never to offend in anyone, beginning with oneself, the personal dignity common to all. (*VS*, §52)

The binding character of negative precepts with respect to the moral evaluation of a proposed action extends to the particular instance of the act and does not remain (as in the positive injunctions) at the level of the mere generic "kinds." Observing a positive injunction affords a flexibility of expression at the level of the particular action in a way that a negative injunction does not. The latter bind not simply in some universal or generic manner, but in the very consideration of the concrete action itself. Its force extends, if you will, down to the level of the uniquely particular act in question. If the particular action under consideration falls under the species of the prohibiting norm, it is immediately to be ruled out as appropriate. No further prudential assessment of the means to the completion of the proposed action is necessary, indeed even appropriate.

While in the case of a positive obligation, if the particular action falls within the parameters of the positive norm, further deliberation about the circumstances of the action is requisite. Consideration of the circumstances might limit the proposed activity in question or it may even suspend the decision to follow through on the act, yielding the conclusion that the action proposed is permissible, but imprudent. On the other hand, when the action proposed falls within the category of those acts prohibited by negative precepts, no further consideration of the circumstances of the action is warranted. It is not to be done.

In this sense, the negative moral norms enter the arena of moral analysis with a far greater authority, a far greater power of illuminating the particular instance than the positive moral precepts.[8] In this sense, there is no room for appropriating a good or a virtue in one's person, for there is no prudential reasoning involved in the determination to commit an intrinsically evil action.[9] One might consider the various means of completing an act of murder, but such deliberations bear only a material resemblance to prudential reasoning, lacking the formal necessity of deliberation about means toward rightly ordered ends.

To speak about the moral life, the formation of conscience, the development of the virtues and growth in holiness, then, without giving due attention to the very real, existential difference between the positive and negative injunctions of the moral law as promulgated by the Church, is to ignore an important facet of moral formation. For in the one instance, a kind of creative expression of one's deepest inclinations is called upon as the requisite appropriation of the Christian virtuous life, the dramatic appeal to love knowing no limits to its fulfillment and expression. Each person writes in him or herself the story of God's call to beatitude and the dramatic character of one's response. In no way does individual temperament fall to the wayside under some bloodless, objective morality, immune to the vicissitudes of time and place, culture and context. The call of the gospel is a garden in which one's soul comes to flower under the warming light of the Divine Creator. All of this and more is true of the moral life considered in its positive dimensions.

In regard to its negative proscriptions, however, all nuance is to be set aside. There will be some acts which by their very nature are to be rejected out of hand as violating the negative precepts of the moral order. Here there is no room for "style," no consideration of context and culture, as the binding character of the negative precepts cut to the very heart of the human person as such. In contrast to its positive complement, the negative precepts enter the horizon of one's deliberation with an illuminating authority unparalleled by the positive demands.

Recognizing the distinctive way in which negative and positive injunctions shape consciences helps shed light on the perplexing criticism frequently launched against Catholic moral tradition: namely, that it lacks a consistent approach to the moral life, that its social tradition gives rise to an historically sensitive analysis, while the sexual teachings apparently do not.[10] A further consideration of the situation shows, however, that the pertinent distinction is not between social and sexual teachings, but rather the positive and negative dimensions of the natural law. For in both social and sexual matters, positive precepts concerning the love of neighbor, the pursuit of justice, the nature of responsible parenting, and the gift of self, give rise to a necessary and abundant exercise in prudential reasoning among the people of God. The magisterium provides an authentic service in handing on to the faithful the rich tradition of reflection on precisely what the love of another demands in each historical epoch and cultural circumstance. At the same time, the negative proscriptions (against theft and murder, fornication and adultery) have an unyielding character about them, binding on consciences regardless of culture or circumstance. Such proscriptions lack the on-going, open-textured character of the positive demands, binding consciences in both social and sexual matters. An authentically "consistent ethic of life" would ground its consistency on the universality of the moral order and would seek especially to maintain the very real distinctions to be made between negative and positive precepts, the prohibition against killing the innocent and the call to respect life. The latter is subject to historical nuance in a manner that the former is not.[11]

Does this mean that the negative precepts of the moral order are more important than the positive? That avoiding evil is more important than doing good? Of course not, to affirm otherwise would be to retreat to the very deformations noted in the opening of this essay. It would be to fall prey to the caricature of overbearing moralizers, to betray the deeper, positive invitation to life in Christ. Sensitive to this potential criticism, the Holy Father reminds us:

> The fact that only the negative commandments oblige always and under all circumstances does not mean that in the moral life prohibitions are more important than the obligation to do good indicated by the positive commandments. (*VS*, §52)

And yet, it needs to be noted that "important" can be understood in many ways and that there are very good reasons to entertain the notion that the negative moral precepts can indeed be considered "more important" than the positive injunctions. We have already noted their asymmetrical status in the moral life with regard to their positive counterpart, the existential clarity they bring to the situation of the acting person. There remain other dimensions of this asymmetrical condition, namely: the cultural and anthropological.

The promulgation of negative precepts points to the "objective" pole of the human person within the historically transcendent order of morality. One can begin to discern the health of a particular culture based upon an analysis of the further articulations of the negative formulations put forward by the Church. In other words, while the general negative formulation of the natural law as articulated in the commandment "thou shalt not kill" reaches to the depths of all human consciences and communities, one can nonetheless begin to wonder what kind of culture it is that needs to be instructed more specifically *not* to murder the child in the womb, *not* to murder the handicapped or elderly. Like a photographic negative, the outlines of the heart of the human community come to the foreground in a consideration of its negative proscriptions. What will later ages come to think of a community which needs to be instructed concerning the negative precept to denounce child trafficking and homosexual unions; cloning and in-vitro fertilization; torture and genocide? Granted, as general formulations, the negative precepts of the Ten Commandments have a transcultural character about them, applying to all peoples at all times. In the further articulation of their secondary principles on the part of the teaching Church, however, the negative precepts of the moral law provide something of a barometer of the human community to which they are addressed. Ironically, it seems, evil has a remarkably historical, culturally conditioned character in a way that love does not.

Finally, negative moral precepts shed light on the unique conditions of human willing itself, its splendor and pathos in this "valley of tears." In other words, not only does a consideration of the negative precepts bring to light the cultural conditions of moral deliberation, the demands of prudential reasoning and the particular judgments of conscience incumbent upon believers in a particular age, a consideration of their place in the divine law also yields insights into the anthropological dimensions of man as well: principally the profound depths of the power of human willing and the overall context of the fall.

Negative moral precepts, their place in the divine law, their promulgation in the Church gives witness to, if only indirectly, the power to refuse. It is precisely in his refusal that man is capable, if only negatively, to give witness to the higher order of love to which he has been called since his conception. The presence of negative precepts, prohibitions against certain actions, indicates that there is something about the creature to whom such commands are issued. For only a creature who is capable of resisting an impulse is worthy of being subject to a negative command. In a roundabout way, it is precisely our dignity as beings capable of rising above inclinations which belies our higher capacity to set our hearts on something greater. Only a creature capable of discerning the higher good is capable of refusing a lesser. Negative moral norms, their absolute and binding character, far from diminishing our dignity, actually announce its fundamental splendor and power. For only a creature who has the capacity to rise above the immediate context, capable of apprehending in an intimate way the transcendent nature of the good to which he or she is called, is capable finally of saying "no." It is possible that one's supreme gift of self will find its most intimate, personal and unrepeatable expression of love not in some enactment of a life positively ordered toward the good, but in a raw and unmitigated act of refusal, a final refusal to do that which is prohibited by God.

This is the principal reason that the encyclical ends with an extended meditation on martyrdom. The martyrs are the living witness to the unsurpassable dignity of man, his vocation to beatitude and the depths of his power to will the sovereign good in the face of seemingly insurmountable odds. The martyrs bear in their persons the dignity of all persons for all times. For while "it is always possible that man, as the result of coercion or other circumstances, can be hindered from doing certain good actions; ... *he can never be hindered from not doing certain actions, especially if he is prepared to die rather than to do evil.*" (*VS*, §52; emphasis added) This text appears early in the document, but signals to the reader an important direction toward which the overall meditation on the dignity of the human person before the divine moral order will be brought. The positive precepts have an historical character; they are conditioned by circumstance and are mutable in their enactment. The negative, in contrast, bear a timeless character about them. To honor them, even to the point of giving up one's very life, points to something transcendent about the human person, its radiant dignity at all times in every instance. Circumstance will determine how one fulfills the positive precepts of love of God and neighbor, as scholars, as students, as parents, as priests, as young or old, as rich or poor. But the negative injunctions reflect no such subtlety or inflection; they bind us all in the common mission to refuse to do that which is intrinsically disordered. "The unacceptability of . . . ethical theories, which deny the existence of negative moral norms regarding specific kinds of behavior, norms which are valid without exception," the Holy Father states, "is confirmed in a particularly eloquent way by Christian martyrdom, which has always accompanied and continues to accompany the life of the Church even today." (*VS*, §90)

Martyrdom in its most concrete instantiation binds diverse peoples together in their witness to the transcendent character of the good and the power of the human person to fix his or her will precisely upon it. One comes to know personally, in every instance to refuse to do that which is intrinsically evil, the universal dignity of every human being before God, the supreme good.

> Martyrdom rejects as false and illusory whatever "human meaning" one might claim to attribute, even in "exceptional" conditions, to an act morally evil in itself. Indeed, it even more clearly unmasks the true face of such an act: it is a violation of man's "humanity," in the one perpetrating it even before one enduring it. Hence martyrdom is also the exaltation of the person's perfect humanity and of true "life." (*VS*, §92)

While many of us will not be called to witness in the dramatic circumstances of surrendering our very blood in a moment of truth and refusal, even in its analogous expression of a life surrendered over time in living witness to a moral truth, the "martyr" gives witness to the objective moral order. In this sense, one's refusal to participate in that which is intrinsically disordered, (at the risk of losing one's name, friends, family, livelihood or security) marks for so many the path of martyrdom in contemporary society. In an overall anti-culture of death, one's witness to the moral order is likely to consist not so much in a single moment of heroic sacrifice, but in on-going efforts to refuse to yield to its ideology.

Veritatis Splendor offers to the human community a valuable cultural lesson concerning the universal, timeless character of the moral order: that our human community suffers from habitual inclinations to do that which is disordered; that the promulgation of negative precepts is the necessary aid to remedy such defects; and most importantly, if only to avoid the putative errors of our predecessors in moral theology, that "no darkness of error or of sin can totally take away from man the light of God the Creator. In the depths of his heart there always remains a yearning for absolute truth and a thirst to attain full knowledge of it." (*VS*, §1) Were it not the case that there remains in each one of us a yearning for absolute truth, there would be no conditions for refusing—at the cost of our livelihoods if not our very lives—to violate the dignity of the person in oneself or another. There would be no grounds for the absolute character of the negative precepts and the cross of Christ would be emptied of its power.

NOTES

1. Cf. Servais Pinckaers, O.P., *The Sources of Christian Ethics*. Trans. Mary Thomas Noble, O.P. (Washington, D. C.: 1995) especially Part Two: A Brief History of Moral Theology.

2. See Russell Hittinger, *The First Grace: Rediscovering the Natural Law in a Post-Christian World*. (Wilmington: ISI Books, 2003). For an engaging reflection on the implications locating the natural law within the divine law see Guy Mansini, OSB, and Lawrence J. Welch, "Revelation, Natural Law, and Homosexual Unions," in *Nova et Vetera* 2 (2004): 337—366.

3. Cf. Livio Melina, *Sharing in Christ's Virtues: For a Renewal of Moral Theology in the Light of 'Veritatis Splendor.'* (Washington: The Catholic University of America Press, 2001).

4. Many dimensions of the encyclical are brought to light in the helpful volume by J. A. DiNoia, O.P. and Romanus Cessario, O.P., *Veritatis Splendor and the Renewal of Moral Theology*. (Chicago: Midwest Theological Forum, 1999).

5. Indeed, there are so many instances in which the Holy Father reflects on the negative precepts of the moral order and their unique status in the moral life as such that it is not possible to elucidate them all here in this essay. In varying degrees of emphasis, the distinction is alluded to in the following sections of the document: *VS*, §§13; 50; 52; 53; 56; 66; 67; 75; 76; 82; 84; 87; 90; 96; 97; 99; 115.

6. The rules of education allow for the universal affirmative proposition to be obverted to a universal negative, and vice versa, without changing the meaning of the proposition, provided that the contradictory of the original predicate is also supplied.

7. For a consideration of this notion in the *Summa Theologiae* of St. Thomas Aquinas see: I-II, q. 71, a. 5, ad 3; I-II, q. 88, a. 1, ad 2; II-II, q. 140, a. 2, ad 2; II-II, q. 3, a. 1.

8. One classic formulation: "Thus negative or prohibitory laws have precedence over affirmative or preceptive laws." In John A. McHugh, O.P., and Charles J. Callan, O.P., *Moral Theology: A Complete Course* (London: Herder, 1929) Sect. 291c.

9. On vices resembling prudence in St. Thomas, see *Summa Theologiae* II-II, q. 55.

10. For an accessible overview of such criticisms see Richard Gula, *What Are They Saying About Moral Norms?* (New York: Paulist, 1982) 38—48. For a critical analysis and response to this perspective see John S. Grabowski and Michael J. Naughton, "Catholic Social and Sexual Ethics: Inconsistent or Organic?" *The Thomist* 57, no. 4 (1993) 555—578. However, Grabowski and Naughton do not make use of the distinction I'm employing here.

11. This is why some Catholics opposing abortion become frustrated with efforts to place that specific political objective within a broader, more consistent ethic of life. Abortion is most certainly a matter of social justice and should be seen in the broader context of the overall value of the human person. And yet, in practical matters of political prudence, persuasion, and conscience formation a different kind of reflection is warranted when considering violations of negative over and against positive precepts. Because the latter demand significant prudential reflection and rightly allow for a diversity of opinions, this more diffuse atmosphere runs the risk of undermining the very focused efforts to overturn policy which violates a negative precept in a grave manner.

Chapter Eleven

Veritatis Splendor and the Fundamental Option: Seeking Guidance from Thomas' Doctrine of Infused Cardinal Virtue

William C. Mattison

In the third part of Chapter II of the encyclical *Veritatis Splendor*, Pope John Paul II outlines the deficiencies of certain articulations of "fundamental option" approaches to moral theology that starkly dichotomize one's fundamental option and "deliberate choices of a concrete kind of behavior" (§65, cf. 68). He goes on in this section to reject a certain understanding of the distinction between mortal and venial sins, in which mortal sins are possible only at the level of fundamental option. Discussions of this part of *Veritatis Splendor* have since focused on whether or not the pope presents an accurate portrayal of fundamental option theory, and relatedly but distinctly, whether or not fundamental option theory does indeed divide attention to the person's stance before God from the person's concrete moral choices.

The first section of this paper briefly examines this debate on the relationship between persons and acts. But its primary purpose is to identify two features of the discussion of fundamental option in *Veritatis Splendor* that are often untreated in debates over persons and acts. Given these two considerations, it is argued here that an examination of St. Thomas' doctrine on the infused cardinal virtues would help illuminate the present discussion. For the question at hand is not simply about the relationship between persons and acts, but also about how God's grace transforms people's lives, particularly their concrete moral choices in the natural realm. To that end, Thomas' doctrine is briefly explicated in the second section with the help of some of his historical predecessors. A contemporary misinterpretation of infused cardinal virtue is identified to demonstrate what is at stake in one's doctrine of infused cardinal virtue. What emerges in this discussion are striking parallels between a contemporary misread of the infused cardinal virtues and the thought of those whom Pope John Paul II criticizes in *Veritatis Splendor*. Those similarities point us back in the third and final section to examine what this investigation of infused cardinal virtue contributes to the debate over fundamental option. Thomas' doctrine of infused cardinal virtue will illuminate how fundamental option theory, as applied to moral theology, improperly dichotomizes "inner-worldly" activities from one's relationship to God by conflating two different categorizations of virtue that Thomas is careful to distinguish. In doing so, they also imply a doctrine of grace—and of nature as recipient of God's grace—that is gravely deficient.

VERITATIS SPLENDOR AND FUNDAMENTAL OPTION

The pope begins his discussion of fundamental option theory by affirming one of its central insights: there is an important difference between a *"decision about one's self* and a setting of one's own life for or against the Good, for or against the Truth, and ultimately for or against God" and "particular everyday choices".[1] However, it quickly becomes clear that the pope thinks several theologians have taken this distinction too far, such that what is a helpful "distinction" between fundamental option and deliberate particular choices has been misunderstood as a "division" or "separation" (*VS*, §65).[2] Several commentators sympathetic with fundamental option theory have retorted that the pope mischaracterizes the more nuanced presentation of this theory.[3] Yet even those sympathetic to the goals of fundamental option theory demonstrate that there is a real difference between the pope's position in *Veritatis Splendor* and even nuanced versions of fundamental option theory.[4] That real difference is best identified in the following quotations:

> According to the logic of the positions mentioned above, an individual could, by virtue of a fundamental option, remain faithful to God independently of whether or not certain of his choices and his acts are in conformity with specific moral norms or rules. By virtue of a primordial option for charity, that individual could continue to be morally good, persevere in God's grace and attain salvation, even if certain of his specific kinds of behavior were deliberately and gravely contrary to God's commandments as set forth by the Church (*VS,* §68). The conclusion to which this [theory] eventually leads is that the properly moral assessment of the person is reserved to his fundamental option, prescinding in whole or in part from his choice of particular actions, of concrete types of behavior (*VS,* §65).

All participants in this debate grant that it is important to distinguish between a person and her acts, since all recognize that it is possible for a person to commit grave sin and yet not sever one's relationship with God.[5] The question at hand is whether fundamental option theory helps one better explain this fact of moral theology, or whether it actually confounds this dilemma by distinguishing persons and acts at the high cost of severing the tie between particular moral choices and abiding states of character.

In order to determine which of these is the case, it is necessary to examine how fundamental option theory explains the relationship between acts and persons. The focus in this piece is on the work of Josef Füchs, who uses the term "basic freedom" for what is more commonly called fundamental option.[6] Füchs makes the distinction between persons and acts clear in the following extended quotation:

> [I]t is not the good and evil aims and actions themselves or the measure of good in man's exercise of his freedom of choice [as opposed to basic freedom] that determine his goodness or wickedness. Here the decisive factor is rather the extent to which an individual as a person, in his freely chosen good or evil aims and actions, determines himself as a whole, i.e., in basic freedom, thus determining himself as good or evil, and ordering his aims and acts in accordance with that determination.[7]

Basic freedom is the "self-determination of the person as a whole."[8] Fuchs is clear that this commitment of the whole person is intimately tied to particular actions. As the above quotation states, it is determined "in his freely chosen good or evil actions." Though "the basic freedom of a person as a whole in the face of the Absolute should not be confused with freedom of choice in particular moral acts," Fuchs also claims one's basic freedom "takes shape in successive acts."[9] While "more than any particular action or actions and more than the sum of them, [basic freedom] underlies them, permeates them, and goes beyond them, without ever being actually one of them."[10]

Fuchs cannot be accurately accused of failing to note the intricate connection between acts and persons. Nor can Fuchs be faulted for failing to neatly solve the difficult question of the relationship between a person and her acts; this has been a moral problem since, and likely before, Aristotle's quixotic claim that only the virtuous person commits truly good acts, and one only becomes virtuous by committing good acts. Fuchs *can*, however, be accurately accused of articulating an inherently problematic understanding of how that connection exists. The problem with Fuchs' approach is that he defines the two levels of freedom in such a way that it is impossible to see how they, as he continually asserts, are inextricably tied together. One's basic freedom can "exist *only in* the concrete act," and yet must "not be confused with particular moral acts" because that deeper freedom is "athematic," without an object.[11] Since one cannot understand one's self or the Absolute as an object, the "surrender or withholding of the self as a basic free act is not a specific but a transcendental process."[12] This division of levels of human freedom does indeed achieve the goal of securing basic freedom from being identified with particular free actions. Yet described as such, it is unclear how basic freedom can "permeate" and "underlie" particular actions. What is the basis for that relation when there is no specified or determined "content," if you will, to one's basic freedom?

At times it seems that Fuchs does wish to give basic freedom an "object," though rather broadly understood. He speaks of it as surrendering or withholding the self.[13] Though at times he says it is wrong to label basic freedom a "decision,"[14] at other times he speaks of it as a "free self-commitment of ourselves"[15] (to what?), or a "full, personal decision that is made."[16]

> Christian intentionality [which equals basic freedom] refers concretely to an actual presence in the particular attitude and conduct of various spheres of life, a living, conscious presence in the daily shaping of life and the world, so that this

daily life in its manifold particularity... represents at the same time and in its depths the living, conscious, and free actualization of the decisiveness of Christian intentionality.[17]

The problem is employing two uses of freedom defined in opposition to each other (with and without specifying object), while trying to claim the two are intimately related and shape each other. One cannot define basic freedom athematically, or without specified content, and simultaneously insist that basic freedom is not independent of particular choices, when what identify the latter is precisely their objects.

Jean Porter voices a similar critique, claiming such a view of basic freedom

> employs the language of freedom while at the same time stripping that language of the context which alone could give it meaning and point. Transcendental freedom ... is a capacity which is exercised apart from any categorical act, and which furthermore has no object, since it concerns the agent's self-disposition as such.[18]

Previous critiques of fundamental option theory propose alternative ways of relating, while not equating, a person and her acts. For example, Benedict Ashley, O.P., claims that the pastoral intent of fundamental option theory—distinguishing a person's general state and particular actions—is better accomplished by traditional attention to objective and subjective features of morality than it is by positing realms of basic freedom and free choice.[19] Porter argues that the Thomistic notion of charity as a virtue achieves this desired distinction, while guarding the relationship between the virtue and specific actions.[20]

The primary purpose of this section is not simply to engage and contribute to the abovementioned debate. Rather, the goal of this section is to identify two features of the debate over the relationship between persons and acts in fundamental option theory that suggest a comparison with Thomas' doctrine of infused cardinal virtue. The first feature that suggests inquiry into Thomas' doctrine of infused cardinal virtue will be fruitful is the fact that fundamental option theorists distinguish the transcendental and categorical realms by object. Since ethicists such as Füchs generally claim that the transcendental level of basic freedom does not properly have an "object," let us say that the transcendental level concerns one's *stance* before God directly, while the categorical level concerns one's engagement with activities of this world, accessible to human reason. As any Christian would resist labeling God an "object" of one's freedom, we could say that transcendental freedom concerns God directly, while categorical freedom concerns created goods directly. The pope himself notes this distinction when he claims that The immediate object of [particular] acts would not be Absolute Good (before which the freedom of the person would be expressed on a transcendental level), but particular (also termed "categorical") goods (*VS*, §65).

The "object" of one's fundamental option is the Absolute Good, or God. The objects of categorical actions are "particular 'inner-worldly' kinds of behavior: those, in other words, concerning man's relationship with himself, with others, and with the material world" (*VS*, §65). Once the source of the distinction between categorical and transcendental is named, the relevance of the infused cardinal virtues is apparent.

The infused cardinal virtues deal precisely with how one's relationship with God transforms one's actions regarding created goods such that they are directed ultimately to God as one's final end.

The second feature of the fundamental option debate which warrants further investigation of the infused cardinal virtues involves the "location," if you will, of grace. Since one's relationship with God concerns the transcendental level, according to fundamental option theorists, sanctifying grace is only lost in a direct rejection of God. This is how ethicists such as Füchs can claim that evil actions need not impact the state of grace marking one's relation with God. However, describing grace in such a manner as to "protect" it from being abolished by evil categorical actions also has the converse effect: categorical actions are unable to be transformed by the grace of God. The very function of infused cardinal virtues is the transformation of "categorical" actions by God's grace. For these two reasons, examining Thomas' doctrine of infused cardinal virtue will help illuminate further deficiencies of fundamental option theory. Describing that doctrine is the task of the following section.

THOMAS AQUINAS ON THE INFUSED CARDINAL VIRTUES

Thus far the term "infused cardinal virtue" has been employed repeatedly but without clarification. The purpose of this section is to unveil Thomas' understanding of infused cardinal virtue. There is need for "unveiling" since Thomas utilizes several different categorizations of virtue and is easily misunderstood if not attended to closely. In fact, this section concludes with an example of a contemporary misread of infused cardinal virtue.

Thomas employs many different categorizations of virtue, three of which are important for this project. The basis of each of these distinctions is described here, followed by an examination of the different possible permutations of virtue given these categorizations. The first way Thomas distinguishes acquired from infused virtues is by way of efficient cause. Some virtues are caused in people by repeated acts or habituation.[21] Others are caused directly by God.[22] The former are called acquired, the latter infused.

A second way of categorizing virtue is by the final end, or ultimate goal, of the activity toward which the virtue disposes one. Following Aristotle, Thomas claims that all properly human activity is directed toward an end, or goal.[23] The ultimate end of humanity is union with God in the beatific vision.[24] However, since this end transcends the unaided capacities of human nature, humanity's ultimate end is properly called supernatural.[25] Humanity also possesses a true, albeit imperfect, natural end.[26] For instance, practical reasoning and ordering of temporal affairs are within natural human capacities, and may be done without further reference to humanity's final end of union with God. Virtues disposing one toward this imperfect end are called natural. Thus virtues may be categorized by the natural or supernatural end toward which they direct a person.[27]

A third way of distinguishing virtues concerns neither the efficient cause nor end, but rather the object of virtue. Virtues, which are ordered dispositions of the person toward good actions, may be differentiated by the types of activity toward which they dispose a person. Thus there are virtues which concern eating, others concerning right belief about God, etc. Of the manifold types of activity that may be governed by a virtue, certain activities are comprehensible to unaided reason (eating, practical decision-making, allotting goods, etc.).[28] Others have God's very self as an object, who transcends unaided human reason.[29] Thomas labels these latter virtues, whose immediate objects are God, "theological." Those virtues whose objects are comprehensible to human reason are called here "cardinal."[30]

Having established these three Thomistic categorizations of virtue, we may now explore the relationships between these different types of virtues. How many permutations are there based on these three distinctions of virtue? One could imagine eight, if all different combinations of each of the terms were possible. However, this is not the case. One can reliably graft the acquired/ infused distinction by efficient cause onto the natural/supernatural distinction by end. In other words, all acquired virtues are directed to the natural end of humanity. Conversely, all infused virtues are directed toward the supernatural end of humanity. Thus these two categorizations yield two, not four, types of virtue: acquired natural virtues and infused supernatural virtues.

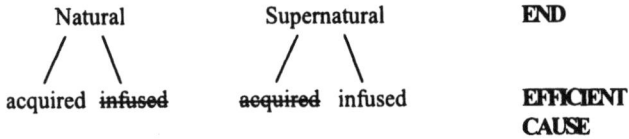

Consider next the categorization by object, cardinal/theological. Can one similarly graft this distinction onto the other, resulting in just two types of virtue, each with three qualifiers? Initially it may seem so. Are acquired natural virtues never theological and always cardinal? The answer is clearly yes. One cannot acquire (on one's own) virtuous inclinations to actions that are ultimately directed to humanity's natural end, but pertain immediately to God. For God is ever enjoyed and never used.[31] In other words, actions pertaining to God are never subordinated to some greater final end.[32] Thus all acquired natural virtues are cardinal, pertaining directly to objects comprehensible to reason.

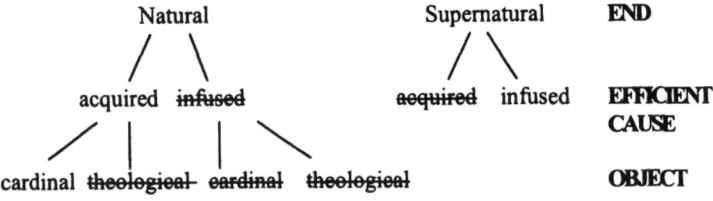

Yet does the same correspondence of categories obtain regarding the infused supernatural virtues? Are infused supernatural virtues always theological and never cardinal? Clearly theological virtues are infused by God; from where else could humans obtain the dispositions to actions that pertain immediately to God? Furthermore, since they do pertain directly to the Divine as their object, it is obvious that they are ultimately directed to God, since again, only God is ever enjoyed and never used.[33] However, it is *not* the case that *cardinal* virtues are never infused supernatural virtues. In other words, it is not the case that all virtues pertaining to objects comprehensible by reason are ultimately directed to humanity's natural end and acquired by repeated acts. Thomas affirms this himself in an article on the existence of infused cardinal virtues:

> The theological virtues direct us sufficiently to our supernatural end inchoatively: i.e., to God Himself immediately. But the soul needs further to be perfected by infused virtues pertaining to other things, yet in relation to God.[34]

Virtues dealing with "other things, yet in relation to God" *are* infused cardinal virtues.

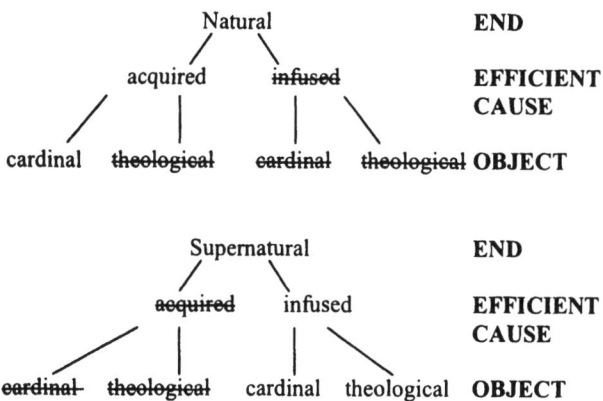

Despite the alluring simplicity of a bipartite categorization of virtues into acquired (natural) cardinal virtues and infused (supernatural) theological virtues, the existence of infused (supernatural) cardinal virtues eliminates such a possibility.[35] What is at stake in maintaining the importance of this odd category of virtues? First, on an historical level, it should be noted that Thomas' categorization of virtue, while innovative in offering a more coherent set of distinctions, is not at all innovative in affirming the presence of cardinal virtues that are infused by God and directed to humanity's supernatural end. To name but two, Alan of Lille and William of Auxerre speak of chastity and justice, respectively, in service to God. Clearly chastity and justice are cardinal virtues, since they concern activities accessible to unaided reason. Yet in this case they are also directed to humanity's supernatural end.[36] Similar affirmations may be found regarding the possibility of cardinal virtues being infused by God as well as acquired by repetition. Regarding Thomas' predecessors, Lottin asks, "Are cardinal virtues infused just as theological virtues are infused? On this point, agreement [among the predecessors] is complete." Each one replies positively.[37]

Thus one reason why Thomas affirms the possibility of infused cardinal virtue is the consistent presence of such virtues in Scripture and tradition.[38] But more is at stake than continuity with tradition. Or better, there are important reasons undergirding this continuity. In the following, some reasons are offered. After examining these reasons, we turn back to the question of fundamental option, bolstered by any insight gleaned from this exploration of the importance of infused cardinal virtue.

Thomas himself indicates what he deems a major reason for affirming the necessity of infused cardinal virtues when he asks whether virtue acquired by habituation belongs to the same species as infused virtue.[39] In his response Thomas recognizes that both acquired and infused, say, temperance, govern the same human capacity regarding pleasures of touch. This is why both are properly called the cardinal virtue temperance. However, both set the mean of temperance using different standards. Acquired temperance disposes one to eat, drink, etc. in a manner according to the rule of human reason. Infused temperance, which directs one to one's supernatural end, disposes one to eat, drink, etc. in a manner according to the Divine rule. Now the mean in each of these cases may differ, as when acquired temperance disposes one to eat simply healthily, and infused temperance disposes one to fast during Lent. In fact, even when the means set by acquired and infused temperance do not differ, the acts of those virtues still do differ in formal object, and thus belong to different species. In Thomas' words, "Both acquired and infused temperance moderate desires for pleasures of touch, but for different reasons . . . wherefore their respective acts are not identical."[40] Given that temperance disposes one differently based on its source and end, the infused cardinal virtues are essential to the Christian life if grace at all changes not only how one stands directly before God, but how one acts in the world on the basis of that relationship with God.

The beauty of Thomas' response is that it simultaneously reveals how grace transforms one's direct relationship with God, as well as one's ongoing involvement in the natural order. This point is perhaps best explored by asking a question that has occupied moral theologians for eight centuries: does charity suffice for guiding the virtuous Christian moral life by providing a new supernatural end for the person's earthly activities acquired by habituation, or need there be infused with charity also a set of infused cardinal virtues?[41] Thomas obviously holds the latter position. The believer becomes directed toward eternal beatitude by sanctifying grace, but Thomas also recognizes that those whose lives are transformed by grace continue to live and work in the world. They continue to reason practically, allot goods, desire pleasures, and persevere through trial. Charity elevates the person to direct friendship with God. Since the object of charity is God's very self, charity is directly concerned with God and not particular inner-worldly activities. Of course, Thomas also recognizes that charity is the "form" of all other virtues, elevating those virtues to be directed to humanity's supernatural end.[42] However, charity and acquired virtue do not alone suffice. In actions concerning objects accessible to reason (i.e., cardinal virtues), acquired virtues alone do not suffice for the believer since they only dispose one to one's natural end. Once these actions become directed to one's final end via charity, one is no longer rightly said to act out of acquired natural virtues. Since one cannot acquire dispositions toward eternal beatitude on one's own, and since one is no longer acting simply toward one's natural end, acquired natural virtues are stretched well past their breaking point. Thus the new principles out of which one acts, which concern activities in the world (as opposed to God's very self) as undertaken in reference to one's supernatural end, are given with charity and rightly called infused cardinal virtues. Through them, the believer's life is completely transformed by love of God. That love is expressed not simply toward God directly, but in one's actions in the natural realm as well. Though the believer's life is founded upon love of God, one must continue to live virtuously in the natural created order. The infused cardinal virtues equip one to do so.

It may seem odd that a set of cardinal virtues infused with charity may direct one toward activities in the natural order. But this was not at all odd for the scholastics, who insisted upon the axiom "grace perfects, not destroys, nature." The key to understanding this scholastic axiom is attending to how one defines "natural." If one understands natural as signifying that which is comprehensible to unaided human reason, one is in accord with scholastics such as Thomas. However, rightly noting that the supernatural is that which exceeds the grasp of unaided human reason, one could then wrongly conclude that the natural is defined as mutually exclusive with the supernatural. In other words, any relation to the supernatural disqualifies an action from being called in any way natural. This would be a drastic error. For the scholastics, particularly under the influence of Augustine, nature is rightly understood as that which is "used," while the supernatural (i.e., God) is that which is enjoyed. Thus the natural is most properly understood in reference to the divine, though of course only the natural is accessible to human reason unassisted by grace.

What does all this matter for the infused cardinal virtues? These are called cardinal because their objects (eating, judging, practical decision-making, etc.) are all activities that are natural, as in accessible to reason. Yet this is **not** to say that such actions concerning activities accessible to reason cannot be guided by infused grace, and undertaken in a manner transformed by one's relationship with God. To the contrary, as activities undertaken with ultimate reference to the divine, this is actually the most perfect type of cardinal virtue.

If one were to rightly recognize both the accessibility of the cardinal virtues' objects to reason, and the existence of a natural end of such actions, but *further* assert that such a natural end precludes the possibility of the cardinal virtues being supernaturally oriented, one would commit a serious scholastic error. Observe such an error in the following passage from a contemporary moral theologian:

> The [cardinal] virtues have, therefore, the same context as their objects. . . . First, the end that specifies the virtue as [cardinal] is not the last end. Second, these virtues have objects presented by reason, comprehensible to reason, and measured by reason. . . . Thus the context of the moral virtues as distinct from

the theological virtues [in object] excludes Thomas' concepts of the last end and charity.[43]

The cardinal virtues are rightly described by Keenan as having objects accessible to reason, but wrongly assumed to be therefore unrelated to the last end of humanity, supernatural beatitude. It is true that cardinal virtues are not necessarily directed to that end. But it is also true that they may be. Indeed, for Thomas and his predecessors, that is the primary sense of cardinal virtue.[44] But Keenan never refers to cardinal virtues as infused and directed to humanity's supernatural end. In the above quote he claims cardinal virtues are not specified by the last end and that their objects are measured by human reason. But neither of these is true when the cardinal virtues are infused. Furthermore, he claims: "Thus, the [cardinal] virtues are produced in us by humanly reasoned acts, while the theological virtues, being beyond our capabilities, are produced in us by God."[45] Again, this may be the case but is not always so. In this bipartite vision of virtue, there is no room for infused cardinal virtue, and it is thus difficult to see how the believer's actions regarding inner-worldly activities are transformed by grace.

What is the likely cause of the erroneous presentation of a bipartite vision of virtue in this theologian's discussion of virtue? There is a conflation of Thomas' categorizations of virtue based on object and end. All theological virtues are rightly assumed to be supernatural. But all cardinal virtues are wrongly assumed to be directed toward humanity's natural end and acquired. The above discussion of Thomas' categorization of virtue reveals how and why this is a mistaken understanding of virtue.

The infused cardinal virtues thus serve two related roles in Thomas' vision of virtue. First, they enable him to argue how the life of grace transforms one's whole life and not simply one's relationship with God. Second, they reveal the scholastic view of the natural order as not necessarily, but nonetheless most perfectly, further directed toward one's final end. Thomas' doctrine of infused cardinal virtue reveals that virtuous activity in the natural order is not only possible in new ways in, but remains necessary for, the graced Christian life if one believes that nature is not destroyed or left behind, but actually perfected, by God's grace.

INFUSED CARDINAL VIRTUES AND THE FUNDAMENTAL OPTION

What has all of this discussion of infused cardinal virtue to do with the fundamental option? Recall that proponents of fundamental option theory make a crucial distinction based upon object. They label the person's stance in freedom before God the "transcendental" level, and one's freedom regarding particular choices the "categorical" realm. What drives this distinction is their claim that only actions at the transcendental level can sever one's relationship with God in mortal sin. Since categorical actions immediately concern worldly goods, they themselves cannot constitute a rejection of God. This is precisely the error of a bipartite vision of virtue that conflates categorizations by end and object. The assumption here is that since (the *objects* of) categorical goods are accessible to reason; they are not further related to the supernatural (*end*). Fundamental option theorists of course recognize that categorical actions *may* involve a rejection of God. But when that happens, it is not a feature of the inner-worldly activity that constitutes a rejection of God. The categorical act only constitutes a rejection of God to the extent that it "carries" such a rejection at the level of one's fundamental option. Thus the rejection is not a feature of the act itself but only of the basic freedom of the person acting. There are several problems with this analysis. First, as discussed in the first section, it is unclear to what extent free categorical acts can "carry" one's fundamental option if the latter is not specified by any object. Second, as should be clear from Thomas' doctrine of infused cardinal virtue, it is *not* the case that actions immediately concerning worldly activities and not God's very self are unrelated to God. That approach assumes that only actions whose *object* is God (or, equally, actions which are expressions of freedom directly toward God) can constitute a rejection of God. This neglects attention to the *end* of an action whose object is not God, but which is nonetheless directed ultimately toward or away from God. Further, whether acts are further related to God or not is not some accidental feature "carried" by the action at hand. The end is determinative of the formal object of the action.[46] Recall Thomas' claim that acts of infused and acquired virtue differ in species, since the formal object of each varies according to the different ends of each. Thus one must attend to both the end and object of inner-worldly activity in order to fully understand its meaning, and determine whether or not it constitutes, rather than "carries" a rejection of God or not.

This failure to adequately attend to the end/object distinction is revealed in Füchs' work when he examines religious actions. Füchs divides the planes of Christian living into the theological (i.e., transcendental, directly toward God) and moral (i.e., categorical). As noted, this division attends only to the object of a particular activity and not to the end. Yet this presents a problem when Füchs examines acts of religion, such as prayer, liturgy, or other religious observances. Such actions clearly concern God, but they are just as clearly categorical, involving inner-worldly goods. Füchs recognizes that such actions are not properly called transcendental, and yet they must also be distinguished from "the moral life which is horizontally determined." So Füchs must posit a sort of middle ground between the moral and theological planes. Füchs claims that "religious life is closer to theological existence than is moral life," since "religious life brings the reality of Christian existence into the sphere of reflective and thematic consciousness."[47] This is the closest Füchs comes to recognizing anything like Thomas' infused cardinal virtues. Here we have inner-worldly activity that is further related to one's stance before God. Unfortunately, Füchs never takes the next step (as Thomas does) of recognizing that *all* moral action can be further related to one's supernatural end and thus "bring the reality of Christian existence into the sphere of reflective and thematic consciousness." But with Füchs' stark object-based division that does not attend also to the end of an activity, a moral action is only able to accidentally "carry" one's basic freedom, rather than be inherently related to God as the ultimate end of the action. Füchs concludes his argument noting that "religiousness promotes Christian existence in a more forceful and immediate way than does the moral life."[48] It is suggested here that for the Christian animated by grace, *all* inner-worldly actions, religious observance or not, are "forcefully" and "immediately" related to one's stance before God.

It should be noted that Thomas' categorization of virtue handles the question of religious observances much more easily. People often wonder why the virtue of religion is placed under Thomas' treatment of justice.[49] Activities of the virtue justice, which is a cardinal virtue, are categorized as such because their objects are inner-worldly activities comprehensible to reason. However, since Thomas attends to both the object and the end of virtue, he is able to claim that while religion involves inner-worldly activities, these are further related to one's supernatural end. When they are, they constitute infused cardinal virtues. In this analysis, it is not an accidental feature of worldly action that relates it to God. Rather, the relation of the worldly activities to one's ultimate end transforms the very formal object of the activities.

This point raises the contested question of intrinsic evils, a question distinct from, yet closely related to the analysis in this article. Can all categorical actions "carry" a fundamental "yes" toward God? For Füchs, it would seem the answer is yes, since that "yes" is an extrinsic feature of the categorical act itself. For Thomas, this is not the case. He notes that certain inner-worldly actions are not only *not* referred to one's last end (God), but are also *incapable* of being thus referred.[50] These acts not only do not carry a self-surrender to God, but are incapable of doing so, and thus lead one away from God due to the very nature of the act itself. Thomas says that while some acts are unable to be further referred to one's last end, other acts are simply not thus referred, even though they could be. The former are called counterfeit goods, and the latter are natural goods. Thus we see that only actions which are refer-**able** to union with God are in any sense good. Others, such as the miser's parsimony, actually move one away from God. It is this latter point which Füchs denies, as when he claims that "right behavior in the world . . . directly involves neither the moral goodness of the person nor his salvation."[51]

Attention to the end/object distinction, as evidenced in Thomas' doctrine of infused cardinal virtue, reveals that one must not too sharply cleave categorical actions from their relation to one's supernatural end, God. Grafting the object and end distinctions among the virtues results in just such a bipartite vision of virtue. Of course, deciding which inner-worldly actions are capable or incapable of further reference to one's supernatural end must be undertaken with respect to a specific activity under consideration. But the categorical/transcendental distinction, as employed by fundamental option ethicists such as Füchs, precludes such a discussion by failing to attend to what Thomas calls infused cardinal virtues.

This point is related to the second and related insight gained from a look at Thomas' infused cardinal virtues concerning the "location" of grace. Fundamental option theorists insist that grace transforms the person at the level of basic freedom. However, they further claim that grace can only be accepted or rejected at "the centre of the person."[52] Of course, the "effects" of such transformation are seen in categorical actions, but these actions are "superficial signs and effects of grace freely accepted or refused."[53] "Specific individual, moral acts as such are not the acceptance or rejection of grace."[54] This understanding of grace warrants two comments. First, given the way fundamental option theorists define the transcendental level of basic freedom as athematic, it is unclear how a transformation at that level can indeed transform actions at the categorical level. This point is an extension of the first section's critique of fundamental option theorists' ability to relate person and acts. Second, the vision of grace articulated here is a "one-way street" in which grace transforms the person at the transcendental level and the effects are somehow seen in one's actions. Yet in this system a person's actions cannot conversely impact one's acceptance or rejection of grace. Rather, categorical actions can only signify, and never constitute, a rejection of God at the transcendental level. Recall this was the whole point of positing the two levels of freedom, to be able to claim that certain actions at the categorical level do not impact one's freedom at the level of basic freedom. Fundamental option theorists such as Fuchs limit the action of grace to the transcendental level. Grace can be seen in categorical action only as a side-effect of its presence at the transcendental level. And one's inner-worldly activities are incapable of informing one's stance before God. Rightly recognizing that "one who does what is unfitting, but who does this in error or in good faith, can be morally good and can be saved in his relationship with God," Fuchs mistakenly concludes (in a classic *non sequitur*) that "behavior in the world of human persons" (clearly the categorical realm) "involves neither the moral goodness of the person nor his salvation."[55] According to Thomas' doctrine of infused cardinal virtue, God's grace is active in inner-worldly activities to lift them toward their orientation to humanity's supernatural end. God's grace, far from being accidentally related to, literally "trans-forms" the inner-worldly act. Conversely, the formal object of an inner-worldly action can be such that it turns one away from that supernatural end. In accordance with the scholastic axiom, activity in the natural order is neither obliterated nor left behind by God's grace. Rather, nature is perfected by God's grace.

Fundamental option ethicists render impossible such an understanding of the relationship between nature and grace by placing one's relationship with God and one's inner-worldly activities in mutually exclusive categories. This is caused by a category mistake in which they conflate distinctions based upon the object versus those based upon the end of activity. It also diminishes the transformative power of grace in the Christian life. It reflects a misunderstanding of how activities in the natural realm persist, but are perfected, in the life of grace. The most specific conclusion this paper offers is that the transcendental/categorical distinction proposed by fundamental option ethicists such as Fuchs not only does not help solve the problem of relating person and acts, but actually complicates it. An examination of Thomas' doctrine of infused cardinal virtue is particularly useful in helping to identify further problems with that distinction. Fundamental option theory conflates classic distinctions based on object versus end of human action, and results in an impoverished notion of grace that operates only at the "centre of the person," rather than also in one's daily activities in the natural order.

NOTES

1. John Paul II, *Veritatis Splendor*, §65, emphasis in original (Daughters of St. Paul edition) unless otherwise noted. Further references to this encyclical (*VS*) will be given parenthetically by paragraph number.

2. Josef Fuchs is widely recognized as a primary target of the fundamental option section of the encyclical. For more on the "unnamed authors," see Joseph A. Selling's "The Context and Arguments of *Veritatis splendor*," in Selling and Jans (eds.) *The Splendor of Accuracy* (Michigan: Eerdmans, 1994), 11—70, esp. 22—26.

3. See, for example, Josef Fuchs' "Good Acts and Good Persons," in John Wilkins (ed.) *Considering Veritatis splendor* (Cleveland: Pilgrim Press, 1994), 21—26; Timothy O'Connell's "The Question of *Grundentscheidung*," *Philosophy and Theology* 10 (1997): 143—168, 158—9.

4. To cite those mentioned above, O'Connell admits that though some of the pope's assertions are caricatures, some of his criticisms of fundamental option theory do accurately grasp that theory (*Grundentscheidung*, 159—61). Fuchs, in the midst of claiming that the pope's charges are unfounded, unwittingly demonstrates the legitimacy of those criticisms when he responds with the following comment, one which exemplifies what the pope critiques: "To repeat: the fundamental option is not an individual act, and particular serious sins do not lead as such to eternal damnation unless embodied in a fundamental option to reject God" ("Good Acts," 25). Jean Porter, not a supporter of fundamental option theory but sympathetic with some of its concerns, argues persuasively that fundamental option theory does indeed suffer from some of the problems the pope identifies (though she disagrees with the encyclical's suggested remedy). See her "Moral Language and the Language of Grace: The Fundamental option and the Virtue of Charity," *Philosophy and Theology* 10 (1997): 169—198, 174ff.

5. For instance, see *VS*, §70 for the pope's recognition of grave sin that may not necessarily sever one's relationship with God.

6. A clear and succinct presentation of Josef Fuchs' position on "basic freedom" is found in "Basic Freedom and Morality," in *Human Values and Christian Morality* (Dublin: Gill, 1968), 92—111. See also his *Personal Responsibility and Christian Morality* (Washington, D.C.: Georgetown University Press, 1983) and *Christian Morality: The Word Becomes Flesh* (Washington, D.C.: Georgetown University Press, 1987). It should be noted that the work of Karl Rahner is clearly formative for fundamental option theorists such as Fuchs. Since this article focuses on the use of fundamental option theory in moral theology, the work of Fuchs, an influential proponent, is examined here. Whether or not critical comments in this piece apply also to Karl Rahner a distinct question not explored further here.

7. See "Basic Freedom and Morality," 93—4.

8. Ibid., 96. Though commitment of the whole person marks basic freedom, Fuchs is careful to note that it is indeed open to revision.

9. Ibid., 97.

10. Ibid., 96. See also *Personal Responsibility and Christian Morality*, 25.

11. See "Basic Freedom and Morality," 97.

12. Ibid., 106.

13. Ibid.

14. See "Good Acts and Good Persons," 24.

15. See "Basic Freedom and Morality," 96.

16. See *Personal Responsibility and Christian Morality*, 56. Here Füchs speaks of "Christian intentionality," which he equates to basic freedom at 57 and 65.

17. Ibid., 56.

18. Porter, "Moral Language," 176. Note that here Porter speaks of transcendental freedom as described by Rahner.

19. See Benedict Ashley, O.P., "Fundamental Option and/or Commitment to Ultimate End," *Philosophy and Theology* 10 (1997):113-141, 131.

20. Porter, "Moral Language," 184ff.

21. *ST* I-II, q. 63, a. 2.

22. *ST* I-II, q. 63, a. 3.

23. *ST* I-II, q. 1, a. 1.

24. *ST* I-II, q. 2, a. 8.

25. This is most clearly explained at *ST* I-II, q. 62, a. 1.

26. See *ST* II-II, q. 23, a. 7.

27. Thomas also uses the term "human" to refer to what are here called "natural" virtues (*ST* I-II, q. 61, a. 1). There he employs "super-human" as the other side of the distinction (*ST* I-II, q. 61, a. 1, ad. 2).

28. See *ST* I-II, q. 62, a. 2.

29. See *ST* I-II, q. 62, a. 1 and 2.

30. Thomas actually distinguishes theological from "moral and intellectual virtues," whose objects are comprehensible to reason (*ST* I-II, q. 62,a. 2). The term "cardinal" is employed here as opposite to theological, rather than the more common "moral," so as to include the intellectual virtues. Thomas himself employs "cardinal" in this more general sense in the title of *ST* I-II, q. 61, and identifies the terms "moral" and "cardinal," in the sense meant here, at *ST* I-II, q. 61,a. 1.

31. Though Thomas does not directly cite Augustine's use/enjoy distinction in his categorization of virtue, it is clearly formative in his categorization. It is explicitly formative in the categorizations of Thomas' predecessors. The classic treatment of the categorizations of virtue in Thomas and his predecessors remains Odon Lottin's *Psychologie et morale aux XIIe et XIIIe siècles* (Louvain: Abbaye du Mont Cesar, 1949),III.2, 99-150.

32. For Thomas, God is by definition the final end of humanity. See *ST* I-II, q. 2, a. 8.

33. Thomas himself claims that all theological virtues are supernatural. See *ST* I-II, q. 62, a. 1 and q. 63, a. 3.

34. *ST* I-II, q. 63, a. 3, ad. 2.

35. The natural/supernatural distinction, in reference to final end, is placed in parentheses here since, as noted above, that distinction can be reliably grafted onto the infused/acquired distinction. In further references in this article to infused virtue, supernatural is understood. Correlatively, natural is implied in references to acquired virtue.

36. See Lottin, *Psychologie*, 175ff. Both thinkers also recognized the possibility of cardinal virtues in service of the earthly city, which they both called "political" virtues.

37. Ibid., 184.

38. In his *sed contra* of his article on whether cardinal virtues are in us by infusion, Thomas quotes the scriptural *locus classicus* for the cardinal virtues, Wisdom 8:7: "She teaches moderation and prudence, justice and fortitude, and nothing is more useful for men than these."

39. See *ST* I-II, q. 63, a. 4. Note that since theological virtues cannot be acquired by habituation, and since Thomas' example in this article is the cardinal virtue temperance, his question must refer to cardinal virtues.

40. *ST* I-II, q. 63, a. 4, ad. 2.

41. There is an extensive body of literature on this question. For a helpful overview of this debate since the thirteenth century, see Robert F. Coerver, C.M.'s *The Quality of Facility in the Moral Virtues*, (Washington, D.C.: Catholic Univerity of America, Dissertation, 1946). For more recent treatments, see: Romanus Cessario, O.P., *The Moral Virtues and Theological Ethics*, (Notre Dame: University of Notre Dame Press, 1991); John Inglis, "Aquinas' Replication of the Acquired Moral Virtues: Rethinking the Standard Philosophical Interpretation of Moral Virtue in Aquinas", *Journal of Religious Ethics* 27.1 (1999): 3—27; Renee Mirkes, O.S.F., "Aquinas' Doctrine of Moral Virtue and Its Significance for Theories of Facility," *The Thomist* 61 (1999):189—218; and, Jean Porter, "The Subversion of Virtue: Acquired and Infused Virtue in the *Summa Theologiae*," *Annual of the Society of Christian Ethics (1992)*: 19—41.

42. See *ST* II-II, q. 23, a. 8.

43. See James F. Keenan, S.J., *Goodness and Rightness in Thomas Aquinas's Summa Theologiae*, (Washington, D.C: Georgetown Press, 1992), 95. Interestingly, Keenan was a student of Füchs.

44. As Philip the Chancellor claims, the cardinal virtues are the "four hinges of the door to the Kingdom of Heaven." See Lottin, *Psychologie*, 99—150.

45. Keenan, "Goodness and Rightness," 95.

46. *ST* I-II, q. 63, a. 4.

47. See Füchs, *Personal Responsibility and Christian Morality*, 28.

48. Ibid.

49. See *ST* II-II, q. 81. See especially *ST* II-II, q. 81, a. 5, where Thomas distinguishes the cardinal virtue religion from theological virtues. Note the following ten questions also concern religious activities.

50. This treatment is found in a crucial article asking whether there can be any virtue without charity. Thomas responds affirmatively, but takes the occasion to note that some inner-worldly activity can never be labeled virtuous, even in a limited sense. See *ST* II-II, q. 23, a. 7.

51. See Füchs, *Christian Morality: The Word Becomes Flesh*, 111.

52. See Füchs, "Basic Freedom and Morality," 111.

53. Ibid., 110.

54. Ibid., 109.

55. See Füchs, *Christian Morality: The Word Becomes Flesh*, 111.

Chapter Twelve

The Political Common Good and the Perfection of Human Freedom

John Goyette, Ph. D.

In *Veritatis Splendor* Pope John Paul II asserts that "[t]he human issues most frequently debated and differently resolved in contemporary moral reflection are all closely related, albeit in various ways, to a crucial issue: *human freedom*." (§31) The encyclical addresses various ways in which a false notion of human freedom results in theological and philosophical opinions incompatible with revealed truth. It is concerned principally with the modern notion of freedom as a kind of moral autonomy according to which human reason freely creates its own values or moral norms. This false view of human freedom is opposed to the constant teaching of the Church regarding the existence of a natural moral law that finds its *origin* and *end* in God. The aim of this paper is to further the discussion in *Veritatis Splendor* by discussing the relation between human freedom and the political common good. More specifically, I aim to show that although human freedom is ultimately ordered towards God as a final end, it is also ordered towards a more proximate final end, the common good of the political community.

The paper has three parts. Firstly, I will explain the notion of the political common good. Secondly, I will show that human liberty is naturally ordered towards, and perfected by, the political common good. Finally, I will conclude with some brief remarks regarding the importance of understanding the natural ordination of human freedom towards the political common good. My account will be drawn principally from the discussion of freedom and the common good in the writings of St. Thomas Aquinas.

The Political Common Good

What is the political common good? Let me begin by quoting a key text from the *Summa Theologiae*, I-II, q. 90, a. 2 where Aquinas speaks about the ordination of law towards the common good:

> Now the first principle in practical matters, which is the object of the practical reason, is the last end: and the last end of human life is bliss or happiness, as stated above. Consequently the law must needs regard principally the relationship to happiness. Moreover, since every part is ordained to the whole, as imperfect to perfect; and since one man is a part of the perfect community, the law

must needs regard properly the relationship to universal happiness.... Consequently, since the law is chiefly ordained to the common good, any other precept in regard to some individual work, must needs be devoid of the nature of a law, save in so far as it regards the common good. Therefore every law is ordained to the common good.

The first thing to note here about the common good is that it is a *common end*, not a good that is common by predication.[1] I might be tempted to describe health as a "common good" since everyone desires to be healthy. When I desire to be healthy, however, I am not seeking the same thing that you are when you seek to be healthy; what I seek is the health of *my body* whereas what you seek is the health of *your body*. When you and I say that we seek to be healthy, the predicate "healthy" means the same thing in both cases, but the *reality* that we seek is not numerically the same. A truly common good, however, is a single end sought by many individuals, e.g., the way that the individual soldiers of an army seek victory. As St. Thomas puts it, the common good is "common, not by the community of genus or species, but the community of final cause" (*ST* I-II, q. 90, a. 2, ad 3). The common good, then, is said to be common because it is a universal cause, i.e., a final cause, not because it is a universal predicate.

A common good, then, presupposes common action and desire, many working together for the sake of a single goal. Insofar as many individuals work together for the sake of a single goal they form a kind of community. Thus, in the broadest sense, the common good is simply the end of a community of individuals working together for a common cause.[2]

Note that this notion of the common good—as an end which is the object of common action and desire—does not yet get us to the political common good. St. Thomas sometimes speaks of the end or goal of any joint enterprise as a common good (in this sense, one can speak of victory in battle as the common good of an army, or children as the common good of a family, or wealth as the common good of a corporation), but he also has a more restricted notion of the common good as the end of a *perfect* community, that community which comprehends all other human communities. St. Thomas, following Aristotle, identifies the city or political community as the perfect human community and the political common good is therefore said to be a common good in the narrow sense of the term. Of course, Aquinas also speaks of the common good of other perfect communities. He speaks of the common good of the whole universe of creatures ordered to God as a final end and he also speaks of the community of God and the blessed which forms a perfect community ordered towards friendship with God. My concern here is to focus on the political common good, the common good of the perfect *human* community.

The city is identified as the perfect human community because happiness is man's final end and it is only within the political community that man can attain happiness. This is because happiness, for St. Thomas, is identified with the perfection of man's rational nature through virtuous living *and* because the full perfection of the moral life can only be attained as a part of the political community.[3] This latter point is especially evident when we note that virtue, though in some sense natural to man, does not come to be by nature. It requires external direction. As St. Thomas notes,

> [M]an has a natural aptitude for virtue; but the perfection of virtue must be acquired by man by means of some kind of training. . . . Now it is difficult to see how man could suffice for himself in the matter of this training: since the perfection of virtue consists chiefly in withdrawing man from undue pleasures, to which above all man is inclined, and especially the young, who are more capable of being trained. Consequently a man needs to receive this training from another, whereby to arrive at the perfection of virtue.[4]

Granting, however, that moral virtue presupposes training from another, one might wonder whether moral education might be adequately attained by the family. Both Aristotle and St. Thomas speak of the family or household as existing primarily to attend to man's material and bodily needs—economics in the original sense of the word. They both acknowledge that the family is a distinctively human institution that plays a large role in moral education, but it is only imperfectly concerned with the life of virtue. St. Thomas makes this evident by pointing out the limits of the family as an institution of moral education:

> [A]s to those young people who are inclined to acts of virtue, by their good natural disposition, or by custom, or rather by the gift of God, paternal training suffices, which is by admonitions. But since some are found to be depraved, and prone to vice, and not easily amenable to words, it was necessary for such to be restrained from evil by force and fear, in order that, at least, they might desist from evil-doing, and leave others in peace, and that they themselves, by being habituated in this way, might be brought to do willingly what hitherto they did from fear, and thus become virtuous. Now this kind of training, which compels through fear of punishment, is the discipline of laws. Therefore in order that man might have peace and virtue, it was necessary for laws to be framed: for, as the Philosopher [sic] says (Polit. i, 2), "as man is the most noble of animals if he be perfect in virtue, so is he the lowest of all, if he be severed from law and righteousness.[5]

For those noble-minded individuals who are well-disposed towards virtue, parental admonition suffices; but for some, fear of punishment is necessary to restrain them from evil. It is important to note that even if the latter where a small number of individuals, their crimes would undermine the life of virtue for all the rest since virtuous living presupposes a peaceful society.

Even apart from the threat of civil punishment, however, the law has a kind of moral authority that outranks parental admonition. The disastrous effects of a bad law illustrate this point. The ruling of the Supreme Court in Roe vs. Wade, for example, has changed people's opinions about the morality of abortion. The law is a moral teacher. The notion that one cannot legislate morality is patently ridiculous if one means that the law does not form our opinions about what is morally right and morally wrong. Indeed, according to Aristotle, what makes a political community is shared opinions about the just and the unjust, the noble and the base (*Politics* I.2, 1215a14-19). Thus, it is not a question of whether one can legislate morality, but a question of which morality one legislates. Thus, while one can acknowledge the importance of the family in the early training to virtue, it is a mistake to make the family bear too high a moral load. The political community, then, is the perfect community because only it is competent to direct human beings towards the life of virtue.

FREEDOM AND THE COMMON GOOD

Not only is the common political good not opposed to human freedom—as if law were merely an expedient restriction of the will's natural inclination to refer all things to my own private good—but human freedom is naturally ordered towards, and perfected by, the common good. To see this we must see that human freedom cannot be defined as freedom from external constraint. This kind of freedom is not distinctively human since even an animal can be free in this sense. Rather, human freedom consists in the ability to govern oneself, something that cannot be understood apart from man's ability to reason. The critical distinction here, according to St. Thomas, is that man, unlike the beast, is able to apprehend, and therefore direct himself towards, the universal good:

> The object of the will is the end and the good in universal. Consequently there can be no will in those things that lack reason and intellect, since they cannot apprehend the universal; but they have a natural appetite or a sensitive appetite, determinate to some particular good.[6]

Unlike the beasts, who are more or less determined by their sensible appetite towards a particular good, human beings are free because they are moved by a desire for the good without qualification.[7] The will has an inclination towards whatever the mind judges to be good, not just towards those particular goods that happen to move the sensible appetite here and now. Consequently, a rational agent has a kind of indifference towards particular goods and is therefore able to freely determine his actions:

> A rational nature endowed with free choice, however, is different in its action from every other agent nature. Every other nature is ordained to some particular good, and its actions are determined in regard to that good. But a rational nature is ordained to good without further qualification. Good, taken absolutely, is the object of the will, just as truth, taken absolutely, is the object of the intellect. That is why the will reaches to the universal principle of good itself, to which no other appetite can attain. And for this reason a rational creature does not have determined actions but is in a state of indifference in regard to innumerable actions.[8]

While the human will is free to choose from among particular goods, it is only able to do so in light of its ordination to the good in general as its proper object. The human will, therefore, is not completely autonomous since it is no more able not to will the universal good than the eye is able not to see color.[9]

The good in general, moreover, is not just an abstract notion or a mere collection of particular goods. The desire for the good in general is the desire to have a good that is perfect or complete because it comprehends all other goods as a final end.¹⁰ What Thomas calls the good in general is none other man's ultimate end, viz., happiness. And since human happiness is a good shared in common with other rational agents as part of a perfect community, the will is ultimately ordered towards, and perfected by, the common good.¹¹ Thus, although the notion of the good in general is formally distinct from the notion of the common good, they are ultimately identical *in rerum natura*. This is why Thomas identifies the proper object of the will with the common good:

> [S]ince affection follows knowledge, the more universal knowledge is, so much the more does the affection which follows it look toward the common good; and the more particular the knowledge is, so much the more does the affection which follows it look toward a private good; and hence among us too, individual love arises as a consequence of sense knowledge, but the love of the common and absolute good arises as a consequence of intellectual knowledge.¹²

According to St. Thomas, the more perfect a man's knowledge, the more he loves the common good over his own private good.¹³

Of course, when Aquinas speaks of love of the common good as a perfection of human freedom he is not restricting himself to the political common good. Indeed, according to Thomas, man's ordination to God transcends his ordination to the earthly political community. Nonetheless, man's ordination towards supernatural beatitude does not nullify his natural ordination to the political common good. This is clear from *ST* I-II, q. 94, a. 4 where Aquinas asks whether or not a man is bound in conscience to obey the laws of the earthly city. He answers the question in the affirmative, basing his argument upon man's participation in the political common good: "For, since one man is a part of the community, each man in all that he is and has, belongs to the community; just as a part, in all that it is, belongs to the whole." Notice that he says that each man *in all that he is and has* belongs to the political community. St. Thomas evidently sees no conflict between full dedication to the political community and a further ordination towards God as the object of supernatural beatitude.¹⁴

Indeed, that human freedom is naturally ordered towards the political common good is made clear in Thomas's discussion of man's natural inclinations in *ST* I-II, q. 94, a. 2. Having discussed those inclinations which belong to man as an animal, he turns to those inclinations which belong to him as a rational agent: "[T]here is in man an inclination to good, according to the nature of his reason, which nature is proper to him: thus man has a natural inclination to know the truth about God, and to live in society." (Ibid.) It is important to note, here, that the inclination that belongs to man as a rational agent is nothing other than the appetite that belongs to the will. Indeed, the two specifically rational inclinations mentioned in question 94 correspond to the common good of the earthly and heavenly cities respectively. Because God has created man to be a political animal and because grace does not destroy but rather completes and perfects man's nature, there is no conflict between man's love of the political common good and his love of God as the common good of the city of God.

CONCLUSION

Having discussed the relation between human freedom and the political common good, let me offer two brief remarks about the importance of recognizing the ordination of human freedom towards the political common good. Firstly, the recognition of the primacy of the political common good, at least insofar as it pertains to temporal happiness, should caution us against a withdrawal from a participation in political life in order to retreat to the sometimes more peaceful abode of the family. The deficiencies of our own political order, or any other political order, should not lead us to overlook the lofty end of political life. Indeed, the fact that the question of the end of the city or *polis* is a subject of such heated debate is a sign that it is an institution of a higher order. The city is the best thing there is in the temporal order of human practical affairs.[15] This is why Thomas, following Aristotle, asserts that the man who first founded the city was the cause of the greatest (maxima) of human goods (*Commentary on the Politics*, Bk. I, lectio 1, section 40). Thus, rather than abandon the political life to those who would subvert its proper end, we ought to work to improve civic life.

My second point pertains to the relation between full dedication to the political common good and the love of the transcendent common good necessary for true Christian charity. Citizenship in the earthly city prepares us for citizenship in the heavenly city. If we are not first dutiful citizens of the earthly city, how will we understand what is demanded of us as good citizens of the kingdom of heaven? The point is nicely illustrated by St. Thomas's treatment of the proper ordination to the common good of the heavenly city in his treatise *On Charity*. He there speaks of the love of the political common good in order to instruct us in the proper love of the celestial city. Let me give you one brief excerpt:

> But when man becomes a citizen of a state and is admitted to participating in the good of some state, certain virtues are suitable, necessary even, for doing those things which are a citizen's duty and for loving the good of the state. Therefore man, through grace, becomes as it were a citizen and a sharer in this blessed society which is called the heavenly Jerusalem (Ephes. II, 19). . . . Therefore certain gratuitous virtues, which are infused, are necessary for man when he is enrolled in the heavenly state; for the proper operation of these virtues there is required the love of the common good for the whole society, which is the divine good considered as the object of beatitude.

Thomas goes on to illustrate how the love of the political common good exhibits the appropriate dedication to the heavenly city by contrasting the tyrant's counterfeit love of the city with the citizen who exposes himself to danger and death for the common good. According to Aquinas, one cannot understand or appreciate the virtue of charity without having some sense, some share, in the love of the political common good that motivates soldiers and statesman to sacrifice themselves for the political common good.

NOTES

1. For a helpful discussion of this distinction, see Gregory Froelich, "The Equivocal Status of the *Bonum Commune*," *New Scholasticism* 63 (1989): 38—57.

2. Note that the common good does not presuppose that each individual member of the community does the same thing. St. Thomas makes this clear in his *Commentary on the Politics*, Bk. III, lection 3, n. 366: "[T]he word "sailor" is common to many men. Many men who differ in power, that is to say, by their art and by their function, are called sailors: one of them is a rower, who propels the ship by means of oars; another is a pilot, who steers the ship by means of the rudder; another a look-out or guardian of the prow, which is the forepart of the ship; and others have other names and functions. Now it is obvious that each one of these men has something that belongs to him by reason of his proper competence and something that belongs to him by reason of a common competence. It pertains to the competence of each one individually to understand and look after his own function diligently, steering, for example, in the case of the pilot, and the same for the others. The common competence, on the other hand, is one that belongs to all, for the work of all of them is directed toward one end, namely, safe navigation; for it is to this end that the aim and desire of any sailor is directed and that the common competence of sailors, which is the competence of the sailor as sailor, is ordered." Aristotle makes a similar point at the end of the *Metaphysics* when speaking about the common good of the universe: "...all things are ordered together somehow, but not all alike—both fishes and fowls and plants; and the world is not such that one thing has nothing to do with another, but they are connected. For all are ordered together to one end . . . " (1075a16). The members of a community, then, can have diverse functions even though they share a common goal. Unity does not mean uniformity.

3. This notion of the political community as a perfect community is, of course, rejected by modern political philosophy. Civil society according to Hobbes and Locke serves merely to safeguard individual rights and liberties and to promote economic prosperity. Aristotle considers and rejects this conception of the city in Bk. 3 of the *Politics* where he argues that many individuals who live together for the sake of mutual exchange based upon the division of labor would not form a city. In fact, Aristotle argues that even if many living together for the sake of mutual exchange had laws against committing injustice against one another, they still would not form a city. According to Aristotle, the city is not merely for the sake of living, but for the sake of living well which he identifies with virtuous living. St. Thomas defends this position in *On Kingship* by noting that ". . . only those who render mutual assistance to one another in living well form a genuine part of an assembled multitude. If men assembled merely to live, then animals . . . would form a part of the civil community. Or, if men assembled only to accrue wealth, then all those who traded together would belong to one city. Yet we see that only such are regarded as forming one multitude as are directed by the same laws and the same government to live well."

4. *ST* I-II, q. 95, a. 1.

5. Ibid.

6. *ST* I-II, q. 1, a. 2, ad. 3.

7. It is important to note that St. Thomas is not saying that only an intelligent agent is *ordered* towards a universal good but that only an intelligent agent can consciously *direct himself* towards a universal good. For Aquinas, all creatures are ultimately ordered towards the common good of the whole universe, but only intellectual creatures are able to *direct themselves* towards a good that transcends the particular good.

8. *De Veritate* q. 24, a. 7.

9. "The will is moved in two ways: first, as to the exercise of its act; secondly, as to the specification of its act, derived from the object. As to the first way, no object moves

the will necessarily, for no matter what the object be, it is in man's power not to think of it, and consequently not to will it actually. But as to the second manner of motion, the will is moved by one object necessarily, by another not. For in the movement of a power by its object, we must consider under what aspect the object moves the power. For the visible moves the sight, under the aspect of color actually visible. Wherefore if color be offered to the sight, it moves the sight necessarily: unless one turns one's eyes away; which belongs to the exercise of the act. But if the sight were confronted with something not in all respects colored actually, but only so in some respects, and in other respects not, the sight would not of necessity see such an object: for it might look at that part of the object which is not actually colored, and thus it would not see it. Now just as the actually colored is the object of sight, so is good the object of the will. Wherefore if the will be offered an object which is good universally and from every point of view, the will tends to it of necessity, if it wills anything at all; since it cannot will the opposite. If, on the other hand, the will is offered an object that is not good from every point of view, it will not tend to it of necessity. And since lack of any good whatever, is a non-good, consequently, that good alone which is perfect and lacking in nothing, is such a good that the will cannot not-will it: and this is Happiness. Whereas any other particular goods, in so far as they are lacking in some good, can be regarded as non-goods: and from this point of view, they can be set aside or approved by the will, which can tend to one and the same thing from various points of view" (*ST* I-II, q. 10, a. 2).

10. "Now good in general, which has the nature of an end, is the object of the will. Consequently, in this respect, the will moves the other powers of the soul to their acts, for we make use of the other powers when we will. For the end and perfection of every other power, is included under the object of the will as some particular good: and always the art or power to which the universal end belongs, moves to their acts the arts or powers to which belong the particular ends included in the universal end. Thus the leader of an army, who intends the common good—i.e. the order of the whole army—by his command moves one of the captains, who intends the order of one company" (*ST* I-II, q. 9, a. 1).

11. Of course, while all men agree in desiring the last end, they disagree about the way in which happiness is to be realized: "We can speak of the last end in two ways: first, considering only the aspect of last end; secondly, considering the thing in which the aspect of last end is realized. So, then, as to the aspect of last end, all agree in desiring the last end: since all desire the fulfillment of their perfection, and it is precisely this fulfillment in which the last end consists, as stated above. But as to the thing in which this aspect is realized, all men are not agreed as to their last end: since some desire riches as their consummate good; some, pleasure; others, something else" (*ST* I-II, q. 1, a. 7).

12. *Spiritual Creatures*, a. 8, ad. 5.

13. For an excellent discussion of the primacy of the common good, see Charles De Koninck, *On the Primacy of the Common Good: Against the Personalists*, trans. by Sean Collins, *The Aquinas Review* 4, no. 1 (1997): 14—71.

14. On this point, see Jacques Maritain, *The Person and the Common Good* (South Bend, Ind.: University of Notre Dame Press, 1985).

15. For a discussion of the nobility of the political common good, see Lawrence Dewan, O.P., "St. Thomas, John Finnis, and the Political Common Good," *The Thomist* 64 (2000): 337—74.

CHAPTER THIRTEEN

OUR MERITS, GOD'S GIFTS

W. Matthews Grant

*You are glorified in the assembly of your Holy Ones,
for in crowning their merits you are crowning your own gifts.*[1]

FAITH, REASON, AND THE PROBLEM OF MERIT

It seems that any genuinely Catholic account of the relationship between faith and reason will need to hold with St. Thomas that, while there are divinely revealed truths that surpass natural reason's ability to demonstrate, the truths that natural reason can establish either converge with these revealed truths or are, at least, compatible with them—and further, that (at least in principle) natural reason, by its own natural powers, can defend these revealed truths against any philosophical account that would contradict them.[2] The alternative to the foregoing would be to endorse one of three extremes contrary to the Catholic tradition reaffirmed by Pope John Paul II in *Fides et Ratio*. What these three extremes have in common is their willingness to allow that faith and reason might contradict one another. They differ in how they respond in the event of contradiction.[3]

One extreme, *rationalism*, responds by jettisoning the claims of revelation. On this approach, only what reason can obtain on its own is to be believed. Since the truths proposed by faith are acceptable only where reason itself can establish them, both the need for and authority of divine revelation becomes obsolete. It follows, obviously enough, that where the content of revealed faith contradicts reason, it is revelation that is to be discarded.[4]

A second extreme, *fideism*, would by contrast jettison the claims of reason. For the fideist, it is not simply that the content of faith might surpass what reason can establish on its own. Rather, reason might literally contradict faith. And if and when this happens, the fideist does not assume what the Catholic position demands—that some mistake has been made in the process of reasoning, a mistake which reason itself can in principle uncover and remedy. Rather, the fideist allows that, even at its best, reason might conflict with the faith. And, thus, since the fideist prefers faith to reason, he generally holds reason in suspicion as something fundamentally unreliable.

A third extreme, the extreme of *double truth*, would relativize truth claims to the domain of either faith or reason, allowing that contradictory claims might both be true relative to their particular domains. The proposition "Jesus is present bodily in the eucharist," and the proposition "Jesus is not present bodily in the eucharist" contradict one another, and only one can be true. But if we relativize these claims, if we say "In faith Jesus is present bodily in the eucharist," while "In reason Jesus is not present bodily in the eucharist," then the contradiction dissolves, for one proposition is no longer the negation of the other. Unfortunately, this way of resolving apparent conflicts between faith and reason comes at a price. Faith and reason would no longer be seen as offering absolute truths about the world as such, but only relative truths—truths limited to a particular perspective. The result would be to limit radically the relevance of faith and reason, and to give up any hope that they might be partners in our coming to an integrated account of the real as such.

Contrary to each of these extremes, John Paul II insists on both the autonomy and the mutual harmony of faith and reason. Against the rationalist, he reminds us that "there exists a knowledge which is peculiar to faith, surpassing the knowledge proper to human reason,"[5] and that "reason ... is not asked to pass judgment on the contents of faith, something of which it would be incapable."[6] Contrary to the fideist, he maintains that "reason has its own specific field in which it can enquire and understand,"[7] and that "the content of revelation can never debase the discoveries and the legitimate autonomy of reason."[8] Against the proponent of double truth, he speaks of the "indissoluble unity between the knowledge of reason and the knowledge of faith."[9]

According to this Catholic vision, then, there will be some truths that reason can establish independently of faith and some truths of faith that are beyond reason's competency to establish. Yet, even though reason is not unlimited in its competency, it is generally presumed reliable. What, then, if the results of reasoning appear to conflict with the authoritatively established content of faith? What, for instance, if some line of reasoning appears to suggest that Jesus could not be bodily present in the eucharist? The rationalist, of course, would have us abandon our eucharistic doctrine. The fideist would recommend a withdrawal from the dangerous preoccupation with reason. The proponent of double truth would allow us both our faith and our reason, so long as we abandoned the attempt to integrate these two parts of ourselves. The Catholic position directs us otherwise. Given that the content of faith has as its source nothing less than a divine revelation, rejecting the doctrine is ruled out. Yet, given that faith and reason are compatible, we know better than simply to reject reason altogether. On the contrary, what an apparent conflict between faith and reason signals for one who holds the Catholic position is not the need to reject reason, but rather that a particular line of reasoning has gone wrong. And, since reasoning done well will be compatible with the faith, the Catholic is committed to the ability of reason, at least in principle, to correct itself in matters where it runs counter to what has been revealed. Thus, where a philosophical argument runs contrary to the faith, philosophy can in principle show the argument to be unsound and can do so according to its own philosophical standards. The faith, then, serves as an extrinsic norm for philosophy, indicating that any philosophical argument that contradicts the faith has a problem with it. Yet, philosophy can remedy the problem from its own intrinsic resources.

One of the perennial locations of apparent tension between faith and reason concerns the compatibility of divine grace and human freedom. The Catholic, as a matter of doctrine, is committed to the truths that salvation is a gift and that salvation depends on our merits. In some way or another, therefore, our merits must be God's gifts.[10] Yet, the very notion of "merit" entails that the one meriting does so freely, and it may seem that to the extent that our merits are God's gifts, they cannot be free. Merit, after all, accrues to one in accordance with one's good works. Thus, if our merits are God's gifts, it can only be because our good works are *from* God. Yet, if our good works are *from* God, then it looks as if God is the cause of those works. And if God is the cause of those works, one might think that they can't be free in the sense required if they are to be genuinely meritorious.

Confronted with this difficulty, it will be tempting to conceive of the relationship between divine grace and human action in such a way that our merits can be credited to grace, while our actions remain sufficiently independent of divine causality so as to be free and meritorious. God's grace, it might be thought, comes first, and is that without which it is not possible for us to merit anything. Yet, we must freely respond to God's initiative. And, although this response is itself made possible by God's grace, the responding must be ours and ours alone. Were the responding itself from God, then it would not be free, and, hence, could not be meritorious.

The foregoing proposal, which I suspect captures the gist of a great deal of popular and academic thinking about the relationship between divine grace and human freedom, attempts to preserve the idea that our merits are God's gifts by making God's grace the necessary condition without which any meritorious response would be impossible. Yet, two things should trouble us about this proposal. First, although our merits are from God and depend on Him in the sense that we could not merit anything were it not for God's grace, that by virtue of which we actually merit is precisely that which we do independently of God. This view assumes that if our responding to God's grace were itself from God, then that responding would no longer be free and meritorious. Thus, it can be free and meritorious only insofar as it is *not* from God. Yet, if we merit precisely by that which is *not* from God, then the notion that our merits are genuinely God's gifts becomes attenuated at best. Second, our meriting is not the same thing as the mere *possibility* of our meriting. Yet, isn't God's gift on the foregoing account more the latter than the former? Strictly speaking, wouldn't we have to say, not that our merits are God's gifts, but rather that the *possibility* of our meriting is God's gift?

It seems, then, that in order to affirm in any robust sense that our merits are God's gifts, we will need to say that our meritorious actions are from God, that they are caused by God. But this brings us back to the original difficulty. How can our meritorious actions be caused by God and yet still be free and meritorious? Notice that, although this problem concerns a theological subject matter (the relationship of divine grace and human freedom), the challenge to the theological doctrine has a philosophical genesis. The notion that for an act to be meritorious, it must be free; views concerning the necessary conditions for an act's being free; the contention that these conditions are violated if an act has a cause other than its agent—these ideas do not have their source in divine revelation, but in philosophical reflection on the nature of free action and responsibility. It is only these philosophical notions that, when applied to the theological doctrine that our merits are God's gifts, provoke the judgment that this doctrine is contradictory.

Yet, if my initial remarks concerning the Catholic understanding of the relationship between faith and reason are correct, then philosophy ought to be able to defend the theological doctrine against this criticism, which emanates from philosophy. In fact, I think it can. I will argue first, that apart from considerations of revealed doctrine, natural reason compels us to say that our merits are God's gifts; second, that the very argument by which natural reason is led to conclude that our merits are God's gifts, by extension, also leads to a conception of a God whose transcendence precludes us from thinking of God's grace as acting on us in a way that deprives us of our freedom; and thus third, that natural reason supports a conception of God that both demands that our merits be God's gifts, while also allowing for the freedom that is essential to the very notion of "merit." In short, natural reason supports an account of the co-operation between divine action and human freedom that would enable us to affirm both the giftedness and the liberty of our good works, without sacrificing one to the other. My project, then, exemplifies the auxiliary role that philosophy can play with respect to theology. If I am right, then natural reason converges with Catholic doctrine concerning our merits as God's gifts, while also exposing, as false or unnecessary, conceptions of God or human freedom that would appear to make that doctrine problematic.

OUR ACTIONS AS CREATURES: A CONCLUSION OF NATURAL REASON

My discussion requires me to take something rather significant for granted at the outset; namely, that the cosmological argument establishes the truth of monotheism. Although it will not be possible for me to defend this claim here, I believe that the claim can be defended, and my argument that natural reason compels us to say that our merits are God's gifts, while at the same time precluding our conceiving of God in such a way as to deprive us of our freedom, depends on the claim being true.

If natural reason, *via* the cosmological argument, establishes the truth of monotheism, does it also compel us to say that our merits are God's gifts? It seems that it does. What would it be to establish the truth of monotheism? It would be to show that there is a single being, depending for its existence on nothing outside itself, which is the source of everything else that exists. Since our actions exist, but are other than God, it would follow that they owe their existence to God and that they are from God. Yet, since our merits accrue to our actions, it would also follow that our merits are from God, that they are God's gifts.

That God is the cause of our actions may be a challenging conclusion, but that it is an unavoidable consequence of the cosmological argument is certainly not a claim original to me. Aquinas, for instance, did not shrink from this inference:

Every action is caused by something existing in act, since nothing produces an action save in so far as it is in act; and every being in act is reduced to the First Act, viz. God, as to its cause, Who is act by His Essence. Therefore, God is the cause of every action, insofar as it is an action.[11]

The question, then, is whether the conclusion that our acts are caused by God forces us to conclude, also, that they can't be free.

DIVINE TRANSCENDENCE AND HUMAN FREEDOM

Simply to assert that our actions can't be free if they are caused by God is to beg the question against those who maintain that they can. What has to be shown is that God's causing our actions entails *something further* that is incompatible with those actions being free. For instance, it might be argued that if God causes our actions, then those actions are necessary or unavoidable, and that, since a free action cannot be necessary or unavoidable, God's causing our actions would preclude their freedom. Or, it might be argued that, if God causes our actions, then they are determined by something outside our control, and hence, for this reason, can't be free.

Confronted with either of these non-question begging arguments, someone who thinks that God is the cause of our actions, yet that those actions are nevertheless free, can respond in one of two ways. He can either deny that God's causing our actions entails the *something further* that is incompatible with those actions being free, or, he can allow that God's causing our actions entails this *something further*, but deny that the *something further* is incompatible with free action. In adopting the first sort of approach, one would have to show that God's causing our actions does not entail that our actions are necessary or unavoidable, or that our actions are determined by something outside our control. In adopting the second sort of approach, one would have to show that our actions being necessary or unavoidable, or determined by something outside our control, does not preclude our actions being free. In what follows, I will adopt the first approach. I will attempt to show that it does not follow from the fact that God causes our actions that our actions are necessary, unavoidable, or determined by something outside our control.

Yet, it is critical to the overall structure of my paper to see how I execute this first sort of response. Remember that my goal is to show that natural reason establishes not only that our merits are from God, but also that the claim that our merits are from God does not preclude the freedom of action necessary to the very idea of merit. I've argued above that the cosmological argument has as its implication that our merits are from God, since it has as its implication that our actions are from God. What I want to show now is that the cosmological argument also leads to a conception of God that precludes thinking of our actions as being necessary, unavoidable, or determined simply because they are caused by God. In other words, not only is the claim that our merits are caused by God an implication of the cosmological argument, but so also is a conception of divine transcendence that rules out our thinking of God's causing our actions as taking away their freedom.

How, then, does natural reason, *via* the cosmological argument, force us to renounce thinking of God in such a way that God's causing our actions entails that they are necessary, unavoidable, or determined by something outside our control? And how is this conception of divine transcendence that rules out our thinking of God's causing our actions as taking away their freedom an implication of the cosmological argument, the very argument that prompts natural reason to think that God causes our actions in the first place?

To begin with, one might mean two different things in saying that if God causes our actions, those actions are necessary. One might mean that those actions are necessary absolutely speaking, or one might mean that those actions are necessary relative to God. I will focus, first, on this latter kind of necessity.

One thing, "B", is necessary relative to another thing, "A", only if it couldn't possibly have been the case that "A" obtain and "B" fail to obtain, that is, only if the obtaining of "A" *entails* the obtaining of "B". Thus, the notion of relative or conditional necessity presupposes that the relationship between the thing necessitated and that relative to which the thing is necessary can be construed on the model of logical entailment. It follows, on this model, that had "B" not obtained, "A" must not have obtained either.

Interestingly, the relationship between a cause and its effect on the thesis of *causal determinism* can also be expressed in terms of logical entailment. Where the causes and effects are events taking place in the natural world, the idea is that a certain configuration of events literally entails or necessitates a specific outcome. It follows, according to this logic of determinism, that if the outcome had been different, the cause would have been different also.

Thus, whether we are talking about our actions being necessary relative to God, or whether we are talking about our actions being causally determined by God, we would have to conceive of the relationship between God and our actions on the model of entailment. Consequently, we would be committed to saying that had our actions been other than they are, God, also, would have been different. For if "A" entails or determines "B", then had "B" not obtained, neither would have "A". Yet, it is precisely this inference that will not hold up in the case of God. The cosmological argument leads us to a conception of God that forces us to deny that God would have been different had his effects been different. Since for any one of my actions, had that action not occurred, there would have been no difference in God, it follows that the logic required for our actions to be causally determined by God, or for our actions to be necessary relative to God, breaks down.

Why does the cosmological argument force us to deny that God would have been different had his effects been different? Because the cosmological argument has as its implication the classical teaching that while creatures are really related to God, God is not really, but only rationally, related to creatures.[12] The claim that creatures are really related to God, but not God to creatures, may appear absurd at first glance, since it seems to follow that if x is related to y, then y is related to x. Fortunately, it is not the intent of the classical teaching to deny this commonsense entailment. Rather, the distinction between real and rational relations draws our attention to the fact that x can be related to y without there being any feature, characteristic, or property of x by virtue of which it is so related. Consider, for instance, the relationship between knower and object known. Clearly, the object known is related to the knower, but it is not related because of any property that belongs to the object. What grounds the relation, its *fundamentum in re*, is not something in the object known, but something in the knower. We can see this point by reflecting on the fact that the object would, in itself, be no different even were it not being known.

Why, then, does the cosmological argument force us to deny that there is any intrinsic feature, characteristic, or property of God by virtue of which he is related to creatures? Because any such feature would either have to belong to God essentially or to be in God as an accident. Yet, in light of the cosmological argument, neither alternative works. Keep in mind that the cosmological argument starts out from the recognition that the things we encounter in the world are contingent—that though they exist, they might not have. It, then, concludes to God as a (*per se*) necessary being who accounts for these contingent things. The cosmological argument, thus, naturally gives rise to the following distinction between God and creatures. God is the uncaused, necessary being, which depends on no other, while creatures are caused, contingent beings, all of which depend on God.

From here we can see why God cannot be really related to his creatures either essentially or by virtue of some accident in God. God cannot be really related to creatures by virtue of the divine essence, for if God were by his very essence related to that which is contingent, then God himself would be contingent. Yet, if God himself were contingent, then he could not be that necessary being that the cosmological argument posits to account for that which is contingent.[13] God would be merely one more instance of the very thing he was posited to explain.

On the other hand, neither can God be really related to his creatures by virtue of some accident in God. In the first place, it is at least arguably the case that a *per se* necessary being must be pure act, and that which is pure act can have no accidents. In the second place, all accidents call for some kind of causal explanation, since they do not belong to their subjects simply by virtue of what those subjects are. Thus, all accidents are caused. Yet, anything that is caused falls on the creaturely half of the distinction that the cosmological argument draws between God and creatures. Since any accident would be a creature, rather than giving us that in God by virtue of which he is related to his effects, it would merely give us one more effect. Rather than solving the problem of how God is related to creatures, it would merely reduplicate it.

It seems, then, that the cosmological argument urges us to deny that God is really related to his creatures. But in that case, there would be no difference in God, even were his effects different. Consequently, the logic required to say that God determines our actions, or that our actions are necessary relative to God, breaks down.

What, then, of the claim that if God causes our actions, those actions are absolutely necessary? The foregoing considerations resist this charge as well. God's causing our actions would make our actions absolutely necessary only if God were a necessary being, and God necessarily caused those actions. Yet, while the cosmological argument concludes to God as a necessary being, it precludes God's necessarily causing our actions. For, God would necessarily cause our actions only if it was part of God's very essence to cause the effects that he does. But, it could be part of God's essence to cause the effects that he does only if God were essentially related to his effects, and as we have seen, the cosmological argument rules this out.

Conclusion

Ironically, it is the very argument through which natural reason is compelled to admit that our actions are caused by God that, by extension, also precludes our thinking of God in a way that would deprive these actions of their freedom. The cosmological argument concludes to God as the source of all being other than himself. As a consequence, our actions are from God, and our merits God's gifts. Yet, since the cosmological argument also results in a radically transcendent conception of God, a God who is not really related to his creatures, the freedom that merit presupposes is preserved. As the first cause, God operates in all our actions, without rendering them necessary. Thus, we can say with Aquinas,

> The divine will must be understood as existing outside the order of beings, as a cause producing the whole of being and all its differences. Now the possible and the necessary are differences of being, and therefore necessity and contingency in things and the distinction of each according to the nature of its proximate causes originate from the divine will itself, for he disposes necessary causes for the effects that he wills to be necessary, and he ordains causes acting contingently (i.e., able to fail) for the effects that he wills to be contingent. And according to the condition of these causes, effects are called either necessary or contingent, although all depend on the divine will as on a first cause, which transcends the order of necessity and contingency. . . . The divine will is unfailing; yet not all its effects are necessary, but some are contingent.[14]

How precisely God is able to cause our actions without taking away their freedom, perhaps, remains a mystery. Nevertheless, *that* God is the cause of our actions appears to be something that reason can know given the assumption we have made, that the cosmological argument works. And by reflecting on this argument, reason can also show why the God that it establishes cannot be thought a threat to human freedom. Thus, philosophy, without exhausting all the mystery surrounding divine grace and human freedom, appears to converge with Catholic doctrine concerning our merits as God's gifts. And it also appears capable of defending that doctrine against the philosophical challenges that would contradict it.

Notes

1. This passage is taken from the *Catechism of the Catholic Church* (2006), together with this footnote: "Roman Missal, Prefatio I de Sanctis; *Qui in Sanctorum concilio celebraris, et eorum coronando merita tua dona coronas*, citing the 'Doctor of grace,' St. Augustine, En. In Ps. 102, 7: PL 37, 1321—1322."

2. See, for instance, Aquinas's *Exposition on Boethius's On the Trinity*, q. 2, a. 3.

3. Beware that the names I use to refer to the three extremes have been employed by a number of different authors, not always with precisely the same meaning. In order to avoid getting caught up in controversies concerning the interpretation of particular figures, I have refrained from giving particular examples of each extreme.

4. A modified version of rationalism might deny that there can be any contradiction between reason and *authentic* revelation. Such an account would still be rationalist, however, in making accordance with what reason can establish on its own the litmus test for distinguishing authentic revelation from inauthentic. Such an account would leave no room for two possibilities that the Catholic position insists on: First, for revelation's surpassing what reason can establish on its own, and second, for revelation's indicating places where reason needs to go back and correct its own mistakes.

5. *FR*, §8.

6. *FR*, §42.

7. *FR*, §14.

8. *FR*, §79.

9. *FR*, §16.

10. This teaching is highlighted in the *Catechism of the Catholic Church*, 2006—2011.

11. *ST* I-II, q. 79, a. 2.

12. For this classical teaching on relations, see Aquinas, *De potentia*, q. 7, a. 10.

13. For a similar, though not identical, argument, see Aquinas, *Summa Contra Gentiles* II, 12 (2).

14. *In I Periherm*, lectio 14 (22). Cf. *De Malo*, q. 16, a. 7 ad. 15.

CHAPTER FOURTEEN

EDITH STEIN AND *FIDES ET RATIO*

Catherine Jack Deavel

In *Fides et Ratio*, Pope John Paul II urges that philosophy must reclaim a proper relation to theology. John Paul II calls on teachers and students of philosophy to pursue this goal by committing themselves to three tasks, which will reinstate traditional aspects of their discipline. First and foremost, philosophy must "recover its sapiential dimension as a search for the ultimate and overarching meaning of life" (*FR*, §81). This task encourages philosophy to reclaim its place as an integrating discipline, which clarifies the proper spheres and relations of other disciplines and helps individuals understand how the knowledge available in different disciplines can be directed toward proper human flourishing. Second, in order to embark on a search for ultimate meaning, philosophy must affirm that human reason is capable of knowing objective truth (albeit imperfectly) (*FR*, §82). Such a claim includes knowledge of natural objects, the contents of scripture, and moral goods. Third, philosophy must apply itself with renewed energy to metaphysics, the study of beings precisely insofar as they are beings. This expansive enterprise takes account of empirical data about objects but sets its sights beyond them to a transcendent knowledge of objects, including the natures and ends of objects.

In presenting these tasks for philosophy, John Paul II is not making demands of philosophy that are external to the structure and goal of philosophy as a discipline. Instead, he claims, each of these tasks revitalizes philosophy, helping to restore philosophy's own proper objects, breadth, and method of inquiry. For example, when philosophy directs itself to the consideration of questions of overarching meaning (rather than to the study of particular problems in isolation), the discipline shows itself to be a true love of wisdom, seeking to understand the structure of what is and the human being's place among existents. One might accept that the three tasks named above are indeed proper to the task of philosophy, however, and yet still be uncomfortable with the context of John Paul II's request. Why must a revival of philosophy require a certain relation of philosophy to theology? Does even the suggestion that philosophy in fact has a "proper" relation to theology already undermine the autonomy of philosophy as a discipline? In order to address questions of ultimate meaning, John Paul II argues, philosophy must take into account theology's claims about the nature of God and the nature of the human being. How should philosophers go about this "taking into account"? The proper method by which philosophy should take up the claims of theology depends on what precisely the proper relationship between philosophy and theology. To help clarify this relation, John Paul II names a series of figures whose thought exhibits the abundant insight possible through a proper relationship between theology and philosophy (*FR*, §74). Edith Stein is listed among the twentieth century figures.[1]

The purpose of this essay is to suggest how Stein's thought, in particular her comments on the relation between philosophy and theology and her early work on empathy, can serve as a resource and model for meeting the tasks to which John Paul II calls philosophers. Stein turns the tools of rigorous philosophical analysis to the nature of the discipline of philosophy as well as to problems of the emotional, embodied, and social aspects of human existence that are central to the good life. Here, I will consider two strands of Stein's work. First, I will suggest that Stein's account of the proper relation of philosophy and theology can help us to clarify the precise relationship between these disciplines that John Paul II describes and advocates. Second, I will argue that Stein's account of empathy provides valuable tools for considering questions of human meaning, particularly in the pursuit of self-knowledge.

With respect to the latter strand, Stein recognizes in her account of empathy that individuals may differ in the range and intensity of their experience, but she also defends a universal and objective account of empathy and emotion. I submit that, in order to address questions of ultimate and overarching meaning, Catholic intellectuals must investigate the emotional and deeply social elements of human beings in addition to questions of how and what we know in a strictly abstract and intellectual manner.[2] These former considerations cannot be deemed secondary questions outside real philosophical work or simply topics too messy for philosophical analysis. Such stances would already greatly restrict philosophy's search for meaning.

RELATION OF DISCIPLINES

The question of what is the proper relation between philosophy and theology has been a familiar topic for generations of Christian thinkers, as John Paul II summarizes briefly (*FR*, §36ff.). After her conversion to Catholicism, Stein found herself confronted with the project of attempting to synthesize modern philosophy (here, the phenomenology of her graduate training) with medieval Christian philosophy, in particular, the thought of St. Thomas Aquinas.[3] Before launching into this synthesis in *Finite and Eternal Being*, Stein addresses some particular difficulties of such an undertaking, including the question of whether there is a Christian philosophy. Encouraged by John Paul II's citation of Stein's work as an example of a proper relation between philosophy and theology, I will present Stein's accounts of the nature of philosophy as a discipline and its proper relation to theology as a means of elucidating and reflecting upon the relation of these disciplines described by John Paul II.[4]

In *Fides et Ratio*, John Paul II describes the proper relationship between theology and philosophy as a circle (§73). Theology begins with the word of God and seeks to understand this revealed truth more fully. This task is the individual pursuit of each human person and our pursuit in common: theology's "final goal will be an understanding of that word which increases with each passing generation" (Ibid.). Human love of wisdom finds its formal and systematic expression in the discipline of philosophy. Precisely as truths, the truths of theology are also proper objects of philosophical inquiry. Because all truth is a unified whole, the truths considered and uncovered by philosophy will intersect with revealed truth, though reason alone could not have arrived at certain truths unaided: "The truth made known to us by revelation is neither the product nor the consummation of an argument devised by human reason. It appears instead as something gratuitous, which itself stirs thought and seeks acceptance as an expression of love" (*FR*, §15). Some truths of revelation are beyond the scope of unaided human reason, *e.g.*, the position that God is a Trinity or the redemptive possibility of suffering that Christ makes known on the cross. Other truths are within the potential scope of reason alone, whether or not they have in fact been arrived at through reason alone, *e.g.*, the existence of a divine being. In the latter case, revelation gives the believer certainty independent of one's ability to follow a particular argument and independent of one's trust in the reason of others. As human reason stretches itself toward an increasingly more complete and rigorous understanding of creation, especially the human person, philosophy will also lead to deeper understanding of the truths of faith and to better means of communicating these truths (*FR*, §§5, 103).

This circular relationship is not, of course, a case of circular reasoning, *i.e.*, mistaken logic that attempts to justify one claim by a second claim and to justify the second claim by the first, with the unfortunate result that neither claim has been justified. John Paul II is not claiming that the discipline of theology finds its foundation in philosophy while the discipline of philosophy finds its foundation in theology, leaving the student of either to despair at locating a solid starting point for her studies. To the contrary, John Paul II insists that the autonomy of both philosophy and theology must be respected (cf. *FR*, §77). Faith and reason are twin gifts of God that offer different means for human beings to approach truth: "the truth attained by philosophy and the truth of revelation are neither identical nor mutually exclusive" (*FR*, §9). The starting points of theology and philosophy must remain clearly distinct. Human reason may apply itself to revealed truths (which are proper objects of theology), but revelation must be recognized as a gift of God, the content of which reason could not or did not uncover alone. The truths under investigation will often overlap; however, *e.g.*, investigation of morality is proper both to philosophy and to theology. In the relation between faith and reason, "[e]ach contains the other, and each has its own scope of action" (*FR*, §17). Theology and philosophy will flourish in their own distinct spheres through the insights of the other discipline.

What is the distinct sphere of philosophy? And once the autonomy of the two disciplines has been established, even if one grants that a relation between these disciplines could prove fruitful, why should one accept the stronger claim that philosophy compromises its own goals as a discipline if it does not relate properly to theology? John Paul II describes several possible stances philosophy might take toward theology. The first two stances, *i.e.*, philosophy apart from faith and "Christian philosophy," are explained in similar terms and expanded upon in Stein's treatment of the relation of philosophy and theology.[5] As she introduces her attempt to synthesize Thomistic and phenomenological philosophy, Stein notes that one of the central difficulties of her project is to bridge the radically different positions taken by modern and medieval philosophy toward the relation of philosophy and theology.[6] Is philosophy a purely natural science, *i.e.*, "a discipline resting exclusively on reason and natural experience as its sources of knowledge," as many modern philosophers hold, or can philosophy legitimately "draw additional light from revelation" as the medievals claim?[7]

John Paul II and Stein, both following Thomas Aquinas, note that philosophy as a natural science entirely apart from revelation is surely possible, *e.g.*, the philosophy of Plato or of Aristotle. But this first stance of philosophy to theology has at least two versions. Reason can and does legitimately pursue knowledge of the truth completely apart from the truths of revelation when these revealed truths are unavailable to reason. The insistence of some modern philosophers on a similar isolation of reason from faith belies a different carriage of mind, however. One should not infer that the man who leaves his car at home and the man who has no car hold the same views about efficient and enjoyable transportation simply from the fact that both arrive on foot. If philosophy is true to its own methods and objects of investigation, John Paul II argues, then "as a search for truth within the natural order, the enterprise of philosophy is always open—at least implicitly—to the supernatural" (*FR*, §75). The separatist tendencies of some modern philosophers suggest an unwillingness to search out truth wherever it may be found.

In contrast, the second stance philosophy can take to theology, namely, Christian philosophy, refers to "a Christian way of philosophizing, a philosophical speculation conceived in dynamic union with faith" (*FR*, §76). In investigating truths of revelation, philosophy is not in danger of becoming theology because philosophy maintains its characteristic rational method. Philosophy attempts to understand the truths of faith as fully as possible by means of natural reason. For the individual thinker, "faith purifies reason" (Ibid.). Christian philosophy invites the virtues of humility and courage—humility guards against the temptation to elevate reason to "an absolute and exclusive value" (*FR*, §79) or, worse, to lose sight of the limit of one's own intellect, and courage prompts one to take up thorny philosophical problems that demand consideration of revealed truths (rather than avoiding these questions altogether). Here, we see faith helping reason to regain its sapiential dimension, urging reason to our intellectually honest and thorough pursuit of truth. John Paul II refers to this purification of the individual intellect as the subjective aspect of Christian philosophy. Stein notes that the benefits of grace apply to "philosophy if we consider it as an attitude [*habitus*] and an activity [*actus*] of the intellect."[8] Because grace is always a gift to the human subject who engages in or studies a science, "Christian philosophy" in this first sense describes the practice of philosophy. The term also encompasses advances or concepts in philosophical thinking that have resulted from Christian belief, either directly or indirectly (*FR*, §76), *e.g.*, creation as the free act of a personal God, or the distinction between concepts of person and nature.[9] John Paul II calls the Christian influence of and contribution to the content of philosophy the objective aspect of Christian philosophy. In Stein's terms, "Christian philosophy" in this second sense describes certain manifestations of philosophy as a science.

Stein proceeds by first giving a definition of philosophy and then examining what is designated by "Christian philosophy." According to Stein, philosophy is first and foremost a science (*Wissenschaft*), a "structure of concepts, judgments, and demonstrations, all interrelated and joined together according to definite laws."[10] By this definition, a science "presupposes the existence of an objective reality and of knowing intellects."[11] An objective reality is implied in part because the objects under investigation determine the content and coherence of a science. A science is comprised of concepts, judgments, and demonstrations that are *of* or *about* the objects of investigation. Sciences are distinguished from one another by the different sets of objects under study, and the nature of these objects will determine the method of investigation in each science. As a structure of concepts, judgments, and demonstrations (all of which are mental entities or actions in relation to an object), a science already implies the existence of a mind. Because these concepts are about particular objects outside but accessible to various human minds, a science can be considered as a body of knowledge apart from any individual thinker.

Stein emphasizes the necessary metaphysical basis for any science. The related propositions that make up a science are true insofar as they correctly capture the nature of an object or its activities and interactions with other objects. The latter are "states-of-affairs" which "reveal the object's inner structure and the relative position which it occupies with respect to the total texture of existents."[12] The existence and activities of an object take place in a context, which is illuminated by the object's activities. For example, the propositional sentence 'the cat is jumping' describes a state-of-affairs that allows me to infer from the activity of the cat to features of the inner structure of the cat (*e.g.*, that it can adequately balance and coordinate its movements to execute its leap) and to features of other existents and their relationships to the cat (*e.g.*, that the earth's gravity is in effect, such that the cat must work to leave the ground). Following Thomas, Stein defines truth in terms of the mind's conformity to reality. Truth is the adequate correspondence of a proposition (and, by extension, the mind knowing this proposition) to a mind-independent being: "The truth of the sentence, in short, is founded upon a true being (that is, a being which has its foundation in itself and which provides a foundation for the sentence)."[13] Propositional sentences are not primarily about other sentences nor about human thoughts; they are about the nature of objects. Because propositional sentences are grounded in states-of-affairs, "in this sense it may be said that these propositions are or 'exist' prior to their being conceived by a human mind and prior to their being formulated in the *material* medium of a human language."[14] In the progress of a science, human minds will not formulate all of the possible sentences that describe objects and states-of-affairs, but those propositional sentences that we do formulate must be judged according to the reality in question. The fundamental criterion of whether a propositional sentence should be added to or retained in a science will be its adequacy to these objects and states-of-affairs, *i.e.*, its truth.

Stein's account helps elucidate John Paul II's tasks for contemporary philosophy. As noted above, she insists that the very nature of a science requires an acknowledgement (at least implicitly) of the existence of objects available to be known and minds capable of knowing them. Stein claims

> Every *Wissenschaft* aims at true being. Being antecedes every *Wissenschaft*: [N]ot only every human knowledge and science understood as an arrangement for the elaboration of true propositions and for the description of the tangible total residue of all the endeavors leading up to true propositions, but even *Wissenschaft* conceived as an idea. . . . Sentences express existing states-of-affairs *and have their ontological* foundation in them.[15]

While no actual science will describe its proper objects perfectly, the human mind is indeed capable of some degree of adequate correspondence to objects, that is, we are capable of knowing objective truth. Philosophy is no different from any other science in this regard, but, because of its proper sphere of objects (that is, beings considered as beings), philosophy makes explicit the need for the sciences to assume metaphysical realism. In order for philosophy to operate properly as a science, it must be overtly metaphysical. As John Paul II claims, in order for philosophy to grow as a structure of concepts, judgments, and demonstrations about existing things, organized by laws (and guided by the ideal of the complete, perfectly integrated set of true propositions about these objects), we must recognize that the human mind can study and know existing things precisely insofar as they are existents. If we hold that philosophy is possible as a science, then we cannot shy away from this study and the assumptions that serve as necessary conditions for this or any other science.[16] Given this understanding of philosophy as a science, John Paul II's call for philosophy to affirm the possibility of objective knowledge and metaphysical realism is indeed a call for philosophy to fulfill itself as a discipline, not an imposition of external and optional tasks for a discipline that is complete without these considerations. These tasks are part of the exercise of philosophy as philosophy.

To explain what is Christian about "Christian philosophy," Stein employs a division from Jacques Maritain's account of this same term: a distinction between the nature of philosophy and the actual situation or condition of philosophy.[17] Applying this general division to her definition of a science, Stein distinguishes between science as an ideal and science in its historical setting (or science as it actually is). In our scientific practice and study, human beings are guided by the ideal of a science as the complete set of true statements about the proper objects or sphere of this science, all "causally and logically correlated or . . . integrated into a conclusive scientific theory."[18] This ideal is not, of course, fully attainable by earthly minds. Instead, we find every science in a particular historical setting. At any given time, a science as it actually is will be a fragmentary collection of the truths presently known (through the efforts of various thinkers up to and including those in the present historical context) about the proper objects of the science.[19] Actual science reflects the particular insights and errors of the individual human thinkers who have contributed to the practice of a science and the content of scientific knowledge as it presently stands. Stein concurs with Maritain that, considered purely in terms of its nature, philosophy has no necessary connection to theology or faith (hence, the true autonomy of the discipline and the possibility of philosophy entirely apart from theology noted above). Philosophy will always be developed and studied in some particular historical setting, however, which allows one to refer legitimately to certain manifestations as "Christian philosophy." The actual science of philosophy may be influenced by a Christian setting, which will inform the content and practice of philosophy.[20]

Stein's discussion of philosophy as a science also clarifies why philosophy, as part of its efforts as an independent discipline, will consider the truths of revelation. Because of its focus on truth and existents, philosophy's proper sphere of objects will overlap with those of other disciplines.[21] Philosophy

> aims at ultimate clarity. It wants to give an account (*lovgon didovnai*) of the ultimate attainable causes. . . . [The world of experience, which acts on sense and intellect,] thus points toward the ultimate sphere of intelligibility, that is toward *being as such* and toward the *structure of the totality of that which is* [*das Seiende als solche*] with its *essential divisions according to genera and species*.[22]

Philosophy considers both the foundations and the findings of the other sciences in its own study of what is. As part of the discipline of philosophy, then, reason will consider the claims of theology. Generally, the genera and species that serve as the proper spheres of objects for other disciplines are available to natural reason alone, *e.g.*, atoms and molecules are available to natural reason in the discipline of chemistry. While revelation may supply truths that are unavailable to human reason, God too is an existent and a cause. We cannot have a comprehensive account of what is without including God in this account.

> If philosophers then want to remain faithful to their goal, if they want to understand that which is [*das Seiende*] in the light of its ultimate causes, they will be compelled by their faith to extend their reflection beyond that which is naturally accessible to them. There are existents beyond the reach of natural experience and natural reason but which have been made known to us by revelation; and they confront the receptive human mind with entirely new tasks.[23]

Philosophy cannot achieve "ultimate clarity" if it ignores the claims of theology.

Stein recognizes that this position invites the objection that Christian philosophy as just described ceases to be philosophy. She acknowledges that, to the extent that Christian philosophy as an actual science embraces revealed truths, it ceases to be autonomous; however, this concession does not imply that philosophy has covertly shifted into theology:

> If . . . philosophy in its exploration of that which is meets with questions which it cannot answer by making use of its own devices (as, for example, the question concerning the origin of the human soul) and if, in order to arrive at a more

comprehensive knowledge of things that are, it appropriates for itself the answers given by Christian theology, then we have a Christian philosophy which uses faith as a source of knowledge. In this latter case we can no longer speak of a *pure* and *autonomous* philosophy. Are we justified in calling it theology? I think not.[24]

In defense, Stein offers an argument by analogy. If a historian includes a summary of a scientific theory and its influence in her consideration of a historical period, she incorporates the claims of natural science without herself becoming a natural scientist and without transforming her writing into a work of natural science. Similarly, a philosopher may incorporate the claims of theology without becoming herself a theologian and without transforming her work into theology. Stein cautions that the analogy is not perfect: the historian is concerned with the historical aspects of a scientific theory, regardless of the truth or falsity of this theory, while the philosopher is concerned with the truth of the claims borrowed from theology (and from any other discipline). Nevertheless, the point of commonality in the cases remains. For both the historian and the philosopher, "another discipline must be consulted to make it possible for scholars to progress in their own field."[25] This turn to another science is a necessary condition for completing the work of the first science.

But, an objector might press, the point at which the analogy fails has been passed over too quickly. Perhaps a philosopher might make use of a claim of revelation without thereby compromising his philosophical reasoning, but this kind of borrowing must be acknowledged as a move into the hypothetical. Because natural reason alone cannot ground the claim in question, the line of reasoning remains philosophy only if the argument is treated as an exercise in determining coherence among beliefs rather than truth. If one were to accept certain claims of revelation, then other positions might well follow. To accept the initial claims, however, the objection continues, is to operate outside the realm of philosophy; therefore, an honest philosopher must treat matters of faith as hypothetical suggestions or remain silent.

Stein meets such a challenge with several distinctions. First, she agrees that the honest philosopher will make clear when he or she is borrowing a truth of revelation. Revealed truths and the conclusions based upon them must be acknowledged as less intelligible to the human knower than the claims and conclusions of natural reason alone. This difference in intelligibility is not evidence against the truth of revealed claims nor against incorporating them into one's philosophical thinking, however. Different degrees of intelligibility are to be expected, since the finite human intellect cannot comprehend God.[26] Second, Stein acknowledges that a philosopher certainly could make use of the claims of revealed truth in a hypothetical mode. She suggests that non-Christian philosophers who choose to engage claims of revelation or conclusions dependent upon them will do precisely this: "they will accept the truths of faith not as 'theses' (as do believers) but only as 'hypotheses.'"[27] The point of disagreement comes in Stein's claim that this hypothetical mode is not the only legitimate philosophical stance when examining claims of revelation.

The purpose of philosophy (considered in its nature and, hopefully, in its practice as well) is to investigate beings and to formulate a comprehensive theory of existents and causes. In this pursuit, a contemporary philosopher has before him the claims of the various other disciplines, including theology. A Christian philosopher believes that the claims of revelation are in fact true; these claims provide information about the existence and nature of certain beings. Far from being dishonest as a philosopher were he to take account of revealed truths in his philosophical thinking, as the objector argues, exactly the opposite is true. A Christian philosopher would be dishonest *as a philosopher* were he not to take into account claims that he holds to be true. He would effectively abandon in practice his commitment to philosophy because he would no longer attempt to investigate all beings nor to formulate a comprehensive theory of existents and causes. Again, philosophy makes use of theology but does not become theology:

> While it is the task of theology to establish the facts of revelation as such and to elaborate their specific meaning and interrelation, it is the task of philosophy to harmonize those propositions at which it has arrived by using its own devices together with the truths of faith and theology. Only thus can reality be made intelligible in its ultimate reasons and causes.[28]

If a Christian philosopher were to follow the advice of our objector, he would find himself in an intellectual muddle. He would be committed both to the position that, because of its nature and goal as a discipline, philosophy must incorporate all truths and to the position that, because of its nature and goal as a discipline, philosophy must not incorporate some truths (*i.e.*, revealed truths)— or at least must not incorporate them as truths.[29] Again, a philosopher could treat the truths of revelation as hypotheses, but the Christian philosopher carries out her work as a philosopher in part by taking these truths as theses. In doing so, the Christian philosopher maintains both her commitment to the aim of her discipline and her own intellectual coherence.

Empathy and Self-Knowledge

In the previous section, I sketched the proper relationship between philosophy and theology, as described by John Paul II and elaborated by Stein. In the present section, we turn to another aspect of John Paul II's exhortation to reclaim the sapiential dimension of philosophy. John Paul II calls philosophy to external and internal realignment: to regain the proper external relation of the discipline of philosophy to other disciplines, especially theology, and to broaden the range of topics considered within the discipline, asking questions of ultimate meaning rather than being content to investigate only limited problems in isolation. While Stein's early work on empathy was written as a student of phenomenology and thus does not make use of the resources of Christian philosophy found in her later work, her account offers insight into the relation of persons emphasized by John Paul II.[30] I will argue that Stein's account of empathy provides resources for considering questions of overarching human meaning, particularly in the pursuit of self-knowledge.

John Paul II titles his introduction to *Fides et Ratio* with the admonition from the ancient temple at Delphi: "know yourself." This command, he writes, attests to the basic human desire to find meaning—to know what kind of a being I am, to know the source and the end of human life (*FR*, §1). The command to know oneself also implies a command to act. In part, I wish to know who I am so that I can become more fully myself, a wiser, more contemplative, more virtuous and more loving human being. Self-knowledge provides insight into what I am and prompts me to act: "the answer given to these questions [of the meaning of human life] decides the direction which people seek to give to their lives" (Ibid.). Self-knowledge, then, is also central to proper virtue and moral action.

Stein's account of empathy is directly related to John Paul II's call to take up these questions of self-knowledge and ultimate meaning in two important ways. First, because humans are inherently social creatures, self-knowledge must include the knowledge of how I am related to other human beings. Our affective relationships to other human beings are at least as fundamental to the good human life as our intellectual relationships to objects of knowledge. We are conscious of ourselves as already bound to other human beings, who are other selves, other "beings like me." As John Paul observes, "[h]uman beings are astonished to discover themselves as part of the world, in a relationship with others like them, all sharing a common destiny" (*FR*, §4). Empathy is one fundamental way in which I relate to other human beings as persons, and my relationships with others powerfully shape my character and my actions.

Second, both John Paul II and Stein make universal claims about human beings, which ground claims about objective meaning. John Paul II unceasingly argues for the importance and possibility of objective (albeit imperfect) knowledge of our world, ourselves, and God. Stein analyzes empathy as a phenomenon. Her conclusions are meant to describe the structure of human experience. At some stage, a thorough philosophical account must be given to ground these universal claims. How do I know that knowledge of myself is also knowledge of thyself? Why should each of us think that our own experience of being human offers insight into objective structures of thought and experience shared by all other human beings?[31] Stein's account of empathy offers a valuable strategy for beginning to answer this kind of challenge.

Stein works within the phenomenological method and begins her account with a brief description of this approach. In the "phenomenological reduction," one brackets the question of whether objects of experience exist in order to focus on the character of these objects as we experience them; that is, the objects of experience are investigated as phenomena. In this respect, the method and goal of phenomenology will be familiar to those acquainted with Descartes' *Meditations on First Philosophy*. The purpose of the reduction is to withhold assent from anything that might be doubtful in order, finally, "to clarify and thereby to find the ultimate basis of all knowledge."[32] In practice, the phenomenologist focuses exclusively on the subject's experience, either an individual experience of a thing (*e.g.*, a perception or a memory of an object) or "the 'full phenomenon of the thing' (the object given as the same in a series of diverse perceptions or memories)."[33] While it could be doubted that an object exists as I presently experience it—or that the object exists at all—it cannot be doubted that I am, in fact, having a particular experience. In other words, the question of whether what I experience is accurate should be bracketed in the phenomenological reduction; however, I can be certain *that* I have an experience, and I can investigate the content and structure of this experience. Like Descartes' radical doubt, the phenomenological reduction extends not just to experience of things in the world outside the subject but to the experiencing subject as well. The existence and the particular attributes of the "empirical I" (who acts in the physical world, remembers her past, answers to my name) are subject to doubt; therefore, this "empirical I" is considered only as a phenomenon. In contrast, the "I" of pure consciousness, *i.e.,* the "I" bound up in present experience precisely as the subject of this experience, cannot be doubted.[34]

Stein focuses on the character of the experience of empathy rather than how the experience comes about. She attempts to describe the kind of awareness of the other person we experience in empathy. Stein defines empathy most broadly as "acts in which foreign experience is comprehended."[35] Empathy is part of the subject's present experience and, therefore, an act of pure consciousness. My empathy and its content, *i.e.,* the foreign experience that I comprehend, are not equally basic. In this respect, empathy is similar to memory. If I remember at this moment an event from my childhood, *e.g.,* swimming in a river, this act of remembering is primordial but what is remembered is non-primordial. I may remember the feel of water, the sound of the current over the stones, and the exhilaration of being able to hold my breath and swim under the water, but I am also aware that I am not sensing or feeling these things in the present. With empathy, too, I am aware that the foreign experience is not my own present experience; however, I also realize that this experience was never my own. In both cases, the content is understood as a primordial experience for some subject— either a past subject or a foreign subject. I recognize that the subject in my memories is the same subject who now remembers.[36] In empathy, I recognize that the foreign experience is the present experience of another subject, another "I" of pure consciousness.

Stein claims that, in empathy, I am aware of the foreign experience of another subject directly: "in empathy we draw no conclusions because the experience is given as foreign in the character of the perception."[37] In an act of empathy, I do not simply infer the experience of another, nor do I study the particular physical cues of the other person, recall a time when I acted in similar ways, and then attribute my own experience to the other person. In these cases, I remain at the level of association. For example, I imagine what my inner experience would be were I in the other person's situation and then attribute this experience to the foreign subject.[38] It is surely possible to infer the experience of another or to associate actions and expressions of the other with my own past experience, but these activities can at best aid empathy; they are not its sum. To the contrary, Stein claims that

> [j]ust as our own individual is announced in our own perceived experiences, so the foreign individual is announced in the empathized ones. But we also see that in one case there is a primordial, while in the other a non-primordial, givenness of the constituting experiences.[39]

Here Stein is following out an implication of the original phenomenological reduction. In the process, she makes an ambitious claim about human experience. The first part is relatively uncontroversial. An experience is always the experience of a particular subject (because an experience involves at least a mental state).[40] We may abstract or generalize from a concrete experience, but experience cannot be thoroughly understood or analyzed without recognition of a subject who experiences. When I empathize, I perceive an experience and, in doing so, recognize the other person as a subject, *i.e.*, the foreign individual is "announced" in empathy. One might accept this explanation thus far even if one assumed that empathy is a form of association; however, as we have seen, Stein claims that empathy is a direct perception of another subject's experience, not the result of a step-wise reasoning process. This claim also seems to stem from the nature of experience. An experience is perceivable or intuitable, albeit in different ways by different subjects, *e.g.*, primordially or non-primordially. When Stein claims that non-primordial experiences are "given" in empathy, she is arguing that our knowledge of other people can include perception of their experience: "empathy posits being [of the other's experience] immediately as a perceived act, and it reaches its object directly without representation."[41] In other words, I can perceive another's joy, anxiety, or pain, not just understand and make intellectual judgments about their experience, *e.g.*, judge correctly that another is in fact joyful, anxious, or pained.[42] Just as I do not comprehend my primordial experience through a process of inference, I need not comprehend the experience of another subject indirectly either: "in my non-primordial experience, I feel, as it were, led by a primordial one not experienced by me but still there, manifesting itself in my non-primordial experience. Thus empathy is a kind of act of perceiving *sui generis*."[43] My knowledge of other subjects, then, is set apart from my knowledge of inanimate objects because it includes direct perception of their experience and this feature is part of knowing subjects as subjects.[44]

This claim that empathy involves direct perception does not entail that I am always correct about another subject's present experience, however, any more than the primordial character of my own experience makes my motivations and emotions transparent to me at all times. Commenting on deception and empathy, Stein argues that when I am mistaken about the experience of others, the problem generally is that I take my own psychic life as the standard for all others, in which case, "I do not reach a deception (i.e., a supposed primordial givenness of what is not actually present), but a false inference on the basis of the false premise."[45] Here, I mistake a bad inference on my part for empathy. Stein further argues that my faulty inferences are in fact corrected by empathy. When, for example, I assume that a friend finds my favorite hobby fascinating, my initial conclusion is refuted by her boredom. We should remember, too, that empathy is not mind-reading for Stein. The living body is part of the foreign individual and Stein recommends that we attend carefully to the other people's bodily expressions and carriage in order to avoid deception.

Through empathy, human beings also gain several important forms of self-knowledge. According to Stein, empathy is necessary for knowledge of myself as a psycho-physical individual (*i.e.*, a unity of mind and body).[46] The physical parts of my body, united with the "I" who is the subject of experience, are a living body. Although the "I" is non-physical and, therefore, does not have a spatial location, properly speaking, it acts as a "zero point of orientation" for the living body that surrounds it and for physical things outside my body, though in different ways.[47] I encounter other people not only as physical things outside me but also as subjects with whom I empathize, and I realize that others encounter me in the same way. Stein claims,

> From the viewpoint of the zero point of orientation gained in empathy, I must no longer consider my own zero point as the zero point, but as a spatial point among many. By this means, and only by this means, I learn to see my living body as a physical body like others. At the same time, only in primordial experience is it given to me as a living body. ... In 'reiterated empathy' I again interpret this physical body as a living body, and so it is that I first am given to myself as a psycho-physical individual in the full sense. The fact of being founded on a physical body is now constitutive for this psycho-physical individual.[48]

"Reiterated empathy" is reflexive empathy, or empathizing with empathy. Various kinds of activities are capable of reiteration, in which the activity can be applied to itself indefinitely, *e.g.*, I can take pleasure in taking pleasure, or think about thinking. In the case of reiterated empathy, "among the acts of another that I comprehend empathically there can be empathic acts in which the other comprehends another's acts."[49] While the other person could be empathizing with a third person's acts, the reiterated empathy that Stein has in mind above is the case in which the person with whom I empathize is empathizing with me. In this scenario, I see myself as the other person sees me, so to speak, while at the same time I empathize with the other from my own zero point of orientation.

One of the more striking features of Stein's account above is her emphasis on the human body. In empathy, I am impressed with the fact that other human beings are also subjects. I learn that I am one "I" among many. The understanding of the human person is not of a purely mental self, however; indeed, Stein insists that an individual is not simply the pure "I" but mind and body together. Here, she threads her way past two tempting errors: the notion that we experience others as physical objects and then must infer their subjectivity from their physical behavior, and the notion that empathy is the rarified connection of one mind to another, a pipeline into the pure thought of another person. Stein comments,

> This individual is not given as a physical body, but as a sensitive, living body belonging to an 'I,' an 'I' that senses, thinks, feels, and wills. The living body of this 'I' not only fits into my phenomenal world but is itself the center of orientation of such a phenomenal world. It faces this world and communicates with me.[50]

Initially, from my encounter with others, I understand that my body is a physical object. Although I will always experience my body primordially as a living body, it is not experienced in this way by others, *i.e.*, no other person can experience my primordial experience in a primordial manner. I learn to imagine myself from without, as another person might observe me, which serves as a condition for empathy.[51] I recognize the possibility of primordial experience and a zero point of orientation within a living body other than my own. I am "given to myself as a psycho-physical individual" in reiterated empathy because I empathize with the other person's encounter with me as "a sensitive, living body belonging to an 'I'." Because the other person experiences me as a mind and body unity, my empathy with this experience underscores for me on a general level that I am an embodied creature and further presents to me particular ways in which I act in the world, which brings us to another way in which empathy furthers our self-knowledge.

Empathy helps an individual to evaluate himself and, hopefully, serves an impetus to build virtue and develop one's abilities. When I empathize with another person, I am aware of another's experience, which I might then evaluate on its own or use to evaluate myself. For example, if I empathize with someone who exhibits remarkable patience, I can make the judgment that this person is virtuous in this regard. I might also realize, with chagrin, that I would not be so patient were I faced with a similar situation. Likewise, in a case of reiterated empathy, another person's empathy with me could help me recognize that I am being selfish. In both cases, I have gained knowledge of my moral character through empathy. Stein notes,

> We see the significance of knowledge of foreign personalities for 'knowledge of self' in what has been said. We not only learn to make ourselves into objects ... but through empathy with 'related natures,' i.e., persons of our type, what is 'sleeping' in us is developed. By empathy with differently composed personal structures we become clear on what we are not, what we are more or less than others. Thus, together with self knowledge, we also have an important aid to self evaluation.[52]

For present purposes, we can consider "types" of persons as general characters or personalities.[53] When I empathize with someone of the same general temperament as myself, I may gain a model of how I can best develop my tendencies, *e.g.*, I might learn how to shape my enthusiasm for conversation into an aptitude for asking good questions. Through empathy, I can come to a clearer and more complete assessment of my strengths and weaknesses of character. Here again, the importance of the sapiential dimension of philosophy becomes apparent. I further may be challenged to change or to live more fully my own system of meaning (in Stein's phrase) when I empathize with someone who has a different system of meaning and value or simply a different personality.

In this essay, I have sketched how two aspects of Stein's thought, namely her description of the relation between philosophy and theology and her early work on empathy, serve as models and resources for meeting John Paul II's challenge to philosophers in *Fides et Ratio*. Stein's account of the proper relation of philosophy and theology helps to clarify the precise relationship between these disciplines urged by John Paul II. In order to fulfill its nature as a discipline and to operate as a true love of wisdom, philosophy will take into account all truths available to it, including the truths of revelation. Further, even in her early phenomenological work, Stein's account of empathy provides valuable tools for considering questions of human meaning, particularly in the pursuit of self-knowledge, because it attends to the way in which self-knowledge is itself possible only in a community of persons. This attention to the relation of human beings with one another and with God is further developed in her turn from strict phenomenological method to an encounter with the tradition of Christian philosophy. In her mature work, in which she turns to the integration of phenomenology and Thomism and reflects directly on truths of faith, Stein offers a practical model of the relation of philosophy and theology she defends above. Her own philosophical development and work across different schools of philosophy manifest a clear and careful desire for wisdom.

NOTES

1. Stein studied phenomenology under Edmund Husserl, one of the founders of this branch of philosophy. A Jewish woman, Stein converted to Catholicism and became a Carmelite nun. She and her sister Rose died in the death camps of Auschwitz. In 1998, Stein was canonized St. Teresa Benedicta of the Cross. She is one of five recent Western thinkers—and the only woman philosopher—named in *Fides et Ratio*. Sarah Borden includes a short biography of Stein as well as an overview of her thought in *Edith Stein*, Outstanding Christian Thinkers Series (New York: Continuum Books, 2003).

2. After all, the ultimate object of knowledge, God, is also the ultimate object of love. John Paul II notes that it is by loving God, as well as knowing Him, that human beings come to true knowledge of themselves.

3. Stein explicitly takes up this project in her *Finite and Eternal Being*, which considers "the *inquiry into the meaning of being*" in a comparative study of Thomistic and phenomenological thought (xxviii, original italics). Stein provides an interesting example of the philosophical synthesis that John Paul II urges because her education in phenomenology is her systematic home, so to speak. She comes to scholastic philosophy with her new Catholic faith but without years of formal philosophical training in these systems. For many contemporary Catholic thinkers, the project of synthesis works in reverse, *viz.*, exploring modern schools of philosophy from a background in the Catholic intellectual tradition, often Thomism. *Finite and Eternal Being: An Attempt at an Ascent To the Meaning of Being*, trans. Kurt F. Reinhardt, The Collected Works of Edith Stein, vol. 9 (Washington, D.C.: Institute of Carmelite Studies, 2002).

4. In objection to this approach, one might point out that John Paul II is careful to distance himself from any particular aspect of a philosopher's thought: "in referring to these [thinkers] I intend not to endorse every aspect of their thought but simply to offer significant examples of a process of philosophical inquiry which was enriched by engaging the data of faith" (*FR*, §74). Given the context, however, as well as the content of Stein's account (which, as we will see, draws heavily on Catholic tradition, particularly Thomism), I take it that the majority of Stein's explanation can serve as one acceptable guide for understanding the relation of philosophy and theology that John Paul II wants to rekindle.

5. The third stance is philosophy as a partner in and foundation for theological thought (*FR*, §77). I will touch on this stance as an implication of Christian philosophy as Stein understands the term.

6. *Finite and Eternal Being*, 12.

7. Ibid.

8. Ibid., 21. Stein notes these two considerations as ways of interpreting Maritain's account of the nature of philosophy (Ibid., 14).

9. The first example is from *Fides et Ratio* (76) and echoed by Stein. The second example is Stein's (*Finite and Eternal Being*, 23). She points out that questions posed by matters of faith, *e.g.*, how best to understand the Eucharist, have occasioned distinctions among concepts and careful reasoning that then become part of the general vocabulary and discourse of philosophy itself.

10. *Finite and Eternal Being*, 15. I have passed over Stein's initial discussion of Maritain's account. See note 8.

11. Ibid. Stein claims that this definition also implies that the knowing intellects are discursive, meaning that they come to knowledge by stepwise reasoning. Presumably, only a discursive intellect would have need of the demonstrations that partially comprise a science, for example, or a structure of concepts informed by a method of inquiry.

12. Ibid., 17.

13. Ibid.

14. Ibid., 17—18.

15. Ibid., 17.

16. One could presumably avoid this conclusion by objecting that Stein's definition of science or her account of truth is incorrect. The definition itself does not seem particularly controversial, however. The challenge for such an objector is to define "science" in such a way that philosophy and the other disciplines are adequately described while at the same time avoiding talk of a division of disciplines based on the difference of objects (which appears to imply reality of these objects) or talk of the minds that know these objects. (The latter approach seems precluded if one wants to affirm, at minimum, that different disciplines assert theories in propositional sentences that have meaning.)

17. Ibid., 13. This distinction can be applied to any science. In Stein's initial discussion of Maritain (which I do not discuss), she notes that Maritain's definition of philosophy as a "formal structure of the mind" implies both "a vital intellectual activity and an enduring intellectual habit," *e.g.*, the act of judging as well as the ingrained disposition to judge with a certain logical precision or according to certain criterion (14). Stein quotes and comments on a German translation of Maritain: *Von der Christlichen Philosophie*, trans. Balduin Schwartz (Salzburg, 1935).

18. *Finite and Eternal Being*, 16. "*Wissenschaft as an idea*—that enduring substrate of every concrete human knowledge and science—is then to be understood as the 'pure' (quasi, as yet bodiless or disincarnate) expression of all those states-of-affairs in which that which is [*das Seiende*] unfolds itself according to its own inner necessity" (Ibid., 18).

19. Ibid., 15—16.

20. As noted above, philosophy may be "Christian" subjectively and objectively, in its practice and its content. Thinkers are purified by faith and motivated to address questions that arise from faith or that can be thoroughly answered only through attention to revealed truths. The claims of revelation introduce categories, concepts, or problems for philosophical analysis, *e.g.*, the natural world as creation, which then become part of the discipline of philosophy.

21. "It is one of the functions of philosophy to elucidate the fundamental principles of all the sciences [*Wissenschaft*]" (*Finite and Eternal Being*, 19). Other disciplines generally take their objects of study and methods as starting-points; philosophy examines these starting-points. Insofar as someone considers the basis of his or her discipline, this person is acting as a philosopher.

22. Ibid., 19. Original italics.

23. Ibid., 21. Or again: in light of the data of Christian revelation, "it appears impossible for a pure philosophy to perfect itself. . . . It needs for its completion the aid of theology without, however, becoming theology." (23)

24. Ibid., 24.

25. Ibid., 24.

26. "Since the ultimate ground of all existence [alles Seienden] is unfathomable, everything which is seen in this ultimate perspective moves into that 'dark light' of faith, and everything intelligible is placed in a setting with an incomprehensible background" (Ibid., 25). In a related move, Stein claims that some proofs for God's existence, including her own, are not strictly speaking proofs in a demonstrative sense. Sarah Borden gives a clear and concise account of Stein's proof for the existence of God in her chapter on Christian philosophy in *Edith Stein*, Outstanding Christian Thinkers Series (New York: Continuum Books, 2003).

27. *Finite and Eternal Being*, 28.

28. Ibid., 23.

29. Our objector might further think that truths of theology are inadmissible on the grounds that natural reason must be the gatekeeper of philosophy. But such an objection needs to be clarified. The position might be a complaint about reasonableness of the content of the revealed truths, the reasonableness of one's criteria for accepting such truths, or both. If the former is the case, then one would need to proceed proposition by proposition, showing that the content of each claim is in fact irrational. If the problem is the criteria according to which one accepts revealed truths, our objector needs to show that the various criteria are below the rational standards of the criteria under which we accept other sorts of truths. (Above, when I speak of the Christian philosopher accepting revealed truths, I assume that our philosopher has some reasons for doing so.) In either case, an appeal to reason in general is not persuasive; an objector would need to make particular arguments in each case.

30. I am proceeding out of chronological order. *On the Problem of Empathy* is Stein's doctoral dissertation, written as a student of phenomenology before her conversion to Catholicism. Thus, the account of philosophy given above was written after her work on empathy, which we are about to discuss. For purposes of clarity, it seemed best to consider more global questions about the discipline of philosophy before giving an example of how the discipline might pursue insight into the relation of human beings.

31. Depending on the aspect of the human being under consideration, we might speculate that certain faculties or even experiences could be shared to some extent with purely spiritual beings. In her dissertation, Stein claims that, at least hypothetically, we might ascribe a variety of emotional experiences to God or other spiritual beings. Cf. Edith Stein, *On the Problem of Empathy*, trans. by Waltraut Stein (Washington, D.C.: ICS Publications, 1989), 11.

32. *On the Problem of Empathy*, 1. Like Descartes, the phenomenologist does not deny the existence of the objects of experience. Instead, the method calls us to suspend judgment, *i.e.*, neither to affirm nor to deny. (Affirming or denying the existence of an object of experience puts one at equal risk of believing what is false, since one could incorrectly affirm the existence of a nonexistent object or incorrectly deny the existence of an existing object.)

33. Ibid., 2.

34. Ibid., 3. Obviously, this claim is controversial. Arguments that the existence and character of this "I" are far from certain may be very similar to arguments against Descartes' intuition of the *cogito*. For the latter, Georges Dicker provides a handy summary of some contemporary analytic arguments in *Descartes: An Analytic and Historical Introduction* (New York: Oxford University Press, 1993). This essay is not the place for

taking up such arguments, however.

35. Ibid., 4. Stein also describes empathy as "the experience of foreign consciousness in general, irrespective of the kind of experiencing subject or of the subject whose consciousness is experienced" (Ibid., 10). Stein later develops this notion of "kinds" of subjects. For present purposes, we can think of "kinds" of subjects as general characters or personalities. While this aspect of Stein's account seems false—her "kinds of subjects" seem to give too much import to the fact that certain human traits tend to be found together—I take Stein's general point to be correct: I can perceive that another person experiences joy or distress even if I would react differently in a similar situation.

36. The same is true of the subject whom I imagine in my daydreams or consider in my plans for the future. Stein comments that I am joined to my remembered or imagined self "by a consciousness of sameness or a continuity of experience" (*On the Problem of Empathy*, 10). One might reject these bases for identifying the subject of memory or fantasy with the "I" of present experience on the grounds that they are subject to doubt through the phenomenological reduction, *i.e.*, I have no indubitable reason for thinking that the subject of my memory and the subject of present experience are both "me." If this were true, one might continue, we have no good reason to think that empathy is a distinct kind of present experience (distinct from imagined experiences, for instance). This argument underestimates the role of phenomena, however. Stein is investigating empathy as a phenomenon, which means that she need not establish the existence of foreign subjects nor the identity of the subject through time in order to advance her analysis. For her purposes, if the consciousness of sameness or a continuity of experience is part of one's experience of memories, then these elements are part of the phenomenon of memory. Likewise, the awareness that the content of empathy is a foreign experience is already part of the phenomenon of empathy. These differences at the level of phenomena are enough to maintain empathy as a distinct phenomenon and act of the "I." Further arguments might help establish the accuracy of the analysis, *e.g.*, by showing that we have good reason to believe in the existence of foreign subjects, but they are not necessary to demonstrate that empathy is a category of present experience.

37. Ibid., 26.

38. Ibid., 14.

39. Ibid., 39.

40. Presumably, human experience generally involves a physical state as well, *e.g.*, surprise involves a quickened heart rate and wide-eyed expression.

41. In this passage, Stein is discussing the theory of association. In this context, a representation might be the memory of my emotional state when I engaged in behavior similar to the other person's present behavior. The bracketed addition constitutes an interpretation on my part.

42. For my purposes, a brief summary will suffice here. Stein describes three possible levels of empathy as "(1) the emergence of the experience, (2) the fulfilling explication, and (3) the comprehensive objectification of the explained experience" (Ibid., 10). An act of empathy may (but need not) involve all three levels. Stein provides the following illustration: "When [the content of empathy] arises before me all at once, it faces me as an object (such as the sadness I 'read on another's face'). But when I inquire into its implied tendencies (try to bring another's mood to clear givenness to myself), the content, having pulled me into it, is no longer really an object. I am no longer turned to the content but to the object of it, am at the subject of the content in the original subject's place. And only after successfully executed clarification, does the content again face me as an object" (Ibid., 9).

43. Ibid., 10.

44. This claim does not, of course, preclude other significant ways in which our

knowledge of other subjects may be set apart from our knowledge of inanimate objects.

45. Ibid., 98-99. Interestingly, Stein claims that God comprehends human experience through empathy and that humans can empathize with God to some degree as well. God, of course, is not subject to mistakes about a human person's experience. Stein writes, "The experience which an 'I' has of another 'I' looks like this [*i.e.,* empathy]. This is how human beings comprehend the psychic life of their fellows. Also as believers they comprehend the love, the anger, and the precepts of their God in this way; and God can comprehend people's lives in no other way. As the possessor of complete knowledge, God is not mistaken about other people's experiences, as people are mistaken about each others' [sic] experiences. But people's experiences do not become God's own, either; nor do they have the same kind of givenness for Him" (Ibid., 11).

46. Empathy also aids knowledge of myself as a spiritual being (*i.e.,* a subject who transcends the bounds of physical and psychological causality and whose actions are motivated by meaning, value, and feeling).

47. Ibid., 46. I am borrowing from Stein's more complicated discussion of body space and outer space, *i.e.,* space outside my body: "[T]he living body is constituted in a two-fold manner as a sensed (bodily perceived) living body and as an outwardly perceived physical body of the outer world. And in this double givenness it is experienced as the same" (47). Generally speaking, the "I" is the zero point of orientation for bodily experience. Stein observes that I experience bodily sensation as spatially located, *e.g.,* a pain in my foot, or a taste in my mouth (which I experience as just below my field of vision). The "I" and the living body taken as a whole form the zero point of orientation with respect to outside physical objects, though the proximity of an object to my body does not translate into corresponding proximity to the "I."

48. Ibid., 70—71.

49. Ibid., 19.

50. Ibid., 3.

51. "This reiterated empathy is at the same time the condition making possible that mirror-image-like givenness of myself in memory and fantasy. . . . If in a childhood memory or fantasy I see myself in the branch of a tree . . . , I see myself as another or as another sees me. This makes empathy possible for me" (Ibid., 70—71).

52. Ibid., 130.

53. Cf. endnote 35 above.

CHAPTER FIFTEEN

MAN AS IMAGO DEI AND CAPAX DEI: MAN'S SPECIFIC OBEDIENTIAL POTENCY

Professor Lawrence Feingold

MAN AS *IMAGO DEI* AND *CAPAX DEI:* MAN'S SPECIFIC OBEDIENTIAL POTENCY FOR GRACE AND GLORY

In this paper I would like to focus on a fundamental notion of Christian anthropology, our *specific obediential potency* to receive supernatural gifts, and to consider its relation to man's being made in the "image of God." I hold that this term is a key to the formulation of Catholic doctrine on man's capacity for grace and glory. Like the terms "consubstantial" and "transubstantiation," it has the merit of enabling an essential element of revealed doctrine to be precisely formulated and defended.

Although effectively shared by a consensus of Catholic theologians for over 400 years, this view is not shared by all contemporary theologians, to say the least. Henri de Lubac, more than anyone else, opposed the use of this notion as a central element in the formulation of Catholic doctrine on our capacity for grace and glory. He held that obediential potency for St. Thomas is a notion applicable principally to miracles, and that to use it to describe the relation of our spiritual nature to the supernatural order was a grave reduction of the openness of our nature, made in the image of God. Furthermore, he held this view to be a deviation from the authentic thought of St. Thomas and high Scholastic theologians in general, a deviation attributed to the classical sixteenth- and seventeenth-century commentators of St. Thomas, beginning with Cajetan, who plays the role of the villain. In *Mystery of the Supernatural*, although recognizing the legitimacy of the term "specific obediential potency,"[1] de Lubac writes:

> But it remains quite clear . . . that for St. Thomas particularly, the simple idea of *potentia obedientialis* conceived not "to express the condition in which God's gift places us of being able to become children of God," but to account for the possibility of miracle, is not adequate as a definition of the relationship of human nature to the supernatural. It does not lay sufficient stress on "the absolutely special case of spirit." Now for Cajetan the idea of *potentia obedientialis* is adequate. . . . In other words, Cajetan rejects St Thomas's principle: "the soul is naturally capable of grace" . . . and reduces the case of the supernatural destiny of created spirit to a particular instance of miracle. The fundamental reason for this reversal is that he has first reduced human nature itself to a case merely of one species among others in his consideration of natural be-

ings. And this double mistake has very grave consequences.[2]

As I hope to show, de Lubac came to these conclusions because of a lack of understanding of what is meant by an obediential potency *specific* to the spiritual creature, in the Thomistic tradition. Secondly, I will try to show how this notion is useful in showing both the distinction and harmony between the natural and supernatural orders.

Before speaking of the *specific* obediential potency of spiritual creatures, let us examine the meaning of the term *obediential potency* in general. For theologians of the thirteenth century, obediential potency is used to indicate a capacity in the creature to receive a perfection directly from the power of God, working above the order of natural causes. The creature has the capacity to obey God when He wills it to transcend its own nature, for before God's omnipotent power, all creatures obey. In the words of the centurion in the Gospel (Mt 8:8): "Only say the word, and my servant will be healed. For I am a man under authority, with soldiers under me; and I say to one, 'Go,' and he goes, and to another, 'Come,' and he comes." And after the miraculous calming of the sea, the Apostles exclaim: "What sort of man is this that even winds and sea obey him?" (Mt 8:27). Obediential potency is a thoroughly Biblical notion.[3]

Is there a limit to this potency? It is as wide as God's omnipotence itself. God's omnipotence stretches to all being. However, even God's omnipotence cannot realize something contradictory, for such a "thing" cannot *be*. Thus the only "limit" to obediential potency in general is contradiction. All creatures are open to receive, above their nature, whatever is not intrinsically contradictory.

This capacity to obey God above the course of nature is used in contrast with natural passive potency, which is the capacity to receive a perfection through *natural* active powers. Thus natural passive potency and obediential potency are two different kinds of passive potencies, corresponding to two different kinds of active powers: natural and divine. In the *Summa fatris Alexandri*, obediential potency is defined in precisely this way: "Active potency is twofold: created and uncreated. *Passive potency is also twofold: with respect to created power and with respect to the uncreated power.*"[4] The latter is referred to as a potency of obedience. For example, the capacity of Adam's rib to be made into a woman is said to be an obediential potency.

St. Thomas inherited this term from his predecessors, and defines it in the same way as Alexander of Hales. A good example is given in *Summa Theologiae* III, q. 11, a. 1:

> It must be borne in mind that in the human soul, *as in every creature*, there is a two-fold passive power. One is in comparison with a natural agent; the other in comparison with the First Agent, which can bring any creature to a higher act than a natural agent can bring it, and this is usually called the *obediential potency* of a creature.[5]

In this article, St. Thomas brings in this distinction in order to establish the particular kind of potency that existed in Christ's human soul for receiving infused knowledge of all revelation.

NATURAL ACTIVE AND PASSIVE POTENCIES AND OBEDIENTIAL POTENCY

This distinction of natural passive potency and obediential potency depends on a general Aristotelian principle according to which active and passive powers correspond to each other and belong in the same genus.[6] If the active power is natural, then the passive power will likewise be natural. If the active power is God alone working above the nature, then the passive power will not be natural but *obediential*.

St. Thomas explains this in his article from the commentary on the Sentences (*In III Sent.*, d. 2, q. 1, a. 1) dealing with the possibility of the Incarnation. He says that the capacity for a human nature to be assumed by God "does not signify a natural passive potency of the creature, for *there is no natural passive potency in nature which does not correspond to the active power of some natural agent*. Therefore, we must say that there is only an *obediential potency* in the creature according to which the creature can become whatever God wishes, as from wood a calf can be brought forth, through the operation of God. This obediential potency corresponds to the divine power, according to which it is said that the creature can become whatever God can make from it."

Understood in this way, the notion of obediential potency is a simple concept. It is the creature's passive receptivity to being moved *directly* by God above the course of nature. We have two types of passive potency: *natural passive potency* to be moved by secondary causes, and *obediential potency* to be moved by the will of God above secondary causes. The notion of obediential potency is especially important in the context of rationalism and naturalism, in which God's capacity to intervene in His creation is denied. Naturalism denies the very existence of obediential potency.

OBEDIENTIAL POTENCY IS NOT LIMITED TO MIRACLES

In order to illustrate the notion of obediential potency, St. Thomas uses the simplest examples taken from sensible things, which are miracles: the conversion of water into wine; the conversion of Adam's rib into Eve or the dust of the earth into the body of Adam; the conversion of bread and wine into the Body of Christ; the conversion of stones into sons of Abraham; the conversion of dead bones into living bodies in the Resurrection. In all of these cases there is a substantial change, worked directly by God without the intervention of secondary causes disposing the matter to receive the new form.

As mentioned above, de Lubac objected vehemently to the use of the category of obediential potency in Christian anthropology to refer to our capacity for the supernatural because he thought it was a category only suitable to refer to miracles.[7] If this were the case, he would be absolutely right to object! He is right to defend the sublime dignity of man that makes him uniquely capable of grace and glory.

However, not all obediential potency should be understood as the mere capacity of a given nature to be turned into something else by God. To repeat, these are the simplest examples to illustrate the notion, because they can be grasped by our senses. It is always helpful to use sensible examples to illustrate metaphysical notions. For example, philosophers illustrate the notion of *form* with the *figure* of a statue. But we don't reduce *form* to external figure! The metaphysical notion extends analogously beyond the sensible.

Likewise, although the medieval masters such as St. Albert and St. Thomas illustrate the category of obediential potency with examples of miracles, they employ it above all to refer to the capacity of spiritual creatures to receive supernatural perfections from God. For example, St. Albert uses it during the time that St. Thomas was his student in Cologne to describe our capacity to receive the vision of God. In his commentary on Dionysius's *Divine Names*, St. Albert writes:

> Our intellect comprehends all those things to which it is in potency according to its natural proportionality, in analogy with prime matter. However, with regard to the vision of God, our intellect is not in potency according to natural proportionality, but only according to *obediential potency*, like prime matter with regard to the form of glory [in the resurrection].[8]

St. Thomas himself explicitly uses the category of obediential potency to refer to *(1)* the capacity of human nature to be assumed in the Incarnation;[9] *(2)* the capacity of Christ's soul to receive the fullness of infused knowledge of supernatural Revelation and the gifts of the Holy Spirit;[10] *(3)* the capacity of Christ's soul to receive the fullness of sanctifying grace;[11] *(4)* the capacity of our souls to receive supernatural infused virtues;[12] *(5)* the capacity of the angels to receive revealed knowledge of anything going beyond the power of the natural light of their intellects;[13] *(6)* and the capacity of our soul to receive the light of prophecy.[14] *(7)* Like St. Albert, he denies that the capacity of our soul to see God is a natural passive potency.[15] Using his definitions of obediential potency, it is clear that this too is an obediential potency.

In summary, the great thirteenth-century theologians use the category of obediential potency to refer to the capacity of a spiritual nature to be elevated above its natural powers by the intervention of God working in and above that nature, infusing sanctifying grace, faith, hope, and charity, the gifts of the Holy Spirit, and the light of glory. This is not a sinister innovation of Cajetan.

SPECIFIC OBEDIENTIAL POTENCY

Let us now look more closely at the notion of specific obediential potency. As mentioned above, obediential potency, since it is based on God's omnipotence, extends to everything that does not imply a contradiction. It is not contradictory for a stone to be turned into a son of Abraham, but it would be contradictory for it to remain a stone and simultaneously be a son of Abraham. Non-spiritual natures cannot receive spiritual perfections without losing their irrational nature and receiving a new spiritual nature. Spiritual creatures, on the contrary, can receive new spiritual perfections above their nature without losing their nature. This is the most sublime dignity of man. Thus spiritual creatures have *transcendent obediential potencies that are unique to them*.

To say that the rational creature has an obediential potency to receive grace and glory is to say something very specific and *mysterious*. It means that the reception of grace and glory does not violate or contradict human nature, making it into *another nature*. A lion or a rock, for example, is not capable of receiving grace and glory *without first ceasing to be a rock or lion* and becoming a rational creature. Balaam's ass could be made to speak, but not to receive grace while remaining an ass.

This capacity of a rational creature to receive supernatural perfections without losing his own nature and identity has come to be called *specific* obediential potency.[16] Thus we distinguish obediential potency in the generic sense and *specific obediential potency* proper to the spiritual creature. The former simply refers to the capacity of a thing to be changed into something else in obedience to the omnipotent will of God. The latter refers to the capacity of a spiritual creature to be elevated to share in some prerogatives of the divine nature *without losing his specific nature and identity*. In other words, grace perfects and elevates spiritual nature without destroying it.

As we said above, obediential potency extends to everything that is not contradictory. This criterion of non-contradiction can be considered in two ways: *(a)* with regard to any possible nature; or *(b)* with regard to the *specific* nature of the creature. If non-contradiction is taken in the former sense, then any nature has an obediential potency to be changed into any other nature, "as a calf can be brought forth out of wood, through the operation of God."[17] If, however, non-contradiction is taken in the latter sense, then it indeed poses a very significant limitation on obediential potency.

In other words, the criterion of non-repugnance or non-contradiction is not an entirely negative principle. Obediential potency that is *specific* to a nature can only be oriented towards the *further perfection of that nature*. When an intellectual nature realizes an act on a higher level not in contradiction with that nature, the act will unfailingly perfect that nature.[18] To define obediential potency by means of a criterion of non-repugnance is not at all to overlook the question of the enormous perfection that it imparts.

Only a spiritual creature created in the image and likeness of God has the *specific obediential potency to be perfected further in that image*, by being carried from a natural to a supernatural likeness, without losing his nature. It is the unique privilege of every intellectual creature to possess a nature capable of this elevation, and hence to possess this specific obediential potency. An intrinsic consequence of being created in the image of God is the capacity to be further perfected in that image through supernatural elevation (deification), while retaining one's essential identity.

In summary, the notion of specific obediential potency has the merit of establishing three things. First, it indicates the revealed truth that the rational creature has a capacity to be elevated by God above his nature to receive supernatural perfections, and thus ultimately to share in the divine life, knowing and loving God as He knows and loves Himself. Secondly, it distinguishes this capacity to receive supernatural perfections from natural passive potencies, to which there always correspond natural active forces. Finally, the term indicates that this capacity is proper to the spiritual creature alone, and is somehow rooted in spiritual nature, created in the image of God. Thus it *simultaneously asserts man's unique capacity for the supernatural, rooted in his spiritual nature, and protects its gratuitousness*, keeping it from being seen to be due to nature.

HISTORY OF THE NOTION OF SPECIFIC OBEDIENTIAL POTENCY

Let us look briefly at the history of the notion of specific obediential potency.

St. Augustine

St. Augustine refers to this notion, without using this terminology, by speaking of man as *capax Dei*, in that he is *imago Dei*. In *De praedestinatione sanctorum*, he writes: "To be capable of having faith and charity belongs to man's nature; but to have faith and charity belongs to the grace of the faithful."[19] In other words, the capacity to receive faith and charity is proper to the spiritual creature alone and is rooted in his spiritual nature. Nevertheless, these perfections are not *from* his nature, but from grace. This perfectly describes the idea of an obediential potency specific to the spiritual creature. It is obediential in that grace is not from man, but from God alone. However, it is specific to man in that it is rooted in his spiritual nature.

In *De Trinitate*, XIV, 8, St. Augustine connects this specific capacity to be elevated to a supernatural possession of God to the fact that man is made in God's image: "It [the soul] is His image insofar as it is capable of Him and can participate in Him. Indeed, how could it achieve so great a good except by being His image?"[20] In more technical Scholastic language of a later age, we could say that man has a specific obediential potency for grace and glory because, as a spiritual creature, he is made in the image of God.

St. Thomas Aquinas

We have seen that St. Thomas uses the category of obediential potency to explain man's capacity for supernatural gifts. He sometimes expresses the idea that this capacity is *specific* to the spiritual creature, using the language of St. Augustine. In fact, he cites both of the above-mentioned texts of St. Augustine several times to indicate the *specific* capacity of the spiritual creature for supernatural participation in God.

In the *Summa Theologiae* III, q. 9, a. 2, ad 3, he says that although "the beatific vision is in some way above the nature of the rational soul, inasmuch as it cannot reach it of its own strength," we are nevertheless "*capable of it by nature, having been made to the likeness of God.*" In other words, although it transcends our natural active and passive potencies, we have a specific capacity rooted in our spiritual nature for the beatific vision. This expresses the notion of *specific* obediential potency.

However, he goes on to add that we are not capable by nature of receiving the uncreated knowledge of God, or of comprehending God, for that would imply a contradiction with the finite nature of the creature. Thus the human soul has no obediential potency at all for comprehensive knowledge of God.

Another very interesting text is *ST* I-II, q. 113, a. 10, on whether the justification of the sinner is miraculous. Here he cites both of the afore-mentioned texts of Augustine in support of his position. He cites the former in the *sed contra*, and the latter text in the body as follows: "In certain miraculous works it is found that the form introduced is beyond the natural power of such matter, as in the resurrection of the dead, life is above the natural power of such a body. And thus the justification of the ungodly is not miraculous, because the soul is naturally capable of grace; since from its having been made to the likeness of God, it is capable of God through grace, as Augustine says."

The notion of the miraculous is closely linked to obediential potency in the generic sense, in which something often receives a substantial change directly by the agency of God. For example, in the resurrection, the scattered bones and dust are converted into a living body, undergoing substantial change.

St. Thomas is saying that the justification of the sinner is not miraculous in the sense of generic obediential potency, for it involves a capacity *specific* to the nature of the spiritual creature, and in this sense is natural, in a certain way. The soul is naturally capable of grace by being the image of God. It is capable of a transformation into a closer likeness with God which *elevates without destroying the specific nature and identity* of the creature. Furthermore, this capacity finds a foothold of some kind in the nature of the creature itself.

Some scholars, such as de Lubac[21] and Laporta, have taken this text of St. Thomas as a repudiation of the notion of obediential potency as a category to refer to our openness to the supernatural. In reality, it repudiates only the *generic* notion of obediential potency but not the obediential potency *specific* to the spiritual creature. For example, de Lubac accuses Cajetan of repudiating the Augustinian/Thomistic principle that "the soul is naturally capable of grace." Why? Simply because Cajetan has said that the soul's unique capacity for the supernatural is *obediential*. De Lubac comes to this conclusion because he identifies obediential potency with the capacity for miracles and seems to be unaware of the notion of specific obediential potency. This explains his zeal in vilifying Cajetan. Nevertheless, although St. Thomas has not used the term, he is clearly expressing the idea of *specific obediential potency* with an Augustinian language.

St. Thomas also refers to the idea of specific obediential potency by borrowing a metaphor from Aristotle's *On the Heavens*.[22] He poses the objection that man should be capable of attaining his perfect beatitude through his own forces, because lower creatures attain their end through their connatural active powers. To this he responds that

> a nature that can attain perfect good, although it needs help from without in order to attain it, is of more noble condition than a nature which cannot attain perfect good, but attains some imperfect good, although it need no outside help in order to attain it, as the Philosopher says.[23]

In other words, man's great nobility is seen in that he has a capacity (surely an obediential potency) *specific* to his spiritual nature, to attain to a disproportionate and divine beatitude through the aid of grace.[24] Spiritual nature is unique in having a capacity for further perfection in likeness with God, that can only be brought about through His aid.

Theologians after St. Thomas

The notion of specific obediential potency is found in an early follower of St. Thomas, Bernard of Auvergne.[25] Writing in the last decade of the thirteenth century with regard to the capacity of the will to receive charity or other infused virtues, this early Thomist expressed himself as follows:

> The creature has no natural receptivity for supernatural habits. . . . For both nature and her receptivity do not extend beyond natural things by means of natural potency. Therefore, the capacity of the will for charity or other supernatural habits is an obediential potency, according to which God can put in the creature anything He wishes that does not imply a contradiction. Therefore, *because . . . it does not imply a contradiction if a habit of the love of God is placed in a creature who can love God by nature, only the intellectual creature has an obediential potency for charity.* Other creatures do not have this potency, by which God could make charity in them while they remain in their nature, because it would imply a contradiction.[26]

The text of Bernard of Auvergne cited above makes the very interesting point that obediential potency is *not the same in all creatures*, even though God can do whatever He wishes in them. Only the rational creature has the obediential capacity to receive the supernatural perfections of grace, the infused virtues, the gifts of the Holy Spirit, the light of glory, and the vision of God, *while yet retaining its nature.*

Capreolus (1380-1444), the greatest Thomist of the fifteenth century, expressed this idea in his commentary on the text of St. Augustine from *De praedestinatione sanctorum*:

> Augustine does not intend to say that the potency of human nature for faith and charity and other things of this type is a natural potency in the proper sense.... Indeed, human nature has an *obediential potency for this kind of supernatural habit from the fact that it is an intellectual nature*. Therefore, this potency is improperly said to be natural.[27]

The notion of specific obediential potency could hardly be more clearly stated.

Cajetan makes this same point in his interpretation of this Augustinian text: "That obediential potency to receive faith and charity is *in the nature of man* because he is intellectual. It is not in the nature of a lion, because such perfections are incompatible with its nature."[28] Sylvester of Ferrara echoes Cajetan: "To have faith or charity is not contrary to the nature of man, as it would be to the nature of a rock."[29]

Báñez also develops the notion of specific obediential potency. Interestingly, he cites the two texts of St. Thomas that we have discussed above:

> In man there is a *capacity and aptitude of nature according to obediential po-*

tency to be elevated to the vision of God. This is proved first as follows. A rock cannot be elevated to that operation, nor any irrational creature. Man, however, can be elevated. Therefore, there is a *natural capacity in man for this dignity which is not in other creatures*. Secondly, it is proved from St. Thomas, *ST* I-II, q. 113, a. 10, in which he says that by the fact that the soul is made in the image of God, it is naturally capable of grace. It should be observed that sometimes St. Thomas asserts that that beatitude [i.e. supernatural] is in accordance with the nature of man on account of this capacity, as he says, for example, in *ST* III, q. 9, a. 2, ad 3.[30]

The notion of specific obediential potency is developed along the same lines and beautifully expressed by Matthias Scheeben:

> The notion of obediential potency in general—parallel with that of natural potency in the strict sense, which is its opposite—is not restricted to expressing the aptitude of spiritual natures for grace. Instead, it can be applied to all created natures to the extent that they are capable of receiving an effect of God which is elevated above the level of law of nature. . . . However, since not all created natures are capable of receiving the *same* effect of God, it remains true that the *particular potentia obedientialis* with which we are concerned here, is a specific privilege of spiritual nature as such, and coincides with the capacity for a supernatural similitude of God to be brought forth out of the simple image of God.[31]

More recently, the notion of specific obediential potency has been skillfully expounded by Steven Long:

> Inasmuch as creatures can be said to be in potency to that which only the divine power can bring forth in them, it nonetheless remains true that God can bring about certain effects only in certain natures. For example: only a knowing and loving creature can, through the active agency of God, be brought to graced knowledge and love of God. If God can raise up sons of Abraham from the very rocks, this can only be by rendering them no longer to be rocks. By contrast, the life of grace through the active agency of God perfects human persons, uplifting human nature without destroying or mutating it.[32]

Or again:

> A rock cannot know and love God without ceasing to be a rock—it cannot even be 'helped' to know and love because it lacks any such faculties that might so be helped. By contrast while a human person cannot know and love God in direct vision and embrace without supernatural aid, with such aid the human person may partake in intrinsically supernatural divine friendship: and this is the specific notion of obediential potency as applied to the relation of grace to nature. It is a wholly passive potency that yet presupposes as its subject some determinate nature that is such that when aided by the active agency of God it may achieve a certain specific range of actuation. It is because of man's essentially spiritual nature that he has an obediential potency to the supernatural life.[33]

The Controversy Concerning Obediential Potency in the Twentieth Century

We are now in a position to give a preliminary response to the criticism leveled by de Lubac against the use of the category of obediential potency to refer to our capacity to receive supernatural perfections.

First of all, this category was clearly used in this context above all by St. Thomas himself, as well as St. Albert, and other thirteenth-century masters. Secondly, St. Thomas does not exclusively or primarily identify obediential potency with the capacity for the miraculous, but uses it especially to explain the capacity of the spirit for supernatural elevation. Third and most importantly, the notion of specific obediential potency does not treat the spiritual creature as if it were no different from any other natural thing. This was de Lubac's most serious charge against the Thomistic commentators. On the contrary, the Thomistic tradition consistently recognizes that the spiritual creature has sublime obediential potencies not shared by any lower nature, rooted in the nature of the spirit.

St. Thomas lays down the wise rule that one should never fight over terminology alone, but rather keep the mind focused on the content that it expresses. It is clear that Thomists such as Capreolus, Cajetan, Sylvester of Ferrara, Báñez, Scheeben, etc., are all in profound agreement with St. Augustine and St. Thomas in speaking of a specific capacity of the spiritual creature for supernatural perfection, rooted in the fact that we are made in the image and likeness of God. Why vilify them for this?

The ironic thing is that one would have thought that the notion of specific obediential potency should have been attractive to de Lubac, because it underlines the spiritual creature's unique capacity for the supernatural extension of his natural privilege to attain to God by means of his own acts.

Finally, a common objection against the thesis that man has an obediential potency for grace and glory is that it would make the supernatural order a second story, separated from the natural order and parallel to it, without any intrinsic connection.[34] This, I maintain, is utterly false and completely misrepresents the traditional Thomist understanding of the unique openness of spiritual nature to the supernatural.

The Thomist tradition affirms that the *specific obediential potency for the supernatural is based on the natural power of a spiritual nature to attain to God in some way (although imperfectly), which can then be extended and elevated.* Thus there is a fundamental intrinsic link between the two orders, which are related as imperfect to perfect: imperfect contemplation of God through the light of reason to perfect contemplation through the light of faith and glory; imperfect happiness to perfect; imperfect natural religion to perfect supernatural worship; imperfect natural virtue to the perfection of supernatural virtue; imperfect free will to its perfection through grace and glory; imperfect communion through natural friendship to perfect communion through grace and glory.

The imperfection of spiritual nature in realizing these goods is due simply to the fact that natural knowledge and love of God, and happiness in Him, is necessarily *proportionate* to our limited nature and the limitation of its active powers. The imperfection of the natural image of God in man, intrinsic to our creaturely status and aggravated by sin, is healed and elevated by grace and divinized by glory.

ELEMENTS OF THE *IMAGO DEI* IN MAN CAPABLE OF SUPERNATURAL ELEVATION

We have seen that our specific obediential potency to receive grace and glory is connected by St. Augustine, St. Thomas, Báñez, and Scheeben, with our having been made in the image and likeness of God. St. Thomas understands this image above all in terms of our capacity to know and love God.[35] Just as God's eternal beatitude lies in knowing and loving His infinite Goodness, so man also finds happiness in knowing and loving God. However, this can be done in two fundamentally distinct ways: imperfectly according to the proportionality of our nature; or perfectly above the forces of our nature, with the very power of God. Thus man is in the image of God both on the natural and supernatural levels. Man is made into a supernatural image of God by participating in God's own knowledge and love of Himself.[36]

Our capacity for elevation, by which we are *capax Dei*, is rooted in the fact that loving contemplation of God is our *natural end*. This natural end makes us capable of a supernatural end consisting in a divine elevation of our mode of contemplating God. If we could not naturally know and love God in any way, we could not be brought to a supernatural knowledge and love of God without changing our nature. That is, if we were not created in the image of God, we would not have a specific obediential potency for sharing in God's inner life through grace and glory. This is what St. Augustine and St. Thomas mean when they say that "having been made to the likeness of God, man is capable of God through grace." Our naturally being in the image and likeness of God is the foothold and foundation for the elevation to a supernatural image, so to speak. Let us look at this more closely.

Natural Knowledge of God Transformed

First of all, the natural capacity of our reason to know God through creation provides the foothold for a supernatural extension of that capacity, through faith, infused knowledge, and the beatific vision. Natural knowledge of God attains to Him as First Cause, whereas by supernatural knowledge we can know Him also in His inner life. If we had no capacity for natural knowledge of God, then we would be unable to understand God's revelation of Himself. *Our natural capacity to know God "through the things that are made" is the natural foundation for our specific obediential potency to become "hearers of the Word,"* when God supernaturally reveals Himself to us. The capacity to receive the theological virtue of faith is rooted in our intellectual nature which can naturally grasp the *praeambula fidei*. Hence the great importance of the Church's teaching in Vatican I that the mind is capable of certain knowledge of God through reason.[37]

Natural Love of God Transformed into Supernatural

Secondly, our natural capacity to love God as Author of nature can be elevated into a supernatural love for the God who has revealed Himself in His inner life and His plan of salvation for man. Once man knows the existence of God through reason or instruction, it is natural for him to love and revere God as the author and end of nature. This natural capacity to love God provides the basis for a supernatural love of God in the theological virtue of charity, which extends the natural love, and is directed to God not just as Creator or First Cause, but as He is known by faith as Redeemer and Father, who adopts us into the divine intimacy. St. Thomas contrasts the natural love for God, directed to Him as "principle and *end* of all natural being,"[38] with the supernatural love directed to God "insofar as He can be participated through glory by His friends."[39] The existence of a natural love of God, and its distinction from supernatural charity, is a fundamental thesis of St. Thomas and Thomism.[40] It is of crucial importance, for if we were incapable of loving God by our natural powers alone (as held by Luther and Jansenism), then it would seem that we could not be elevated to a supernatural love of God without substantially changing our nature. Charity would have no foothold in our nature. Clearly our capacity for natural love for God is the foundation for our obediential capacity to receive the most precious gift of charity. This capacity for natural love of God, and especially the distinction of the two loves, needs vigorous defense today.

The same considerations can be applied to love of neighbor. Man has a natural desire for communion with others and oblative love. Pope John Paul II, for example, has shown eloquently how, through this beautiful dimension of human existence, man (even on the natural plane) is in the image of the Holy Trinity. This natural desire for communion is capable of supernatural transformation into the virtue of fraternal charity and the communion of saints in Christ's mystical body, and ultimately into communion with the Blessed Trinity in Heaven. Our natural capacity for communion in society and in the family is the foundation for our obediential potency to enter into the intra-Trinitarian communion itself.

Natural End Transformed into the Beatific Vision

Being able to naturally know, freely love, and worship God, man is naturally capable of true although imperfect beatitude, lying in the loving contemplation of God through creation. Man can have no other end than God, because no finite goodness or truth can satisfy man's intellect and will, which are faculties open to unlimited goodness and truth. This natural capacity for happiness in the contemplation of God lies at the center of what is meant by man being made in God's image.

Precisely because man's happiness naturally lies in God, it can be elevated to a more perfect contemplation of God through grace and glory. At the beginning of his first major work, the *Commentary on the Sentences*, St. Thomas wrote:

> All who have thought rightly have held that the end of human life lies in the contemplation of God. However, the contemplation of God is twofold. One type is through creatures, and this is imperfect.... There is another contemplation of God, by which He is seen immediately in His essence, and this is per-

fect. It will be realized in heaven (*in patria*) and is possible for man according to faith.[41]

The difference between man's connatural and supernatural end lies in the *way in which God is contemplated*: *by our natural powers* in the case of our natural end, and *by the light of glory* in the beatific vision in the case of our supernatural end. Our connatural end is *elevated and immeasurably perfected* by our supernatural end.

The relation between the two ends is in no way extrinsic. Supernatural beatitude carries the natural trajectory to God, constituting natural happiness, infinitely farther, enabling it to attain to the secret of God's inner life and intimacy.

This shows us the great importance of the traditional Thomist thesis that beatitude is twofold: connatural and supernatural. The supernatural elevation is possible only because our natural end, as can be known by philosophy, already lies in a contemplation of God. The denial of the possibility of a natural end for man, as is very common today, would take away the foothold in nature for a supernatural extension of happiness through the beatific vision. Paradoxically, the denial of the possibility of a natural end for man would create a kind of "extrinsicism" (!), for it would mean that our supernatural end would not be the superabundant and divine continuation or extension of nature's proportionate tendency.

Natural Desire to See God Transformed into Theological Hope

Another beautiful and profound foundation for specific obediential potency is our natural desire to see God in His essence, which is surely one of the aspects in which we are made in His image. St. Thomas demonstrates that this desire is naturally aroused in man through the consideration of the existence and mystery of God, the First Cause. Nevertheless, this desire is in itself conditional and disproportionate without grace.

Now this natural desire to see God provides the foundation for a supernatural elevation. Precisely because we have a *natural* desire to see God, this desire can be elevated by grace. The effect of this elevation is the transformation of an inefficacious wish into the theological virtue of hope: a *supernatural* desire to see God. Because we naturally desire to see Him, we can be brought to efficaciously hope to see His face through the force of His promise given in revelation, and the aid of His grace.[42]

St. Thomas says that "God produces natural and supernatural desires in us. He gives us natural desires when He gives us a natural spirit belonging to human nature. . . . He gives us *supernatural desires* when he infuses in us a supernatural spirit, namely the Holy Spirit."[43] Through grace, our natural desires are elevated into supernatural ones.

Henri de Lubac thought that the natural desire to see God was incompatible with man having *only an obediential* potency for the vision of God, and he severely faulted the Thomist tradition starting with Cajetan for minimizing that desire. Nevertheless, the natural desire to see God is used by St. Thomas and the Thomistic tradition precisely as the *sign* of an *obediential potency* to see God, *specific* to the intellectual creature. This is the whole purpose of St. Thomas's argument in *Summa Contra Gentiles* III, 50 and *Summa Theologiae* I, q. 12, a. 1. It would be extremely unfitting if we did not have the root capacity for what we naturally desire. The natural desire to see God and man's specific obediential potency for supernatural gifts are in perfect harmony, for the former is a sign of the latter.

It should also be clarified that the Thomistic commentators of the sixteenth and seventeenth centuries who affirmed a specific obediential potency in man for the vision of God and other supernatural gifts did not deny a natural desire to see God. On the contrary, they all affirmed it, interpreting it as an elicited natural desire. The thesis that our capacity for the vision of God is a specific obediential potency in no way implies that man is closed in on himself, self-sufficient, or deprived of a natural desire to see God, as is said in much recent theological literature. In fact, these two doctrines together—the natural desire to see God and our specific obediential potency for it—provide the most adequate framework for understanding the harmony and distinction between nature and grace.

CHRIST REVEALS MAN TO HIMSELF

I would like to conclude by relating man's specific obediential potency for grace and glory with the text of *Gaudium et Spes* 22, which affirms that "only in the mystery of the Incarnate Word does the mystery of man take on light.... Christ, the final Adam, by the revelation of the mystery of the Father and His love, fully reveals man to man himself and makes his supreme calling clear."

Christ reveals man to himself above all by revealing the hidden dimension of his specific capacity to obey a divine call—a call to be elevated to a supernatural image and likeness of God and to a supernatural communion with Him.

Philosophy can never discover the mysterious dimensions of our obediential potency to be raised up to share in the divine life, nor, much less, God's plan to actually fulfill that potency. What it can do, however, is investigate the natural dimensions of our being made in God's image: our natural ability to know and love God, our social nature, our capacity for communion, our natural religiosity, our free will, our natural desire to see God. These serve as *praeambula fidei* with regard to supernatural anthropology. One of the great merits of the philosophy of Karol Wojtyla was his masterful analysis of aspects of the natural image of God in man, which then provides the categories to theological anthropology for understanding the supernatural elevation of that image.

Steven Long has used the analogy of a stained glass window in this regard.[44] Philosophy can show the outlines of the structure viewed from without. The eyes of theology can see the window from within, lit up by the light brought to us by Christ. The theologian can show how the fact that we are naturally in the image of God provides the foothold for the elevation of these faculties to an undreamed-of dimension.

Using the analogy of proper proportionality, which we have presented here with regard to understanding man as the image of God in the levels of nature, grace, and glory, we can go on to investigate the intimate relation between natural and supernatural virtue; between natural love of God and supernatural love; between natural religiosity and supernatural religion; between the natural societies of the nations, and the supernatural society of the Church; between the natural desire to know the essence of God, and the supernatural desire of infused hope; etc.

The more we contemplate the exquisite relation between the natural and the supernatural image of God in man, the more we will be struck by the intrinsic relation between the two, despite the awesome and ultimately ungraspable disproportion between them. Here we see the condescension of God: He takes our extremely finite spiritual faculties, and transforms them from within without destroying them, so that they can not only touch God the Creator, but God in His own inner life, God's own intimacy. In the words of Psalm 8: "What is man that thou art mindful of him, or the son of man that thou visitest him?"

NOTES

1. *The Mystery of the Supernatural*, trans. Rosemary Sheed (New York: Crossroad Pub./Herder & Herder, 1998), 140 [182 in the 1967 ed.]. "To avoid any confusion between the supernatural gift and the mere fulfillment a nature receives from some natural agent, we may join some of the moderns ... in specifying that the 'passive potentiality' which characterizes human nature in relation to that supernatural gift can be called 'specific obediential power'."

2. Ibid., 140—143 [182-185].

3. See also Ps 148:8: "Fire and hail, snow and frost, stormy wind fulfilling his command!"; Ps 104:30. See Florent Gaboriau, *Thomas d'Aquin en dialogue* (Paris: FAC éditions, 1993), 52.

4. Lib. I, pars 1, inq. 1, tract. 4, q. 3, c. 1, ad 2 (contra tertiam opinionem) (Ad Claras Aquas [Quaracchi], 1928), 1:233a-b.

5. See also *ST* III, q. 1, a. 3, ad 3; *De Veritate*, q. 8, a. 12, ad 4; *De Veritate*, q. 29, a. 3, ad 3; *De Veritate*, q. 8, a. 4, ad 13; *De Virtute*, q. un., a. 10, ad 13; *In III Sent.*, d. 1, q. 1, a. 3, ad 4.

6. St. Thomas often cites Averroes (in his commentary on IX *Metaphysics*) as the authority for this principle, as in *III Sent.*, d. 26, q. 1, a. 2. In *IV Sent.*, d. 43, q. 1, a. 1, qu^a. 3 (*Suppl.*, q. 75, a. 3), he attributes the principle directly to Aristotle in book IX of the *Metaphysics*, which would refer to ch. 1, 1046a19: "The potency of acting and being acted on is one." In *De pot.*, q. 6, a. 1, obj. 18, he explains the axiom as a consequence of Aristotle's principle according to which act and potency divide every genus, as stated in the *Physics* 3.1.201a10. For this principle in St. Thomas, see *SCG* III, c. 45, n. 6, Marietti 2222.

7. Denis Bradley follows de Lubac on this point, in *Aquinas on the Twofold Human Good* (Washington, DC: Catholic Univ. of America Press, 1997), 449: "Miracles, then, serve as the Thomistic prototype for understanding the obediential potency of a creature." Gilson also came to agree with de Lubac on this. See his letter to de Lubac of June 20, 1965, published in *Letters of Étienne Gilson to Henri de Lubac, Annotated by Henry de Lubac* (San Francisco: Ignatius, 1988), 81.

8. Cap. 1, n. 27, ad 7, in *Opera omnia*, vol. 37/1, ed. Paulus Simon (Monasterii Westfalorum in Aedibus Aschendorff, 1972), 13b, lines 58-66: "Ad videndum Deum non est in potentia secundum proportionem naturalem, *sed tantum secundum potentiam oboedientiae.*" St. Albert is responding to an objection arguing that the created mind should be capable of comprehending God, just as prime matter is capable of receiving every form. See L.-B. Gillon, "Aux origines de la 'Puissance Obédientielle'," *RT* 47 (1947): 304. This commentary was composed c. 1250 (see *Opera omnia*, 37/1:vi). See also G. Frénaud, "Esprit et grâce sanctifiante (Notes d'histoire doctrinale sur les premiers théologiens de l'École thomiste)," *La pensée catholique* 5 (1948): 25—47, for other early Thomists before Cajetan who teach that the capacity of the human soul for supernatural perfections is properly an obediential potency.

9. *ST* III, q. 1, a. 3, ad 3; *In III Sent.*, d. 1, q. 1, a. 3, ad 4; *In III Sent.*, d. 2, q. 1, a. 1.

10. *ST* III, q. 11, a. 1. For a discussion of this text, see Feingold, *Natural Desire to See God According to St. Thomas Aquinas and His Interpreters*, 2nd ed. (Ave Maria, FL: Sapientia Press of Ave Maria Univ., forthcoming), 141—146.

11. *De Veritate*, q. 29, a. 3, ad 3; see Feingold, *Natural Desire to See God*, 138—141.

12. *De Virtute*, q. un., a. 10, ad 13. For a discussion, see Feingold, *Natural Desire to See God*, 260-265; Mark Johnson, "St. Thomas, Obediential Potency, and the Infused Virtues: *De virtutibus in communi*, a. 10, ad 13," in *Thomistica*, ed. E. Manning (Leuven: Peeters, 1995), 27—34; Steven Long, "On the Loss, and the Recovery, of Nature as a Theonomic Principle: Reflections on the Nature/Grace Controversy," *Nova et Vetera* (English ed.) 5, no. 1 (2007): 163.

13. *De Veritate*, q. 8, a. 4, ad 13; see Feingold, *Natural Desire to See God*, 146—148.

14. *De Veritate*, q. 12, a. 3, ad 18.

15. *Comp. Theol.*, I, c. 104; see Feingold, *Natural Desire to See God*, 149—150.

16. This *terminology* is found only in the twentieth century, but the *notion* goes back to the thirteenth-century, as can be seen by the text of Bernard of Auvergne quoted above. Báñez, *Scholastica commentaria in Primam partem angelici doctoris D. Thomae usque ad 64 qu.* (Lyon, 1588), q. 12, a. 1, col. 213—214, also clearly expresses this notion. For the term "*specific* obediential potency," see P.A. Raineri, "De possibilitate videndi Deum per essentiam," *Divus Thomas* (Piacenza) 40 (1937): 3: "The potency for the vision of the divine essence is an obediential potency specific to man, insofar as he is an intellectual creature."

17. See *In III Sent.*, d. 2, q. 1, a. 1.

18. See *ST* III, q. 11, a. 1. Here St. Thomas is speaking about the obediential potency in the soul of Christ to receive all the gifts of wisdom and the other gifts of the Holy Spirit, as well as all knowledge of Revelation.

19. Cap. 5, 10 (*PL* 44, 968): "*Proinde posse habere fidem, sicut posse habere charitatem, naturae est hominum: habere autem fidem quemadmodum habere charitatem, gratiae est fidelium.*" Peter Lombard cites this in his *Sententiae*, II, d. 28, c. 3, n. 5, and comments: "*Quod non ita dictum est, tanquam ex libero arbitrio valeat haberi fides vel caritas, sed quia aptitudinem naturalem habet mens hominis ad credendum vel diligendum: quae Dei gratia praeventa, credit et diligit; quod sine gratia non valet.*"

20. Lib. 14, cap. 8 (*PL* 42, 1044): "*Eo quippe ipso imago ejus est, quo ejus capax est, ejusque particeps esse potest; quod tam magnum bonum, nisi per hoc quod imago ejus est, [intelligi] non potest.*" St. Bernard also expresses this idea of specific obediential potency in *De gratia et libero arbitrio*, chap. 1 (PL 182, 1002b): "God is the author of salvation; free will is only *capable* of it. No one could give it except God, nor is anything capable of receiving it, except free will."

21. *Mystery of the Supernatural*, 1998, 143.

22. *On the Heavens*, II, 12, 292a22.

23. *ST* I-II, q. 5, a. 5, ad 2. See the parallel text, *De malo*, q. 5, a. 1: "Therefore, the rational creature transcends all other creatures in this, that he is capable of the supreme good through the vision and enjoyment of God, although the proper principles of his nature are insufficient to attain this end, for which he needs the aid of divine grace."

24. The same idea is expressed in *ST* I-II, q. 109, a. 4, ad 2: "What we can do with the divine assistance, is not completely impossible for us; for according to the Philosopher: 'What we can do through our friends, in a certain sense we can do by ourselves'" (*Nich. Ethics*, III, 3, 1112b27).

25. Bishop of Clermont in the late thirteenth and early fourteenth century.

26. *Impugnationes*, Ms. Vat. Borgh. 298, fol. 74rb, in L.-B. Gillon, "Aux origines de la 'Puissance Obédientielle'," *RT* 47 (1947): 308. See also fol. 74va (Gillon, 309): "Whether this obediential potency or capacity is the same as the being of the will? One should reply in the affirmative, except that this capacity adds to the essence a relation to the divine power such that God can do in it whatever He wills. . . . This potency is not natural to the will, except in a broad sense, according to which we say that obediential potency is natural in that, improperly speaking, it is natural that God do whatever He wills in and with the creature."

27. *Defensiones theologiae divi Thomae Aquinatis*, vol. 1, in Prol., q. 1, a. 2, B, n. 5 (Turin, 1900), 18b-19a. At about the same time (1430-35), Denis the Carthusian interprets the capacity of the intellectual creature to be raised and properly inclined to the vision of God, as an *obediential potency*: "Therefore certain theologians of not inconsiderable genius say that all created natures have a certain innate obediential power, by which they obey the command of their omnipotent Creator, also in the things that are above nature. This should also be understood to be the case in the created mind. The nature itself of the soul with relation to the supernatural munificence and absolute power of God obtains an appetite and capacity for supernatural beatitude, and is capable and desirous of those things to which it has been supernaturally instituted and ordered." *De puritate et felicitate animae*, a. 59, 40:433a.

28. Commentary on *ST* I, q. 1, a. 1, n. X, Leonine ed., 8.

29. Commentary on *SCG* I, c. 5, n. V/4, Leonine ed., 16b.

30. Báñez, *Scholastica commentaria in Primam partem Summae Theologicae S. Thomae Aquinatis*, q. 12, a. 1, ed. Luis Urbano (Madrid: Editorial F.E.D.A., 1934), 250.

31. Matthias Joseph Scheeben, *Handbuch der Katholischen Dogmatik*, bk. 3, *Schöpfungslehre*, §171, n. 925, in *Gesammelte Schriften*, 3rd ed. (Freiburg: Herder, 1961), 5: 440—441. See also 438: "This receptivity, which among all created natures only belongs to spiritual beings, is *rooted in their specific perfection*, which marks out spiritual natures from all others."

32. "Obediential Potency, Human Knowledge, and the Natural Desire for God," *International Philosophical Quarterly* 37 (March 1997): 45. See also "On the Possibility of a Purely Natural End for Man: A Response to Denis Bradley," *The Thomist* 64 (2000): 214—218.

33. "Nature as a Theonomic Principle," *Nova et Vetera* 5 (2007): 165—166.

34. See, for example, Stephen J. Duffy, *The Graced Horizon. Nature and Grace in Modern Catholic Thought* (Collegeville, MN: The Liturgical Press, 1992), 43.

35. *ST* I, q. 93, a. 4: "I answer that, since man is said to be the image of God by reason of his intellectual nature, he is the most perfectly like God according to that in which he can best imitate God in his intellectual nature. Now the intellectual nature imitates God chiefly in this, that God understands and loves Himself. Wherefore we see that the image of God is in man in *three ways. First*, inasmuch as man possesses a natural aptitude for understanding and loving God; and this aptitude consists in the very nature of the mind, which is common to all men. *Secondly*, inasmuch as man actually and habitually knows and loves God, though imperfectly; and this image consists in the conformity of grace. *Thirdly*, inasmuch as man knows and loves God perfectly; and this image consists in the likeness of glory."

36. The supernatural level itself has two dimensions: grace and glory. St. Thomas therefore speaks of the image of God in man in three dimensions: nature, grace, and glory. This distinction of three senses of *imago Dei* was already traditional. Peter Lombard has this distinction in his *Glossa* on Ps 4:7 (PL 191, 88): "Distinguitur triplex imago: creationis, recreationis, et similitudinis."

37. The *praeambula fidei* require vigorous defense today, as Ralph McInerny has argued in his recent book *Praeambula Fidei: Thomism and the God of the Philosophers* (Washington, DC: Catholic Univ. of America Press, 2006).

38. See *De spe*, q. un., a. 1, ad 9; *ST* I-II, q. 62, a. 1, ad 3; I-II, q. 109, a. 3, ad 1.

39. *In III Sent.*, d. 27, q. 2, a. 2, ad 4.

40. See *ST* I, q. 60, a. 5, ad 4: "God, insofar as He is the universal good, from Whom every natural good depends, is loved by every being with natural love. Insofar as He is the good which of its very nature beatifies all with supernatural beatitude, He is loved with the love of charity"; I, q. 62, a. 2, ad 1; I, q. 63, a. 1, ad 3; I-II, q. 62, a. 1, ad 3; I-II, q. 109, a. 3, ad 1: "Charity loves God above all things in a higher way than nature does. For nature loves God above all things inasmuch as He is the *beginning and the end of natural good*; whereas charity loves Him, as He is the *object of beatitude*, and inasmuch as man has a spiritual fellowship with God"; II-II, q. 26, a. 3: "The good we receive from God is twofold, the good of nature, and the good of grace. Now the *participation in natural goods* bestowed on us by God is the foundation of *natural love*, in virtue of which…man, so long as his nature remains unimpaired, loves God above all things and more than himself.... This is realized much more with regard to the *friendship of charity* which is *based on participation in the gifts of grace*"; *Quodl.*, I, q. 4, a. 3 [8], ad 1: "To love God as He is the principle of all being, pertains to natural love; but to love God as He is the object of beatitude, belongs to gratuitous love"; *De car.*, q. un., a. 2, ad 16: "Love of the supreme good, *insofar as it is the principle of natural being*, is in us by nature. However, *insofar as it is the object of that beatitude* which surpasses the entire capacity of created nature, it is not in us by nature, but is above nature"; *De spe*, q. un., a. 1, ad 9: "To love God above all things can be understood in two ways. One way, insofar as the divine good is the *principle and end of all natural being*… In another way one can love God above all, *insofar as God is the object of beatitude*…and such love is the act of charity, which no creature can realize without grace"; *In I Cor*, c. 13, v. 13, lect. 4 (Marietti 806): "Every love consists in a certain union. ... Now we have a twofold union with God. One is *with regard to the goods of nature*, which we participate in here from Him. The other is *with regard to beatitude*, insofar as here we are participants by grace in the supernal happiness.... And according to the first participation in God, there is a *natural friendship* insofar as each thing, insofar as it is, *desires God as first cause and supreme good*, as its end. Based on the second kind of participation there is the love of charity"; *De malo*, q. 16, a. 4, ad 14 and 15; *De malo*, q. 5, a. 3, ad 4; *Comp. theol.*, I, q. 174, n. 2: (speaking of a natural love for God even in the damned) "Thus it is necessary that the intellect of man placed in that extreme misery have some knowledge of God and some

love of God, *insofar as He is the principle of natural perfections*, which is natural love, but not for Him in Himself, nor *insofar as He is the principle of virtues and graces*"; *In II Sent.*, d. 3, q. 4, ad 1: "To love God as He is the principle of all being, pertains to natural love; but to love God as He is the object of beatitude, belongs to gratuitous love"; *In II Sent.*, d. 33, q. 2, a. 2, ad 5; *In III Sent.*, d. 27, q. 2, a. 2, ad 4. See Gagnebet, M. R., "L'amour naturel de Dieu chez saint Thomas et ses contemporains," *Revue Thomiste* 48 (1948): 432—434.

41. *In I Sent.*, d. 1, q. 1. See also *ST* I, q. 62, a. 1; *De ver.*, q. 14, a. 2.

42. This is beautifully stated by de Lubac, in *Surnaturel*, 483: "The entire problem of the spiritual life is to liberate this desire, and then to transform it: a radical conversion, *metanoia* without which there is no entrance into the Kingdom."

43. Lectio 2 (v. 5), Marietti 160-161. St. Thomas is commenting on 2 Cor 5:2-4.

44. "On the Possibility of a Purely Natural End for Man: A Response to Denis Bradley," *The Thomist* 64 (2000): 236.

BIBLIOGRAPHY

Abbot, Walter, ed., *The Documents of Vatican II: In a New and Definitive Translation, With Commentaries and Notes by Catholic, Protestant and Orthodox Authorities*, trans. by Joseph Gallagher. New York: Herder & Herder, Association Press, 1966.

Aertsen, Jan. "The Circulation-motive and Man in the Thought of Thomas Aquinas." In *L'homme et son Univers au Moyen age I*, ed. Christian Wenin. Louvain-La-Neuve: Editions de l'Institut Supérieur de Philosophie, (1986): 432—39.

Albacete, Lorenzo. "The Relevance of Christ or the *Sequela Christi*." *Communio* 2 (1994): 252—264.

Ashley, Benedict. "Fundamental Option and/or Commitment to Ultimate End." *Philosophy and Theology* 10 (1997): 113—141.

Báñez, Domingo. *Scholastica commentaria in Primam partem angelici doctoris D. Thomae usque ad 64 qu.* Lyon, 1588.

———. *Scholastica commentaria in Primam partem Summae Theologicae S. Thomae Aquinatis*, ed. Luis Urbano. Madrid: Editorial F.E.D.A., 1934.

Barton, John. "Source Criticism: OT," and Dietrich-Alex Koch, "Source Criticism: NT." In *Anchor Bible Dictionary* vol. 6, ed. David Noel Freedman. New York: Doubleday, 1992.

Benson, Robert. *The Paradoxes of Catholicism*. Fort Collins, CO: Roman Catholic Books, 2000.

Boadt, Lawrence. *Reading the Old Testament: An Introduction*. New York: Paulist Press, 1984.

Bonaventure. *Commentarius in Evangelium S. Lucae*, vol. 7, *Opera Omnia*. Quaracchi, 1895.

Borden, Sarah. *Edith Stein*. New York: Continuum Books, 2003.

Bouyer, Louis. *The Spirit and Forms of Protestantism*. Princeton, NJ: Scepter Press, 2001.

———. *Word and Sacraments in Protestantism and Catholicism*. San Franciso: Ignatius Press, 2004.

Boyle, John. "Aquinas' Roman Commentary on Peter Lombard." *Anuario Filosofico* 39 (2006): 477—496.

Boyle, Leonard E. "'Alia lectura fratris Thome.'" *Mediaeval Studies* 45 (1983): 418—429.

Bradley, Denis. *Aquinas on the Twofold Human Good: Reason and Human Happiness in Aquinas's Moral Science*. Washington, D.C.: The Catholic University of America Press, 1997.

———. *Aquinas on the Twofold Human Good*. Washington, D.C.: The Catholic University of America Press, 1997.

Campbell, Antony and Mark O'Brien. "1—2 Samuel." In *The International Bible Commentary: A Catholic and Ecumenical Commentary for the Twenty-First Century*, ed. William Farmer. Collegeville, MN: The Liturgical Press, 1998.

Cessario, Romanus. *The Godly Image: Christ and Salvation in Catholic Thought from Anselm to Aquinas, Studies in Historical Theology VI*. Petersham, MA: St. Bede's Publications, 1990.

———. *The Moral Virtues and Theological Ethics*. Notre Dame, IN: University of Notre Dame Press, 1991.

Chenu, M.-D. *Towards Understanding St. Thomas*, trans. A. M. Landre and D. Hughes. Chicago: Henry Regnery Company, 1964.

Coerver, Robert F. *The Quality of Facility in the Moral Virtues*. Ph.D. diss., Washington, D.C.: The Catholic University of America, 1946.

De Koninck, Charles. *On the Primacy of the Common Good: Against the Personalists*, trans. Sean Collins. *The Aquinas Review* 4, no. 1 (1997): 14—71.

De Lubac, Henri. "Obediential Potency, Human Knowledge, and the Natural Desire for God." *International Philosophical Quarterly* 37 (March 1997): 45—63.

———. *Augustinisme et théologie moderne*. Paris: Aubier, 1965.

———. *Surnaturel etude historiques*. Paris: Aubier, 1946.

———. *The Mystery of the Supernatural*, trans. Rosemary Sheed. New York: Crossroad Pub./Herder & Herder, 1998.

De Molina, Luis. *Liberi arbitrii cum gratiae donis, divina praescientia, providentia, praedestinatione et reprobatione Concordia*. Lisbon, 1588.

Dewan, Lawrence. "St. Thomas, John Finnis, and the Political Common Good." *The Thomist* 64 (2000): 337—374.

DiNoia, J. A., and Romanus Cessario. *Veritatis Splendor and the Renewal of Moral Theology*. Chicago: Midwest Theological Forum, 1999.

———. "Karl Rahner." In *The Modern Theologian: An Introduction to Christian Theology in the Twentieth Century*, vol. 1, ed. David F. Ford. Oxford: Basil Blackwell, 1989.

Dondaine, H.F. "'Alia lectura fratris Thome? *(Super I Sent.)*'." *Mediaeval Studies* 42 (1980): 308—386.

Duffy, Stephen J. *The Graced Horizon: Nature and Grace in Modern Catholic Thought*. Collegeville, MN: The Liturgical Press, 1992.

Dulles, Avery. "Faith and Reason: From Vatican I to John Paul II." In *The Two Wings of Catholic Thought*. Washington, D.C.: The Catholic University of America Press, 2003.

Faricy, Robert. "The Trinitarian Indwelling." *The Thomist* 35 (1971): 369—404.

Feingold, Lawrence. *Natural Desire to See God According to St. Thomas Aquinas and His Interpreters*. Rome: Apollinare Studi, 2001.

Fitzmyer, Joseph. *The Biblical Commission's Document "The Interpretation of the Bible in the Church": Text and Commentary*. no. 18. Subsidia Biblica. Rome: Editrice Pontificio Istituto Biblico, 1995.

Fortin, Ernest. "Augustine, Thomas Aquinas, and the Problem in the Natural Law." *Collected Essays, II: Classical Christianity and the Political Order*, ed. J. Brian Benestad. New York: Rowman & Littlefield, 1996.

Frénaud, G. "Esprit et grâce sanctifiante (Notes d'histoire doctrinale sur les premiers théologiens de l'École thomiste)." *La pensée catholique*. 5 (1948): 25—47.

Friedman, Richard Elliott. "Torah [Pentateuch]." In *Anchor Bible Dictionary*, ed. David Noel Freedman. New York: Doubleday, 1992.

Froelich, Gregory. "The Equivocal Status of the *Bonum Commune*." *New Scholasticism* 63 (1989): 38—57.

Füchs, Josef. *Moral Demands and Personal Obligations*, trans. by Brian McNeil. Washington, D.C.: Georgetown University Press, 1993.

———. "Basic Freedom and Morality." In *Human Values and Christian Morality*. Dublin: Gill, 1968.

———. "Good Acts and Good Persons." In *Considering Veritatis Splendor*, ed. John Wilkins. Cleveland: Pilgrim Press, 1994.

———. *Christian Morality: The Word Becomes Flesh*. Washington, D.C.: Georgetown University Press, 1987.

Gaboriau, Florent. *Thomas d'Aquin en dialogue.* Paris: FAC Éditions, 1993.
Gagnebet, M. R., "L'amour naturel de Dieu chez saint Thomas et ses contemporains." *Revue Thomiste* 48 (1948): 432—434.
Gaillardetz, Richard. "Richard McCormick and the Moral Magisterium." *Louvain Studies* 25 (Winter 2000): 356—361.
Garrigou-Lagrange, Reginald. *Reality,* trans. Patrick Cummins. St. Louis: Herder, 1958.
———. "La nouvelle théologie, où va-t-elle?" *Angelicum* (1946): 126—145.
Gauthier, René. "Quelques questions à propos du commentaire de S. Thomas sur le *De anima.*" *Angelicum* 51 (1974): 419—472.
Geffré, Claude. *Le Christianisme au risque de l'interprétation.* Paris: Editions du Cerf, 1983.
Gese, Hartmut. "Die Herkunft des Herrenmahls." In *Zur biblischen Theologie: Alttestamentliche Vortrage.* Tubingen: J.C.B. Mohr, 1989.
Gillon, L.-B. "Aux origines de la 'Puissance Obédientielle'." *Revue Thomiste* 55 (1947): 304—310.
Gilson, Étienne and Henri de Lubac. *Letters of Étienne Gilson to Henri de Lubac, Annotated by Henri de Lubac.* San Francisco: Ignatius Press, 1988.
———. *Reason and Revelation in the Middle Ages.* New York: Charles Scribner's Sons, 1938.
———. *Thomist Realism & the Critique of Knowledge,* trans. Mark A. Wauck. San Francisco: Ignatius Press, 1986.
Grabowski, John S. and Michael J. Naughton, "Catholic Social and Sexual Ethics: Inconsistent or Organic?" *The Thomist* 57, no. 4 (1993) 555—578.
Gula, Richard. *What Are They Saying About Moral Norms?* New York: Paulist Press, 1982.
Harris, Stephen. *Understanding the Bible.* Mountain View, CA: Mayfield Publishing Company, 2000.
Hill, William. "Uncreated Grace—A Critique of Karl Rahner." *The Thomist* 27 (1963): 333—356.
———. *Proper Relations to the Indwelling Persons.* Washington, D.C.: Thomist Press, 1955.
Hittinger, Russell. "Natural Law and Catholic Moral Theology." *A Preserving Grace,* ed. by Michael Cromartie. Grand Rapids, MI: Eerdmans Publishing Co., (1997): 1—30.
———. *The First Grace: Rediscovering the Natural Law in a Post-Christian World.* Wilmington, DE: ISI Books, 2003.
Hütter, Reinhard. "The Directedness of Reason(ing) and the Metaphysics of Creation." In *Reason and the Reasons of Faith,* ed. Paul J. Griffiths and Reinhard Hütter. London/New York: T & T Clark International, 2005.
Inglis, John. "Aquinas' Replication of the Acquired Moral Virtues: Rethinking the Standard Philosophical Interpretation of Moral Virtue in Aquinas." *Journal of Religious Ethics* 27 (1999): 3—27.
John of St. Thomas. *Cursus Theologicus I.* Paris: Ludovicus Vivés, 1883.
John Paul II. *In Pontificia Universitate S. Thomae Aquinatis, Saeculo Expleto a Datis Encyclicis Aeterni Patris.*
———. *Encyclical Letter, Dominum et Vivificantem: On the Holy Spirit and the Life of the Church in the World.* 1986.
———. *Encyclical Letter, Fides et Ratio: On the Relationship Between Faith and Reason.* Boston: Pauline Books and Media, 1998.
———. *Encyclical Letter, Veritatis Splendor: The Splendor of Truth.* Boston: Pauline Books and Media, 1993.
———. *Motu Proprio Letter, Ad Tuendam Fidem. 1998.*

Johnson, Mark. "St. Thomas, Obediential Potency, and the Infused Virtues: *De virtutibus in communi*, a. 10, ad 13." In *Thomistica*, ed. E. Manning. Leuven: Peeters, 1995.

Justin Martyr. *Second Apology*, 13, *Dialogue with Trypho*, 4. In *Writings of Saint Justin Martyr*, trans. Thomas B. Falls, *The Fathers of the Church*, 6. New York: Christian Heritage, 1948.

Keenan, James F. *Goodness and Rightness in Thomas Aquinas's Summa Theologiae*. Washington, D.C.: Georgetown Press, 1992.

Knox, Ronald. *The Beliefs of Catholics*. New York: Sheed & Ward, 1940.

———. *The Creed in Slow Motion*. New York: Sheed & Ward, 1949.

Komonchak, Joseph A. "Theology and Culture at Mid-Century: The Example of Henri de Lubac." *Theological Studies* 51 (1990): 579—602.

Koterski, Joseph. "The Challenge to Metaphysics in *Fides et Ratio*," in *The Two Wings of Catholic Thought: Essays on Fides et Ratio*, ed. David Ruel Foster and Joseph Koterski, S.J. Washington, D.C.: The Catholic University of America Press, 2003.

Labourdette, M.-M. and Nicolas, M.-J. "L'analogie de la vérité et l'unité de la science théologique." *Revue Thomiste* 55 (1947): 417—466.

———. "La théologie, intelligence de la foi." *Revue Thomiste* 46 (1946): 5—44.

Laporta, Jorge. *La Destinée de la nature humane selon Thomas d'Aquin*. Paris: J. Vrin, 1965.

Levering, Matthew. *Scripture and Metaphysics: Aquinas and the Renewal of Trinitarian Theology*. Malden, MA: Blackwell Publishing, 2004.

Long, Steven. "Obediential Potency, Human Knowledge, and the Natural Desire for God." *International Philosophical Quarterly* 37 (1997): 45—64.

———. "On the Loss, and the Recovery, of Nature as a Theonomic Principle: Reflections on the Nature/Grace Controversy." *Nova et Vetera* 5, n. 1 (2007): 133—184.

———. "On the Possibility of a Purely Natural End for Man: A Response to Denis Bradley." *The Thomist* 64 (2000): 211—237.

———. "Providence, liberté et loi naturelle." *Revue Thomiste* 102 (2002): 355—406.

Lottin, Odon. *Psychologie et morale aux XIIe et XIIIe siècles*. Louvain: Abbaye du Mont Cesar, 1949.

Malloy, Christopher. "Participation and Theology: A Response to Schindler's 'What's the Difference?'" *The Saint Anselm Journal* 3.1 (Fall, 2005): 38—61.

Mansini, Guy. "Balthasar and the Theodramatic Enrichment of the Trinity." *The Thomist* 64 (2000): 499—519.Mansini, Guy and Lawrence J. Welch. "Revelation, Natural Law, and Homosexual Unions." *Nova et Vetera* 2 (2004): 337—366.

Maritain, Jacques. *The Person and the Common Good*. Notre Dame, IN: University of Notre Dame Press, 1985.

Martin, Francis. "Spirit and Flesh in the Doing of Theology." *Journal of Pentecostal Theology* 18 (2001): 5—31.

Martin, Francis and Sean McEvenue. "Truth Told in the Bible: Biblical Poetics and the Question of Truth." *The International Bible Commentary: A Catholic and Ecumenical Commentary for the Twenty-First Century*, ed. William Farmer. Collegeville, MN: The Liturgical Press, 1998.

McCool, Gerald. *From Unity to Pluralism: The Internal Evolution of Thomism*. New York: Fordham University Press, 1989.

———. *Ninetheenth-Century Scholasticism: The Search for a Unitary Method*. New York: Fordham University Press 1977.

McCormick, Richard. "Medicaid and Abortion." *Theological Studies* (December, 1984): 715—721.

———. *The Critical Calling*. Washington DC: Georgetown University Press, 2006.

McDermott, John. "Metaphysical Conundrums at the Root of Moral Disagreement." *Irish Theological Quarterly* 71 (1990): 713—42.

McHugh, John and Charles J. Callan. *Moral Theology: A Complete Course*. London: Herder, 1929.

McInerny, Ralph. *Aquinas and Analogy*. Washington, D.C.: The Catholic University of America Press, 1996.

———. "Scotus and Univocity." *Being and Predication: Thomistic Interpretations*, vol. 16. Studies in Philosophy and the History of Philosophy. Washington, D.C.: The Catholic University of America Press, 1986.

———. *Praeambula Fidei: Thomism and the God of the Philosophers*. Washington, D.C.: The Catholic University of America Press, 2006.

Melina, Livio. *Sharing in Christ's Virtues: For a Renewal of Moral Theology in the Light of 'Veritatis Splendor.'* Washington, D.C.: The Catholic University of America Press, 2001.

Milbank, John. "Intensities." *Modern Theology* 15 (1999): 445—497.

———. *Radical Orthodoxy? A Catholic Enquiry*, ed. Laurence Paul Hemming. Aldershot: Ashgate, 2000.

Mirkes, Renée. "Aquinas' Doctrine of Moral Virtue and Its Significance for Theories of Facility." *The Thomist* 61 (1999):189—218.

Nichols, Aidan. "Thomism and *La Nouvelle Théologie*." *The Thomist* 64 (2000): 1—19.

O'Brien, Thomas. "'*Sacra Doctrina*' Revisited: The Context of Medieval Education." *The Thomist* 41 (1977): 475—509.

O'Connell, Timothy. "The Question of *Grundentscheidung*." *Philosophy and Theology* 10 (1997): 143—168.

O'Meara, Thomas. "Grace as a Theological Structure in the *Summa Theologiae* of Thomas Aquinas." *Recherches de théologie ancienne et médiévale* 55 (1988): 130—153.

———. "Karl Rahner: Some Audiences and Sources for His Theology," *Communio* 18 (1991): 237—251.

Palakeel, Joseph. "The Use of Analogy in Theological Discourse: An Ecumenical Investigation." *Tesi Gregoriana Serie Teologia* 4. Rome: Editrice Pontificia Università Gregoriana, 1995.

Paul VI. *Dei Verbum*. 1965.

Pearce, Joseph. *Literary Converts*. San Francisco: Ignatius Press, 2000.

Peers, E. Allison. *The Complete Works of Saint Teresa of Jesus* vol. 1. New York: Sheed & Ward, 1946.

Pereira, Jose. "Thomism and the Magisterium: From *Aeterni Patris* to *Veritatis Splendor*." *Logos: A Journal of Catholic Thought and Culture* 5, no. 3. (Summer 2002): 146—183.

Pinckaers, Servais. *The Sources of Christian Ethics*. Trans. Mary Thomas Noble, O.P. Washington, D.C.: The Catholic University of America Press, 1995.

Porter, Jean. "Moral Language and the Language of Grace: The Fundamental Option and the Virtue of Charity." *Philosophy and Theology* 10 (1997): 169—198.

———. "The Subversion of Virtue: Acquired and Infused Virtue in the *Summa Theologiae*." *Annual of the Society of Christian Ethics* (1992): 19—41.

Raineri, P.A. "De possibilitate videndi Deum per essentiam," *Divus Thomas* 40 (1937): 3—21; 113—128.

Rhonheimer, Martin. *Natural Law and Practical Reason*, trans. by Gerald Malsbary. New York: Fordham University Press, 2000.

Rocca, Gregory. "Analogy as Judgment and Faith in God's Incomprehensibility: A Study in the Theological Epistemology of Thomas Aquinas." Ph.D. Diss., Catholic University of America, 1989.

———. *Speaking the Incomprehensible God: Thomas Aquinas on the Interplay of Positive and Negative Theology*. Washington, D.C.: The Catholic University of America Press, 2004.

Scheeben, Mathias Joseph. *Handbuch der Katholischen Dogmatik*, Bk. 3, *Schöpfungslehre*, in *Gesammelte Schriften*, 3rd ed. Freiburg: Herder, 1961.

Schindler, D.C. *Hans Urs von Balthasar and the Dramatic Structure of Truth: A Philosophical Investigation*. New York: Fordham University Press, 2004.

Selling, Joseph A. "The Context and Arguments of *Veritatis splendor*." In Joseph Selling and Jan Jans (eds.) *The Splendor of Accuracy*. Grand Rapids, MI: Eerdmans, 1994.

Sheed, Frank and Maisie Ward. *Catholic Evidence Training Outlines*. New York: Sheed & Ward, 1934.

Sokolowski, Robert. *Presence and Absence: A Philosophical Investigation of Language and Being*. Bloomington, IN: Indiana University Press, 1978.

Stein, Edith. *Finite and Eternal Being*. Washington, D.C.: ICS Publications, 2002.

———. *On the Problem of Empathy*. Washington, D.C.: ICS Publications, 1989.

Steinmueller, John E. *Special Introduction to the Old Testament 2, A Companion to Scripture Studies*. New York: Joseph F. Wagner, Inc., 1942.

———. *General Introduction to the Bible*, vol. 1. *A Companion to Scripture Studies*. New York: Joseph F. Wagner, Inc., 1941.

Suárez, Francisco. *Disputationes Metaphysicae*, in *Opera omnia*, vol. 26. Paris: Vivès, 1866.

Sullivan, Francis. "Infallible Teaching on Moral Issues? Reflections on *Veritatis splendor* and *Evangelium Vitae*." In *Choosing Life: A Dialogue on Evangelium Vitae*, ed. Kevin Wm. Wildes and Alan C. Mitchell. Washington, D.C.: Georgetown University Press, 1997.

———. *Magisterium: Teaching Authority in the Catholic Church*. New York: Paulist Press, 1983.

Teresa of Avila. *The Book of Her Life* in *The Collected Works of St. Teresa of Avila*, trans. Kieran Kavanaugh and Otilio Rodriguez.Washington, D.C.: ICS Publications, 1976—85.

Thomas Aquinas. *Lectura romana in primum Sententiarum Petri Lombardi*, ed. Leonard E. Boyle and John F. Boyle. Toronto: Pontifical Institute of Mediaeval Studies, 2006.

Torrell, J.-P. Introduction to Leonard E. Boyle's *Facing History: A Different Thomas Aquinas*. Louvain-La-Neuve: Federation Interantionale des Instituts d'Etudes Medievales, 2000.

Tracy, David. *The Analogical Imagination: Christian Theology and the Culture of Pluralism*. New York: Crossroad, 1981.

Tück, Jan-Heiner. "The Utmost: On the Possibilities and Limits of a Trinitarian Theology of the Cross." *Communio* 30 (2003): 430—451.

Van Steenberghen, Fernand. "Comment être thomiste aujourd'hui?" *Revue Philosophique de Louvain* 85 (1987): 171—197.

Vandervelde, George. "The Grammar of Grace: Karl Rahner as a Watershed in Contemporary Theology." *Theological Studies* 49 (1988): 445—459.

Von Balthasar, Hans Urs. *Dramatis Personae: Man in God*, vol. 2, *Theo-Drama: Theological Dramatic Theory*, trans. Graham Harrison. San Francisco: Ignatius Press, 1990.

Walgrave, Jan H. *Unfolding Revelation: The Nature of Doctrinal Development*. Philadelphia: Westminster, 1972.

Wallace, William. *Causality and Scientific Explanation*. Vol. I: Medieval and Early Classical Science. Ann Arbor, MI: The University of Michigan Press, 1972.

Weisheipl, James. "The Meaning of *Sacra Doctrina* in the *Summa Theologiae* I, q.1." *The Thomist* 38 (1974): 49—80.
———. *Friar Thomas D'Aquino*. New York: Doubleday, 1983.
Wright, N.T. *The Resurrection of the Son of God*. Minneapolis: Fortress Press, 2003.

INDEX OF NAMES

Abbot, Walter, 23n, 217
Aertsen, Jan A., 51n, 217
Alan of Lille, 149
Albacete, Lorenzo, 97, 100n, 217
Albert the Great, St., 200, 206, 212n
Alexander of Hales, 198
Anselm, St., 53n, 77
Aquinas, Thomas, iii, iv, ix—xiii, 20, 26—29, 31—33, 35, 37, 38n, 40—41, 43—53, 55—63, 79—80, 82n, 83n, 85, 88—94, 99n, 100n, 102—105, 111, 113n, 114n, 121, 142n, 143—144, 146—155, 157—165, 170, 174—175, 178, 180—181, 197—200, 202—212, 214—215, 217—223
Aristotle, 17, 20, 47, 52n, 53n, 65, 110, 145, 147, 160, 161, 164, 165n, 180, 203, 211n
Ashley, Benedict, 146, 157n, 217
Athanasius, 51n
Augustine, 64, 90, 100n, 104, 137, 151, 157n, 174n, 202—204, 206—207, 218
Averroes, 211n

Báñez, Domingo, 53n, 204, 206—207, 212n, 213n, 217
Barron, Padre, 53n
Barton, John, 107, 116n, 217
Baum, Gregory, 98n
Benson, Robert Hugh, xii, 119, 121, 125—127, 129, 130n, 217
Berger, David, 60
Bernard de Auvergne, 204, 211n
Biffi, Giacomo, 26
Blondel, Maurice, 18, 38n, 50n, 121
Boadt, Lawrence, 112n, 116n, 217
Böckle, Franz, 98n
Bonaventure, 115n, 217
Borden, Sarah, 191n, 193n, 217
Bouillard, Henri, 41n
Bouyer, Louis, 119, 129n, 217
Boyle, John F., iii, ix, x, 55, 61n, 217, 222, 229

Boyle, John P., 98n
Boyle, Leonard, 55—56, 61n, 217, 222, 229
Bradley, Denis, 41n, 92, 100n, 211n, 215n, 217, 220

Cajetan, 50, 197, 200, 203—204, 206, 209, 212n
Callan, Charles, 142n, 221
Campbell, Antony, 116n, 217
Capreolus, John, 204, 206, 229
Chenu, M.D., 44, 46—48, 51n, 218
Chesterton, G.K., 119
Chirico, P., 98n
Cessario, Romanus, iii, v, ix—x, 43, 53n, 142n, 158n, 217—218, 229
Clement IV, 46
Clement of Alexandria, 21
Coerver, Robert, 158n, 218
Comte, Auguste, 18
Curran, Charles E., 98n

Daniélou, Jean, 41n, 50n
David, J., 98n
De Koninck, Charles, 166n, 218
De Lubac, Henri, 30, 34—37, 41n, 42n, 50n, 63—64, 197—199, 203, 206, 209, 211n, 215n, 218—220
De Molina, Luis, 39n, 218
Dewan, Lawrence, 166n, 218
Deavel, Catherine Jack, iv, xiii, 177, 229
Deavel, David Paul, iii, xii, 119, 229
Demmer, Klaus, 98n
Denis the Carthusian, 213n
Descartes, Rene, 51n, 186—187 193n
Didymus the Blind, 44, 48, 51n
DiNoia, J.A., 50n, 142n, 218
Dionysius, 101, 200
Dondaine, Antoine, 55—57, 59
Dondaine, Hyacinthe, 56—57, 59, 62n, 218
Droge, Arthur, 79, 82n
Duffy, Stephen J., 213n, 218

Dulles, Avery, ii, iii, v, ix—xi, 17, 63, 74, 82n, 98n, 113n, 119—121, 218, 229—230

Ephrem the Syrian, 101

Faricy, Robert, 51n, 218
Feingold, Lawrence, iv, ix, xiii, 197, 212n, 218, 230
Fessard, Gaston, 41n
Feuerbach, Ludwig, 18
Finley, John, 113n
Fitzmeyer, Joseph A., 115n
Fortin, Ernest, 99n, 218
Frege, Gottlob, 59
Foster, David Ruel, 81n, 99n, 113n, 130n, 220
Freedman, David Noel, 116n, 217—218
Friedman, Richard Elliott, 116n, 218
Froelich, Gregory, 165n, 218
Fuchs, Josef, 33—34, 40n, 87, 89, 91, 98n, 99n, 144—147, 153—158, 218

Gagnebet, M. R., 215n, 219
Gaillardetz, Richard, 98n, 99n, 219
Garrigou-Lagrange, Reginald, 31, 35, 38n, 42n, 63, 65, 219
Gauthier, Rene A., 52n, 219
Geffré, Claude, 51n, 219
Gese, Hartmut, 116n, 219
Gilson, Étienne, 41n, 51n, 117n, 211n, 219
Goyette, John, iv, xii, 159, 230
Grabowski, John, 142n, 219
Grant, Matthews, iv, xii, 167, 230
Grisez, Germain, 87, 98n
Gula, Richard, 142n, 219

Häring, Bernard, 34
Harris, Stephen, 108, 112n, 116n, 217
Harrison, Graham, 117n, 222
Hegel, Georg W.F., 18, 30
Heidegger, Martin, x, 18, 43, 64
Hellin, José, 26
Hill, William, 50n, 52n, 219
Hittinger, Russell, 34, 40n, 88—90, 92, 142n, 219
Hobbes, Thomas, 165n
Hugh of St. Victor, 47, 115n
Hume, David, 30

Hütter, Reinhard, 82n, 219

Inglis, John, 158n, 219

James, William, 22
Janssens, Louis, 98n
John of St.Thomas, 219
John Paul II, ix—xiii, 19—22, 23n, 25—27, 29—31, 33, 37, 42n, 59—68, 76, 77, 82n, 84, 86, 98n, 100n, 102, 112n, 113n, 117n, 119—123, 125—129, 143, 156n, 159, 167, 168, 177—182, 185, 186, 190, 191n, 208, 218, 219, 229
Justin Martyr, 79, 82n, 220

Kant, Immanuel, 18, 21, 30, 33
Keating, Karl, 120
Keenan, James F., 152, 158n, 220
Kenney, Sir Anthony, 59
Kierkegaard, Søren, 18
Knox, Ronald, xii, 119—129, 129n, 130n, 220
Koch, Deitrich-Alex, 116n, 217
Komonchak, Joseph A., 50m, 98n, 220
Koterski, Joseph, 81n, 97n, 113n, 130n, 220
Kwasniewski, Peter, 61, 62

Labourdette, Marie-Michel, 31, 35, 42n, 220
Lafont, G., 51n
Laporta, Jorge, 40n—41n, 203, 220
Leo XIII, 121
Levada, William, 98n
Levering, Matthew, 110, 116n, 220
Locke, John, 18, 165n
Lombard, Peter, 55—56, 62n, 212n, 214n, 217, 222, 229
Long, Steven, iii, v, ix, x, 25, 205, 210, 212n, 220, 230—231
Lottin, Odon, 150, 157n, 158n, 220

MacIntyre, Alasdair, ix, 129n
Mackey, J.P., 98n
Maguire, Daniel, 98n
Malebranche, Nicolas, 18
Malloy, Christopher, iii, xi, 101, 112n, 220, 231
Mansini, Guy, iii, xi, 73, 110, 117n, 142n, 220, 231

Mansour, Sr. Agnes Mary, 98n
Marcel, Gabriel, 18
Maréchal, Joseph, 50n
Maritain, Jacques, 19, 166n, 182—183, 192n, 220, 230
Martin, Francis, 112n, 115n, 220
Marx, Karl, 18
Mattison, William, iv, xii, 143, 231
McCool, Gerald, 50n, 220
McCormick, Richard, 87—88, 91, 98n, 99n, 219, 220
McDermott, John, 100n, 221
McEvenue, Sean, 112n, 220
McHugh, John, 142n, 221
McInerny, Ralph, 113n, 114n, 129n, 214n, 221
Melina, Livio, 142n, 221
Melito of Sardis, 101
Meredith, Anthony, 81n
Milbank, John, xi, 73, 81n, 221
Mirkes, Renée, 154n, 220
Mortensen, John, 113n, 114n

Naughton, Michael, 142n, 219
Newman, John Henry, 26, 119, 125, 130n, 230
Nietzsche, Frederick, ix, 18
Nicolas, M-J, 35, 42n, 220
Nichols, Aidan, 41n, 221

O'Brien, Mark, 116n, 217
O'Brien, Thomas C., 53n, 221
O'Connell, Timothy, 156n, 221
O'Meara, Thomas, 43—46, 49, 50n—53n, 221
Origen, 51n

Palakeel, Joseph, 111, 117n, 221
Paul VI, 21—22, 27, 221
Pearce, Joseph, 130n, 221
Peers, E. Allison, 53n, 221
Pereira, Jose, 26—28, 31, 37, 221
Persson, E., 51n
Pesch, O., 51n
Philip the Chancellor, 158n
Pieper, Josef, 60
Pinckaers, Servais, 135, 142n, 221
Pius XII, 65—66, 121
Plato, 17, 46—47, 50n, 79, 82n, 180
Plotinus, 47
Polanyi, Michael, 66, 126

Porter, Jean, 146, 156n—158n, 221
Popper, Karl, 29

Rahner, Karl, x, 18, 20, 34, 43, 46, 50n—52n, 64, 98n, 156n, 157n, 218, 219, 221, 222
Reginald, Antonius, 51n
Reimarus, Hermann, 109
Rhonheimer, Martin, 40n, 221
Ricoeur, Paul, 51n, 115n
Rocca, Gregory, 105, 114n, 221
Rousselot, Pierre, 50n
Russell, Bertrand, 25

Sartre, Jean-Paul, 18
Scheeben, Matthias, 205—207, 213n, 222
Schillebeeckx, Edward, 51n
Schindler, David, 112n, 117n, 220, 222
Schlier, Heinrich, 81n, 119
Schuller, Bruno, 98n
Schoors, Antoon, 116n. 117n
Scotus, John Duns, 114n, 221
Sheed, Frank, xii, 53n, 119, 120, 127—129, 130n, 220—222
Seckler, M., 51n
Selling, Joseph, 156n, 222
Sokolowski, Robert, 82n, 83n, 222
Spinoza, Baruch, 109
Stein, Edith, iv, xiii, 177—178, 180—195, 217, 222
Steinmueller, John E., 112n, 116n, 222
Suárez, Francisco, 20, 26, 37n, 222
Sullivan, Francis, 86—88, 91, 95—96, 98n—100n, 222
Sylvester de Ferrara, 204, 206

Teilhard de Chardin, Pierre, 41n
Teresa of Avila, 50, 53n, 221, 222
Thils, Gustave, 98n
Thompson, Christopher, iv, v, xii, 135, 231
Torrell, Jean-Pierre, 56—59, 62n, 222
Tracy, David, 114n, 222
Tück, Jan-Heiner, 110, 111, 117n, 222

Van Steenberghen, F., 50n, 222
Vandevelde, George, 46
Von Balthasar, Hans Urs, xi, xii, 39n, 41n, 50n, 102, 109—111, 117n, 220, 222

Vonier, Anscar, 119

Walgrave, Jan, 26, 37n, 222
Walker, Adrian, 61, 62
Wallace, William A., 53n, 222
Ward, Maisie, xii, 53n, 120, 127—129, 130n, 220—222

Weisheipl, James, 52n, 53n, 223
Welch, Lawrence, iii, xi, 85, 142n, 220, 231
William of Auxerre, 149
William of Moerbeke, 46
Wright, N.T., 116n, 223
Wojtyla, Karol, x, 20, 59, 62, 65, 210

Contributors

John F. Boyle, M.S.L., Ph.D., is professor of theology and Catholic studies at the University of St. Thomas, St. Paul, Minnesota. He is the editor (with Leonard Boyle, O.P.) of Thomas Aquinas, *Lectura Romana in primum Sententiarum Petri Lombardi*. He has published a number of essays on various topics in the theology of St. Thomas Aquinas.

Romanus Cessario, O.P., is professor of theology at St. John's Seminary, Boston. His books include *The Moral Virtues and Theological Ethics* (2nd edition, 2008), John Capreolus's *Treatise on the Virtues* (2001), *Introduction to Moral Theology* (2001), *A Short History of Thomism* (2004); and *Christian Faith and the Theological Life* (1996). Recently he published an essay, "The Sacraments of the Church," in *Vatican II: Renewal with the Tradition,* edited by Fr. Matthew Lamb (Oxford 2008).

Catherine Jack Deavel, Ph.D., is associate professor of philosophy at the University of St. Thomas in St. Paul, Minnesota and associate editor of the *American Catholic Philosophical Quarterly*. She also serves on the Executive Council of the American Catholic Philosophical Association. Having received her Ph.D. in philosophy from Fordham University in 2000 for her dissertation on formal and final causation in ancient and early modern thought, Deavel has published on various topics in the history of philosophy in academic journals such as *International Philosophical Quarterly, Logos, New Blackfriars, Proceedings of the American Catholic Philosophical Association* and *Review of Metaphysics*. She has also written in several volumes of the Philosophy and Popular Culture Series (Open Court and Blackwell).

David Paul Deavel is an associate editor of *Logos: A Journal of Catholic Thought and Culture* and contributing editor for *Gilbert Magazine*. He has taught at both the University of St. Thomas (Minnesota) and The Saint Paul Seminary School of Divinity. His writing has appeared in academic journals such as *Faith & Reason, Journal of Markets and Morality, Logos, New Blackfriars,* and *Pro Ecclesia;* as well as more popular outlets including *America, Books & Culture, Catholic World Report, The Christian Century, Commonweal, First Things, Touchstone* and elsewhere.

Avery Cardinal Dulles, S.J., S.T.D. (†2008), received his doctorate in Sacred Theology in 1960 from the Gregorian University in Rome. He taught at Woodstock College, the Catholic University of America, and Fordham University, where he was the Laurence J. McGinley Professor of Religion and Society since 1988. He published 750 articles on theology, as well as 23 books. He was named cardinal by Pope John Paul II in 2001, and was the first American Theologian who was not a bishop to receive such an honor. Prior to his entrance into the Society of Jesus, he was a lieutenant in the United States Navy. Cardinal Dulles passed away on December 12, 2008.

Lawrence Feingold, S.T.D., studied Philosophy and Theology at the Pontifical University of the Holy Cross in Rome from 1990 to 1999. He earned a doctorate in Dogmatic Theology, *summa cum laude*, with a dissertation on *The Natural Desire to See God According to St. Thomas Aquinas and His Interpreters*. His scholarly interests center on the theology and philosophy of St. Thomas Aquinas and the Thomistic tradition, the relationship between nature and grace, Christian anthropology, Christology, fundamental theology, and the relationship between Christian faith and culture. From 1995-96 he studied Biblical Hebrew and Greek in Jerusalem at the Studium Biblicum Franciscanum. After completing his studies in Rome, he taught Philosophy and Theology in the House of Formation of the religious order, *Miles Christi*, located in Lujan, Argentina from 1999 to 2004. In 2005 he moved to St. Louis, MO, where he directed and taught the philosophical studium of a new religious institute, the Canons Regular of the New Jerusalem. He has spoken in numerous conferences in Detroit, Buenos Aires and St. Louis.

John Goyette, Ph.D., is a Tutor at Thomas Aquinas College (Santa Paula, CA). He received a Ph.D. in Philosophy from the Catholic University of America in 1998. He was an editor of, and contributor to, a volume of essays on natural law entitled *St. Thomas Aquinas and the Natural Law Tradition* (Catholic University Press, 2004). He has also published essays on Aristotelian/Thomistic natural philosophy, Newman's *Idea of a University*, and Augustine's notion of Christian education in *De doctrina christiana*. His articles, essays, and reviews have appeared in the Catholic University of America Press, St. Augustine's Press, *The Thomist, Nova et Vetera, Maritain Studies*, and *the Review of Metaphysics*.

W. Matthews Grant, Ph.D., is an Associate Professor Philosophy at the University of St. Thomas (St. Paul, MN). Most of his work has been in the philosophy of God, and he has published in such journals as *Faith and Philosophy, Proceedings of the American Catholic Philosophical Association, Religious Studies, The Saint Anselm Journal*, and *The Thomist*.

Steven Long, Ph.D., is Professor of Theology. He has previously taught at the University of St. Thomas, at St. Joseph's College, Christendom College, and the Catholic University of America. His research interests include Thomistic metaphysics and natural law; the theology of grace in relation to human freedom; the philosophy and theology of Law; and such specific moral issues as the death penalty and the nature of the object of the moral act. He has published many articles in such journals as *Communio, The National Catholic Bioethics Quarterly, Nova et Vetera, Revue Thomiste*, and *The Thomist*, as well as chapters on such topics as divine providence, the death penalty and *Evangelium Vitae*, the doctrine of just war, and religious freedom. His book *The Teleological Gram-*

mar of the Moral Act was published in 2007 by Sapientia Press. His work *Natura Pura: On the Recovery of Nature in the Doctrine of Grace* is forthcoming from Fordham University Press later in 2009. A collection of Dr. Long's essays, tentatively titled *Thomistic Disputations: Providence, Freedom, and Law* has been accepted for publication and is forthcoming from Sapientia Press. He holds an M.A. from the University of Toledo and a Ph.D. from the Catholic University of America.

Christopher Malloy, Ph.D., is Acting Chair and Associate Professor of Theology at The University of Dallas. He earned his doctorate in systematic theology from Catholic University in 2001. He is author of eight articles and one monograph, *Engrafted into Christ: A Critique of the Joint Declaration* (Peter Lang, 2005). He serves as Associate Editor of *Nova et Vetera: English Edition*.

Father Guy Mansini, O.S.B., teaches theology at Saint Meinrad Seminary in Saint Meinrad, Indiana. He is the author of several articles and books on a variety of theological topics. Most recently (2005), he published *Promising and the Good*, through Sapientia Press of Ave Maria University.

William Mattison, Ph.D., holds degrees from Georgetown University and Weston Jesuit School of Theology. He earned his doctorate at the University of Notre Dame. He has taught at the University of Notre Dame and Mount St. Mary's University. He is currently an Assistant Professor of Moral Theology at the Catholic University of America. Dr. Mattison researches and teaches in the area of fundamental moral theology, with a focus on virtue and the work of St. Thomas Aquinas. He is the author of the recently published *Introducing Moral Theology: True Happiness and the Virtues* (Brazos Press, 2008). He has articles in several peer-reviewed journals (including *Theological Studies* and the *Journal of the Society of Christian Ethics*) and chapters in several books.

Christopher Thompson, Ph.D., is the Academic Dean and professor of moral theology at The Saint Paul Seminary School of Divinity. Prior to his appointment, he served as Chair and professor of Catholic Studies at the University of St. Thomas, St. Paul, MN. He is the author of several articles in theology, moral psychology and fundamental moral theology, appearing in *The Thomist*, *Proceedings of the American Catholic Philosophical Society*, *The Bulletin of Society of Catholic Social Scientists*, and *Logos: A Journal of Catholic Thought and Culture*.

Lawrence Welch, Ph.D., earned his degree from Marquette University and is a professor of Systematic Theology at Kenrick Seminary in St. Louis, MO. He is the author of several articles in systematic theology and related topics. His work appears in *Theological Studies, Heythorp Journal, New Blackfriars, The Irish Theological Quarterly* and *Nova et Vetera*. Recently, he co-authored a piece with Fr. Guy Mansini, O.S.B., "Commentary on *Presbyterium ordinis*," in *Vatican II: Renewal with the Tradition*, edited by Fr. Matthew Lamb (Oxford, 2008)

CPSIA information can be obtained at www.ICGtesting.com
Printed in the USA
BVOW012120200911

271653BV00002B/6/P